# Tolley's Practical Guide to State Benefits and Personal Injury Awards



by

Alan Robinson

LexisNexis™ UK

**Members of the LexisNexis Group worldwide**

| | |
|---|---|
| United Kingdom | LexisNexis UK, a Division of Reed Elsevier (UK) Ltd, 2 Addiscombe Road, CROYDON CR9 5AF |
| Argentina | LexisNexis Argentina, BUENOS AIRES |
| Australia | LexisNexis Butterworths, CHATSWOOD, New South Wales |
| Austria | LexisNexis Verlag ARD Orac GmbH & Co KG, VIENNA |
| Canada | LexisNexis Butterworths, MARKHAM, Ontario |
| Chile | LexisNexis Chile Ltda, SANTIAGO DE CHILE |
| Czech Republic | Nakladatelství Orac sro, PRAGUE |
| France | Editions du Juris-Classeur SA, PARIS |
| Germany | LexisNexis Deutschland GmbH, FRANKFURT and MUNSTER |
| Hong Kong | LexisNexis Butterworths, HONG KONG |
| Hungary | HVG-Orac, BUDAPEST |
| India | LexisNexis Butterworths, NEW DELHI |
| Ireland | Butterworths (Ireland) Ltd, DUBLIN |
| Italy | Giuffrè Editore, MILAN |
| Malaysia | Malayan Law Journal Sdn Bhd, KUALA LUMPUR |
| New Zealand | LexisNexis Butterworths, WELLINGTON |
| Poland | Wydawnictwo Prawnicze LexisNexis, WARSAW |
| Singapore | LexisNexis Butterworths, SINGAPORE |
| South Africa | LexisNexis Butterworths, Durban |
| Switzerland | Stämpfli Verlag AG, BERNE |
| USA | LexisNexis, DAYTON, Ohio |

First published in 2003



A CIP Catalogue record for this book is available from the British Library.

ISBN 0 7545 1625 3

Typeset by Letterpart Ltd, Reigate, Surrey

Printed and bound in Great Britain by The Cromwell Press Limited, Trowbridge, Wiltshire

Visit LexisNexis UK at www.lexisnexis.co.uk

# Preface

The words 'personal injury' tend to bring to mind obvious injuries which will heal, such as a broken leg. However, the term encompasses a much wider range of physical and mental conditions, not all of which will heal, and some of which are fatal. The different systems of compensation and support available to someone in this situation are complex and inter-related, and it is crucial to identify appropriate sources of financial help at an early stage.

In terms of damages or compensation, English law is based on the law of negligence, which requires the claimant to show that he or she has suffered injury due to the fault of someone else. If the injury is partly their own fault, the rules of contributory negligence will operate to remove a proportionate part of the compensation. In addition to the common law remedies, there are various forms of statutory liability which impose duties, and also schemes which provide compensation to those suffering personal injury such as the Criminal Injuries Compensation Scheme.

On top of schemes which provide compensation, the state provides in various ways for those who suffer personal injury or bereavement. For those killed or injured on military service, the war pensions scheme provides a comparatively generous series of allowances. For those injured at work, or who suffer from disease as a result of their exposure to dangerous working conditions, the industrial injuries scheme provides a pension for disability and additions for constant attention. For those to whom neither of these schemes apply, the 'civilian' schemes of disability living allowance and attendance allowance can help to meet the extra costs of illness or disability, and carers allowance can help to provide for those caring for a person who is so disabled.

Where the person concerned is unable to work, two benefits – statutory sick pay and incapacity benefit – provide state help. Where this is insufficient to meet needs, the working tax credit makes particular means-tested provision for disability, and income support, housing and council tax benefit provide additional sources of income. The social fund can meet needs for capital expenditure and for items such as funeral expenses. Certain benefits are available free or at a reduced cost to those on low incomes-free prescriptions, travel to hospital and so on. In the case of a death, bereavement benefits are available to a bereaved spouse, and guardians allowance to those looking after an orphaned child.

In addition to the state's provision in the form of cash benefits, the community care system places responsibilities on local and health authorities to provide services to meet illness and disability. In some cases there is a duty to make provision. In certain cases funding can be made available directly to the injured person or their carer to enable them to make provision for themselves. Such services as are provided may have to be paid for. There are a number of different funds which assist with the provision of services for those who have become disabled. Finally, there is a range of private schemes available, such as accident insurance, which can help to meet immediate needs for an injured person.

The book is laid out as follows. Chapter One summarises the main causes of personal injury and illness and introduces some of the concepts which are explored later. Chapter Two is an overview of the social security system for those who are unfamiliar with it; it sets out the framework within which decisions on benefit claims will be taken. Chapters Three to Seven cover the principal benefits which may be claimed for injury and illness. Chapter Eight covers other forms of support and other sources of compensation. In Chapter Nine the methods of claiming compensation through the legal system are outlined; the principles of negligence liability, and of different forms of statutory liability. Chapter Ten covers the calculation of damages. All the material regarding fatal accidents is brought together in Chapter Eleven, and Chapter Twelve summarises some recent personal injury cases which help to illustrate the scheme in operation.

In the chapters on social security benefits, principal Acts and regulations are referred to by abbreviations. The key to the abbreviations, and a brief outline of the subject matter of the legislation, is to be found in Appendix 4.

The law is up to date as at 20 June 2003.

# Contents


| | | |
|---|---|---|
| 1. | **Personal Injury and Illness** | **1** |
| | Introduction | **1** |
| | Injury at work | **1** |
| | Illness at work | **2** |
| | Medical negligence | **3** |
| | Vaccine damage | **5** |
| | Road accidents | **5** |
| | Tripping | **6** |
| | Injury in the home | **7** |
| | Injuries sustained on premises under the control of another | **8** |
| | Sports Injuries | **8** |
| | Injuries caused by animals | **9** |
| | Actions for personal injury | **9** |
| 2. | **State Benefits and Personal Injuries** | **10** |
| | Introduction | **10** |
| | The benefit system | **10** |
| | Calculation and amount of benefit | **11** |
| | Claims and payments | **13** |
| | Decisions | **16** |
| | Appeals | **18** |
| | Overpayments | **19** |
| | Personal Injury: the benefits in outline | **20** |
| 3. | **Industrial Injuries Benefits** | **24** |
| | Introduction | **24** |
| | Claiming industrial injury benefit | **24** |
| | Personal injuries | **26** |
| | Prescribed diseases | **31** |
| | Accidents and diseases-assessment | **34** |
| | Decision making and appeals | **38** |
| | The effect of an award on other benefits | **38** |
| | Additions to basic benefit | **38** |
| | Benefits now withdrawn | **40** |

| | | |
|---|---|---|
| 4. | **War Pensions** | **45** |
| | Introduction | **45** |
| | Attributable to or aggravated by service | **46** |
| | Benefits payable | **48** |
| | Awards for death | **49** |
| | Making a claim | **51** |
| | Overlapping provisions | **52** |
| | Appeals | **52** |
| | Medical treatment and care for war pensioners | **55** |
| 5. | **Benefits for Disability** | **57** |
| | Disability living allowance | **57** |
| | Attendance allowance | **69** |
| | Carers allowance | **73** |
| | Severe disablement allowance | **77** |
| 6. | **Benefits for Incapacity** | **80** |
| | Statutory sick pay | **80** |
| | Incapacity benefit | **84** |
| 7. | **Income Based Benefits and Tax Credits** | **96** |
| | Introduction | **96** |
| | Income support | **96** |
| | Tax credits | **113** |
| | Housing benefit | **117** |
| | Council tax benefit | **123** |
| | State pension credit | **124** |
| | The social fund | **128** |
| | Health benefits | **131** |
| 8. | **Other Forms of Support** | **135** |
| | Community care | **135** |
| | Disabled facilities grants | **139** |
| | Criminal injuries compensation | **140** |
| | Motor Insurers Bureau | **148** |
| | Vaccine damage payments | **149** |
| | Other forms of provision | **151** |
| | Private provision | **152** |

| | | |
|---|---|---|
| **9.** | **Liability and Negligence** | **154** |
| | Introduction | **154** |
| | Liability due to negligence | **54** |
| | Statutory liability | **165** |
| | Limitation | **169** |
| **10.** | **Compensation and Damages** | **172** |
| | Introduction | **172** |
| | Awards for damages | **172** |
| | Amounts of awards for general damages | **176** |
| | Recovery of benefits | **176** |
| | Structured settlements | **180** |
| **11.** | **Fatalities** | **181** |
| | Introduction | **181** |
| | Inquests | **181** |
| | Actions by survivors | **182** |
| | Bereavement benefits | **184** |
| | Guardians allowance | **187** |
| | Social Fund funeral expenses payments | **189** |
| **12.** | **Recent Personal Injury Cases** | **192** |
| | Principles of negligence | **192** |
| **Appendix 1** | | **198** |
| **Appendix 2** | | **201** |
| **Appendix 3** | | **222** |
| **Appendix 4** | | **233** |
| **Appendix 5** | | **237** |
| **Table of Cases** | | **241** |
| **Table of Statutes** | | **246** |
| **Table of Statutory Instruments** | | **251** |
| **Index** | | **257** |

# 1 Personal Injury and Illness

## Introduction 1.1

Personal injury can arise in a number of different circumstances. The commonest causes are injuries in the workplace and injuries on the road, and both are the subject of compulsory insurance. Injuries may, however, also occur in other circumstances which may give rise to a claim – in particular, in premises occupied or managed by another, in hospital, and in the home. There may be liability for injuries caused as a result of defects in premises, or as a result of a defective or malfunctioning product. Injuries may be incurred on the sports field, or from an animal. Each of these injuries can raise different questions, which are summarised below.

## Injury at work 1.2

Workplace injuries may arise as a result of defective machinery or equipment, as a result of an employer's failure to take proper care to provide a safe system of work for the employee, or as a result of the actions of others, whether fellow workmates or strangers. In general this discussion is based on the assumption that there is a contract of employment between employer and employee; however, this is not a necessary pre-condition of a claim, and a non-employee such as a visiting consultant may have a claim against an employer on many, if not all of the grounds listed above.

Employers are subject to a series of statutory duties regarding the provision of a safe system of work. Probably the most important of these is that imposed on employers by the *Health and Safety at Work Act 1974*. However, this Act is a criminal statute and gives no grounds for civil liability. In most cases, the employee's claim will be based on negligence, or will be based on the breach of the employers duty under legislation such as the *Factories Acts.*

As well as the obvious cases of injury involving trauma, other types of workplace injury which may need consideration include illness which is caused over a short period (such as poisoning), or over a long period, such as stress or the recognised forms of industrial disease. The latter are considered in the next section.

With workplace injuries, as with most other forms of personal injury, it is advisable to ensure that details of the incident giving rise to the injury are recorded as soon as possible. This is not simply a case of recording the details in the employer's accident book (although the employer has a statutory duty to do this under *Regulation 25* of the *Social Security (Claims and Payments) Regulations 1979 (SI 1979 No 628)*), but also of recommending to the injured person that they should write down at the earliest opportunity the circumstances which gave rise to their injuries. Steps should also be taken to identify witnesses at an early stage. Workplace injuries commonly have witnesses to them, and the names and home addresses of those witnesses should be obtained at the first opportunity. It may also be useful to make sketches and to take photographs of the site of the incident, and of any pieces of equipment which it is alleged were defective.

All these are matters which will be considered by a solicitor who is engaged in making a claim on the injured person's behalf. However, it can be of considerable assistance to the solicitor (and can have consequent financial savings) if this information is obtained at an early stage and can be handed over at the first meeting.

Where medical treatment was obtained, details should be recorded of the hospital or general practitioner providing the treatment, and of any payments made. The claimant should record items such as the number of visits to the hospital and the expenditure incurred in travelling. It is useful for a diary to be kept.

If a claim is to be pursued, the injured person will be asked not merely about his or her financial losses, but also about the effects which the accident has had on his or her life in other respects. This will include issues such as the injured person's social life, sex life, and sporting and recreational activities.

## Illness at work 1.3

Where illness is caused by some momentary exposure to its cause (such as poisoning) a case which results in illness as a result of an incident at work is likely to be little different to a case which results in more obvious physical injury. In addition, however, there are a number of circumstances in which injury can be caused in the workplace as a result of prolonged exposure to the particular cause of damage. This may include, for example, illnesses which are commonly recognised as industrial diseases, such as pneumoconiosis or industrial deafness. In addition, however, claims may result from mental or psychological factors, such as bullying and harassment (or increasingly commonly) stress.

**Appendix 3** includes a list of those industrial diseases for which industrial injury benefits may be available, and the exact circumstances in which a claim for benefit for a prescribed disease can be made are outlined in **Chapter 3**. As regards a claim for damages, however, the list of prescribed diseases is not exhaustive and other forms of illness or disease may give rise to a claim. An employee who seeks to pursue such a claim will need to beware of the possibility of other factors contributing to his or her condition. For example, he or she may live close to an industrial installation which has contributed to the illness. Other factors which may cause problems for the employee in these circumstances are the fact of employment with more than one employer working in the same or similar fields, and also the problem of limitation which prevents an action being brought once a certain period of time has elapsed since its inception. The rules on limitation are considered fully in chapter eight.

Claims based on stress have become more common in recent years, particularly since the case of *Walker v Northumberland County Council [1995] 1 ALL ER 737*. In that case, Mr Walker, a social worker, had already taken time off work due to stress, and his employers undertook to provide him with additional help at work in order that the problem should not recur. It was as a result of their failure to do so that Mr Walker was able to make a successful claim when he suffered a subsequent breakdown. Cases of stress are likely to succeed only where there is a history of complaints being made to the employer about the problems which are causing the stress, to which the employers have not responded or have responded inadequately. There is liable to be difficulty in proving that it was a failure on the part of the employer that gave rise to the stress, especially in the case of someone who has suffered other non-occupational stresses which might have caused the breakdown, or at least have materially contributed to it.

In the case of *Hatton v Sutherland [2002] EWCA Civ 76*, the Court of Appeal summarised the law on stress at work, in particular setting out the extent to which a case of stress must be foreseeable to incur liability. Chapter Nine sets out the effect of the Court of Appeal's judgement on stress cases.

The comments above regarding stress are applicable to cases of bullying and harassment. However, it is worth mentioning that in appropriate circumstances bullying or harassment may give rise to a claim before the employment tribunal for discrimination on the grounds of race, sex or disability. Where discrimination has given rise to personal injury, the employment tribunal has jurisdiction to deal with that claim (*Sherrif v Klyne Tugs (Lowestoft) Limited [1999] IRLR 481 (Court of Appeal*).

## Medical negligence 1.4

As will be seen in **Chapter 9**, claims in negligence depend upon there being a duty of care, breach of that duty, and resultant damage. The question of the nature of the duty of care in medical cases is a contentious one. A general statement of the law is to be found in the case of *Barnett v Chelsea and Kensington Hospital Management Committee [1969] 1 QB 428*. Three night watchmen had been drinking tea at work and all became ill. All attended the casualty department of their local hospital at approximately 8 am, and while one of the three lay on some chairs, one of the others relayed their symptoms to the nurse on duty. The nurse in turn relayed those symptoms to the casualty doctor by telephone. The casualty doctor, who was himself unwell, told the nurse by telephone that the men should all go home and should visit their GP later that day. He did not personally examine any of the men concerned and the person who had been lying on the chairs in the waiting room subsequently died as the result of what was shown to have been arsenic poisoning.

The judge in the High Court found that there was a duty of care owed by the casualty doctor to the night watchmen. He should have arranged to see them personally, or have arranged for some other doctor to examine them on his behalf. The judge quoted with approval the words of Lord Justice Denning in *Cassidy v Ministry of Health [1951] 2 KB 343*, who said of hospital authorities, 'once they undertake the task they come under a duty to use care in the doing of it, and that is so whether they do it for reward or not.' There is therefore likely to be a duty of care which will found a claim in negligence where damage results from breach of the duty.

In point of fact the claim in *Barnett* failed. The court held that the negligence of the doctor was not responsible for the death of the deceased, which would have occurred in any event.

It is important in pursuing a claim based on medical negligence to work with a solicitor specialising in this type of claim. There are considerable complexities in medical negligence claims, and the injured person or their relatives needs competent professional advice at the earliest opportunity. It is however useful (as in all claims for damages) to keep a record which as far as possible is made at the time an incident occurs. This will be particularly important in dealing with a large institution such as a hospital, where a sick person or their relatives may have to deal with a bewildering number of professional staff, and it is helpful to maintain a record of the names of staff dealing with the patient. Relatives' observations of the state of the patient's health, and its progress, are also of use and should be recorded. It will not always be apparent to a patient or their relatives that a procedure should be being followed, or a particular appliance used, and a contemporaneous note of deterioration in health can often prompt a questioner to ask staff why a particular procedure was not followed. If no note is made of the condition, however, the fact that standard procedures were not followed may not be discovered.

One important part of any medical negligence claim is likely to be the hospital records of the patient. Under the *Access to Health Records Act 1990*, an application for access to health records can be made by a patient, a person authorised to apply on the patient's behalf, a person who has parental responsibility for a child, the person appointed to manage the affairs of a person who is not competent to manage their own affairs (for example, under an Enduring Power of Attorney), and (where the information is needed to substantiate a claim arising from the death of the patient) the patient's personal representative.

The Act applies to records created after 1 November 1991. Access to earlier records must be permitted where it is necessary to make the later record intelligible. In the case of a child and an application by a person with parental responsibility, the holder of the record must be satisfied that the child either consents or is incapable of consenting, and that access would be in the child's best interests.

Under *section 5(1)*, the holder need not give access to medical records where it would be likely to cause serious harm to the physical or mental health of the patient or of any other person; or where access to the information would identify some person other than the patient.

## Vaccine damage 1.5

One particular aspect of medicine which has given rise to concern is that of vaccine damage. As a result, there is a statutory scheme providing payments to those who have become severely disabled as the result of a vaccination. Under the *Vaccine Damage Payments Act 1979* as amended, people who have suffered severe disability as the result of a vaccination for one of a number of specified diseases are able to claim a lump sum payment of £100,000. The scheme is outlined in **Chapter 8**. The standard non-industrial disablement and incapacity benefit provisions also apply to those disabled in this way.

## Road accidents 1.6

A person injured in a road accident may be able to claim damages on the basis of the negligence of another road user. This may be the driver of the car in which the injured person was a passenger, or the driver of another vehicle, or a third party whose actions have rendered the motoring environment dangerous. In any of these cases, the basis of the claim will be one of negligence. The driver will be seeking to demonstrate that the party on whom blame is sought to be placed owed a duty of care to the injured party, which has been broken.

Any entitlement to state benefits is liable to be confined to those set out in **Chapters 5**, **6** and **7**. However, if the injured party is in the course of his or her employment (whether as a driver or other party), it may be possible for a claim to be made under the industrial injuries scheme. Where the injured person is driving to or from his or her place of work, it is less likely that a claim will succeed, but the question should nonetheless be considered.

In gathering information to present a claim, it is useful to provide as much available evidence as possible of the circumstances and the time. It is often useful to produce a road map which shows the directions of travel of each of the vehicles involved and of any pedestrians. Traffic signs and signals should also be noted as should issues which may have a bearing on the outcome such as street lighting and parked cars.

Since damaged vehicles will of necessity be cleared away before any claim is pursued, it is often valuable if photographs can be taken first if this is possible.

Names and addresses of witnesses should be noted, as should the insurance details of all parties involved. Where those details are noted on scraps of paper, the original scraps of paper should be retained for production later.

Where a road traffic accident involves personal injury, there is an obligation to report the accident to the police. A copy of the Police Report can be obtained upon application.

Another issue which may have a bearing on the outcome of the case is the weather at the time of the accident. If the injured party is unable to recollect what the weather was like, it may be useful to obtain a report from the meteorological office.

One issue which may need to be addressed in a road traffic accident is the issue of conflict of interest between the driver of a vehicle and an injured passenger. It may be the case that the passenger will have a claim against the driver, in which case it is appropriate for both parties to seek independent representation. Road traffic accidents are also one of the commonest sources of findings of contributory negligence, and the possibility of a claim being made against several of the people involved in an incident should be considered.

## Tripping 1.7

A common cause of personal injury is the poor state of repair of many roads and pavements. The majority of such claims are made by elderly or disabled people who trip over uneven pavements or roadworks. This may found a claim against the Highway Authority under *section 41* of the *Highways Act 1980*, which imposes on the Highway Authority a duty to maintain the highway. In such a case, the onus of proof is on the claimant to show that the highway was not reasonably safe and that it caused the accident. Once this burden is satisfied, the burden shifts to the Highway Authority, who must then prove the statutory defence in order to avoid liability. The statutory defence is available to an authority who can show that it has:

> 'taken such care as in all of the circumstances was reasonably required to secure that of the part of the highway for which the action relates was not dangerous'

[*Section 58(1)* of the *Highways Act 1980*.]

Where the Highway Authority arranged for the maintenance of the highway by a competent person, then the onus is on them to show that proper instructions were given and that the person to whom this was delegated carried out those instructions: *Highways Act 1980, s 58(2).*

It is unlikely that a claim will succeed on the basis of a minor defect in the surface of the pavement. Claimants are required to accept a certain level of a risk, and the success of a claim will depend on issues such as the nature and the position of the defect, and on surrounding circumstances such as warning signs or lighting. It is advisable to note details of the accident site as soon as possible after the injury occurs, and it is often advisable to take photographs using a measuring tape to indicate the size of any defects. The possibility of corroborative evidence from passers by or local shop keepers should also be considered.

For injuries caused on private property as a result of tripping, reference should be made to the *Occupiers Liability Acts 1957* and *1984* (see below and **Chapter 9**) with a view to pursing a claim in negligence.

## Injury in the home 1.8

It has been said that the home is one of the most dangerous places for a person to be. The range of hazards which a person may encounter in the home, and the possible range of preventative measures that can be taken, are well known and do not need repetition.

In a number of instances, there is statutory liability on the person deemed responsible for the damage, for example by the manufacture or sale of dangerous goods. The different forms of statutory liability are outlined in **Chapter 9**. Other claims for compensation following an accident in the home will depend on the claimant's ability to demonstrate that the accident was caused by the negligence of another, and this too is outlined in **Chapter 9**.

Whether a claim for compensation can be made or not, the injured person should consider the possibility of a benefit claim in respect of incapacity for work or disability or both. Reference should be made to the benefits outlined in **Chapters 5** and **6** for this purpose.

## Injuries sustained on premises under the control of another 1.9

In the absence of any statutory liability for an injury sustained on the premises of another (for example under the *Defective Premises Act 1972*), it is likely that a claim for an injury sustained on private property will be based on negligence. The *Occupiers Liability Acts 1957* and *1984* are relevant in determining what degree of care is owed to a person injured on another's premises. Put shortly, the *1957 Act* provides that the occupier of premises owes the 'common duty of care' to lawful visitors – those whose presence on the property is expressly or impliedly accepted. The *1984 Act* deals with the position of trespassers, and provides that the occupier is liable where he or she is aware of a danger or has reasonable cause to believe that it exists, and has reasonable grounds to believe that a non-lawful visitor may come into contact with the danger. The duty is then owed if the risk is one against which it is reasonable to offer protection. This particular statutory provision may be of particular significance when the injured person is a child.

Liability under the Acts is explored further in **Chapter 9**, but it may be noted at this stage that the comments above regarding early action by someone who has sustained an injury are again relevant. The person is well advised to write down what happened, to seek the names and addresses of witnesses, to produce a sketch plan and photographs if possible, and to gather as much information as possible as to, for example, the occupier of the premises.

Where the injury is sustained in the course of employment, the benefits in **Chapter 3** may be relevant; where it is not, those in **Chapter 5** should be considered. In any case the benefits in **Chapters 6** and **7** will be relevant.

## Sports injuries 1.10

Sports injuries are a growing area of litigation. In principle sports injuries are no different from any other – if the injury is caused by the negligence (or, indeed, the deliberate action) of another, compensation is payable. However, there is the problem in a personal contact sport as to how far the claimant invited the contact which has given rise to the injury, and thus can be regarded as having accepted the risk. The problem falls under the heading, discussed in **Chapter 9**, of *volenti non fit injuria*, meaning that a person who voluntarily accepts a risk is not entitled to sue when they suffer injury or damage as a result.

There is case law concerning those who play sport as part of their employment, which is outlined in **Chapter 3**, which sets out their entitlement (if any) to industrial injuries benefits. The position as regards a claim based on negligence is set out in **Chapter 9**.

## Injuries caused by animals 1.11

Actions for injuries caused by an animal may be pursued at common law or under statute. Liability at common law is in accordance with ordinary principles of law. For example, in *Draper v Hodder (CA 1972)* the defendant's terriers escaped from his land and savaged a child. The defendant was held liable for failure to confine them. An owner of animals is likely to be liable if, knowing of the potential danger to the public, he or she did not take steps to minimise the danger, for example by restraining the animals.

There is also statutory liability for damage caused by animals, which is found in the *Animals Act 1971*. Animals are divided into those belonging to a dangerous species and those which do not, and the liability of the keeper for the damage is allocated accordingly. A summary of the statutory and common law position is found in **Chapter 9**.

## Actions for personal injury 1.12

The range of possible actions outlined above is of course subject to the usual caveat. There is no point in pursuing an action against a defendant who lacks the resources to meet any damages awarded. In certain cases recovery can be assumed because of the requirement for compulsory insurance (such as liability of an employer or a motorist), the likelihood that insurance is in place (for example public liability insurance for a large company), or the status of the defendant (for example a local authority). However, an action against an individual referee or opponent in a football match, or against the keeper of a dog, may have no better result than judgement in the claimant's favour which goes unsatisfied because the defendant has no money. In such cases, very serious consideration should be given as to whether such an action should be pursued at all.

# 2 State Benefits and Personal Injuries

## Introduction 2.1

There are two principal systems of financial support for those suffering personal injury or illness. These are the state benefit system, and the award of damages (or compensation) in appropriate cases. There may be an overlap between the two.

## The benefit system 2.2

The system of state benefits is governed by a series of Acts of Parliament, of which the principal (consolidating) Acts are the *Social Security Contributions and Benefits Act 1992* and the *Social Security Administration Act 1992*. Both Acts have been substantially amended.

Most of the detail of the different benefits is to be found in regulations. **Appendix 4** contains a list of the principal Acts and Regulations and their scope.

Entitlement to a particular benefit depends on the rules of that particular benefit. However, benefits operate within a wider framework, which provides rules common to different benefits. For example, the contribution system provides a common framework within which all the contributory benefits operate. The contribution conditions affecting the two principal contributory benefits considered in this book (incapacity benefit and bereavement benefits) are discussed under the heading of each of those two benefits respectively.

Most benefits are the responsibility of the Department for Work and Pensions. A decision maker based in a benefit office takes decisions on departmental benefits in the name of the Secretary of State. Decisions on tax credits (but not the state pension credit), on statutory sick pay, and on child benefit and guardians allowance are taken by the Inland Revenue. Decisions on housing benefit and council tax benefit are taken by local authority officers.

There is a right of appeal against decisions of the Secretary of State, and of a local authority officer, to a tribunal established under the *Social Security Act 1998*. Decisions of the Inland Revenue on tax credits also carry a right of appeal to Appeal Tribunals, although this is an interim measure and it is intended that in due course appeals will be made to the Commissioners of Income Tax. Appeals against decisions on statutory sick pay go to the Commissioners of Income Tax. The appeals procedure is outlined below.

There is a further right of appeal from the Appeal Tribunal, on a point of law only, to the Social Security and Child Support Commissioners, and from there to the Court of Appeal. Decisions of the Commissioners are reported, and are binding on tribunals and on decision makers. Sometimes a Tribunal of Commissioners (three in number) will sit to determine a particularly difficult or contentious point.

## Calculation and amount of benefit

### *Contributory and statutory benefits* 2.3

Contributory and statutory benefits are paid at a flat rate. Until April 2003, some contributory benefits (including incapacity benefit) provided increases for dependants, both children and adults. From April 2003, however, the new child tax credit replaces the existing system of increases for children, as well as working families tax credit and the child tax allowance. From April 2004, it will also replace income support and income based jobseekers allowance payments for children (it will not, however, replace child benefit). Those who were claiming a contributory benefit with a child increase at 7 April 2003 continue to receive the increase to their benefit; those who claim for the first time after that date will not receive an increase, but will need to claim child tax credit if they are not claiming it already. Child tax credit is outlined in chapter seven.

There are no dependants' additions to statutory sick pay. There are no adult dependants additions with bereavement benefits.

### *Contributory benefits – increases for an adult dependant* 2.4

Adult dependants additions ('increases') are payable with incapacity benefit. To claim an increase for a spouse, the claimant must be residing with him or her, or contributing to his or her maintenance at least at the rate of the increase. Additionally, either the spouse must be over 60, or the spouses must be residing together and the claimant must be entitled to an increase of benefit for a child (ie they must have a dependent child).

There is also an earnings rule. If the spouse earns more than the prescribed amount, no increase is payable; if less, then the whole of the increase is payable.

To get an increase for an *unmarried* partner, that partner must care for a child for whom the claimant is entitled to child benefit, and the claimant must either reside with the dependant, or contribute towards their maintenance by at least the amount of the increase. Note that the contributory benefits (unlike the income based benefits) draw a distinction between married and unmarried couples.

### *Increases for child dependants* 2.5

Transitional increases for children are payable with short-term higher and long-term incapacity benefit and bereaved parents allowance where this was already in payment at 7 April 2003. The claimant must be getting child benefit for the child, and either the child must be living with the claimant or the claimant must be maintaining the child by at least the amount of the increase.

The standard rate is reduced for the first child to reflect the higher rate of child benefit payable for the first child.

Where a claimant lives in a couple, the partner's earnings, if any, may affect the amount payable for the child.

### *Income Based Benefits and Tax Credits* 2.6

All these benefits are calculated for the individual or family making the claim. Income support allocates a certain sum (the 'applicable amount') to the claimant and his or her family, if any, and compares this with their actual income. Income support then tops up other income to the income support level. Certain items of income are disregarded.

Housing benefit is based on a figure representing the claimant's eligible rent. There are complex controls over the amount payable. If the claimant is on income support or income based jobseekers allowance, their housing benefit consists of the whole of their eligible rent, less deductions if there are any non-dependants living in the house. If they are not on either of these benefits, a calculation is made which compares income with a threshold. If income is below the threshold, the full amount is payable; if not, then the amount payable is reduced proportionately. The calculation for council tax benefit is similar.

There is a proposal to remove some of the complexities associated with the calculation of eligible rent by introducing a standard rent allowance. The scheme is to be piloted in different areas of the country from late 2003.

Tax credits work in a similar way to housing benefit. A maximum amount of tax credit is calculated, and income is then compared to a threshold; if income is less than the threshold the full amount is payable, whereas if it is more, the amount payable is reduced proportionately. Unlike all other benefits covered in this work, tax credits are calculated and paid on a yearly basis.

## Claims and payments 2.7

All benefits (with one or two minor exceptions) require a claim. (*Social Security Administration Act 1992, s 1*). The claim is normally made by the person who is to receive the benefit. However, in the event of the claimant's incapacity to deal with the claim, the Secretary of State has power to appoint another person (usually referred to as an appointee) to make a claim and/or to manage the claim on the incapable person's behalf (see below).

Claims must be in writing, and are usually made on the appropriate claim form. The Secretary of State can accept a claim made by letter which provides the necessary information (*Social Security (Claims and Payments) Regulations 1987 (SI 1987 No 1968), Reg 4(1)*).

In claiming income support (and jobseekers allowance), the onus of proof is on the claimant. The claim must be made on the appropriate form, and must include all necessary evidence (*Social Security (Claims and Payments) Regulations 1987 (SI 1987 No 1968), Reg 4(1A)*). There are prescribed exceptions to this rule where:

- the claimant has a physical, learning, mental, or communication difficulty and it is not reasonably practicable to seek help from someone else;
- the required information or evidence does not exist, or can only be obtained at the risk of serious harm to the claimant and it is not reasonably practicable to obtain it by other means, or it can only be obtained from a third party and it is not reasonably practicable to do so;
- the Secretary of State concludes on the evidence already supplied that the claimant is not entitled to benefit and it is inappropriate to seek further evidence.

[*Social Security (Claims and Payments) Regulations 1987 (SI 1987 No 1968), Reg 4(1B)*.]

For other benefits, a more relaxed approach is taken to the provision of information. Most benefits now require the claimant to produce a national insurance number ('the NINO requirement') as part of a valid claim (*Social Security Administration Act 1992, s 1(1A)*). A claimant is required to produce such certificates, documents, information and evidence in connection with a claim as the Secretary of State may require within one month (*Social Security (Claims and Payments) Regulations 1987 (SI 1987 No 1968), Reg 7(1)*). The Secretary of State may require a claimant to attend an office to provide documents and information (*Reg 8(2)*).

The date of the claim is the date on which the claim form is received in the benefit office (*Reg 6(1)(a)*). However, for tax credits and for the main income-based benefits, where a claimant notifies the office that they wish to claim a benefit, they are sent a claim form and, provided the claim form is competed within a stated time (usually one month), the claim is treated as made on the date of the request.

Claims for all the non means tested benefits except jobseekers allowance (see below) and disability living allowance and attendance allowance can be backdated for up to three months. Tax credit claims can also be backdated for three months (*Regs 19(2), 19(3)* and *Sch 4; Tax Credits (Claims and Notifications) Regulations 2002 (SI 2002 No 2014), Reg* 7). Where someone claims statutory sick pay and is notified that they do not qualify for it, a claim for incapacity benefit which is made within three months of notification is treated as made on the first day of incapacity (*Social Security (Claims and Payments) Regulations 1987 (SI 1987 No 1968), Reg 10*). A claim for disability living allowance or attendance allowance cannot be backdated, but provided a claim form is completed within six weeks of its being issued, the claim is treated as made on the date the form was issued (*Regs 6(8)* and *6(9)*).

A claim for industrial disablement benefit based on occupational deafness or occupational asthma must be brought within five or ten years respectively of working in a prescribed occupation (*Social Security (Industrial Injury) (Prescribed Diseases) Regulations 1985 (SI 1985 No 967), Regs 2(c), 25, 36*). Industrial disablement benefit generally is covered by the three months backdating outlined above.

Income support can be backdated for up to one month if the Secretary of State decides there are 'good administrative reasons'. If it was not reasonable to expect the claimant to claim before they did, and the delay is for one of a series of specified reasons, the claim can be backdated for up to three months, provided that the Secretary of State is satisfied that it is consistent with the proper administration of benefit to do so. There is no right of appeal. 'Good administrative reasons' consist of the following:

- the office was closed (eg because of a strike);
- there have been difficulties with normal transport arrangements to the office, and there was no reasonable alternative;
- there were adverse postal conditions;

- the claim follows the end of a claim for another benefit, where there have been delays in notification of the cessation of the earlier benefit;
- a claim for income support is being made by a separating partner;
- a claim is being made by someone who had a close relative who died within the month before the claim.

[*Social Security (Claims and Payments) Regulations 1987 (SI 1987 No 1968), Reg 19(6)* and *19(7)*; *Social Security and Child Support (Decisions and Appeals) Regulations 1999 (SI 1999 No 991), Sch 2 para 5*.]

Specified reasons for up to three months backdating include the following. The claimant must also show that he or she 'could not reasonably have been expected to make the claim earlier' (*Social Security (Claims and Payments) Regulations 1987 (SI 1987 No 1968), Reg 19(4)*).

- the claimant has difficulty in communicating because he or she has learning, language or literacy difficulties, or is deaf or blind, and it is not reasonably practicable to seek help to make the claim from another person;
- the claimant is sick or disabled, is caring for someone else, or is dealing with a domestic emergency, and it is not reasonably practicable to seek help to make the claim from another person;
- as a result of information given by an officer of the Department for Work and Pensions, the claimant believed their claim would not succeed;
- the claimant received incorrect written advice from a Citizens Advice Bureau, a solicitor or other professional adviser, a doctor, or a local authority, and as a result believed the claim would not succeed;
- the claimant received written information about income or capital from a current or former employer, a bank or a building society, and as a result believed the claim would not succeed;
- bad weather prevented access to the benefit office or job centre.

[*Social Security (Claims and Payments) Regulations 1987 (SI 1987 No 1968), Reg 19(5)*.]

A claim can be backdated by more than three months in limited circumstances where entitlement results from the backdated award of a qualifying benefit.

Housing and council tax benefits can be backdated by up to 52 weeks if the claimant can show 'good cause for late claim' (*Housing Benefit (General) Regulations 1987 (SI 1987 No 1971), Reg 72(15); Council Tax Benefits Regulations 1992 (SI 1992 No 1814), Reg 62 (16)*).

### *Appointees* 2.8

Where a person is unable to act for themselves, then unless the Court of Protection has appointed a receiver with power to claim benefit, the Secretary of State may appoint a person to act in place of the claimant with regard to the claim. This includes the right to receive benefit and to administer the claim on behalf of the incapacitated person. (*Social Security (Claims and Payments) Regulations 1987 (SI 1987 No 1968), Reg 33*). An appointment by the Secretary of State is retrospective in effect and validates any earlier actions of the appointee *(R(SB) 5/90)*.

## Decisions 2.9

Before changes introduced by the *Social Security Act 1998*, decisions were mainly a matter for adjudication officers, with certain decisions being taken by the Secretary of State. There were also separate procedures to determine medical questions. Social Fund decisions were taken by a social fund officer. From 1998, all these decisions are taken in the name of the Secretary of State (*Social Security Act 1998, s 8(1)*). As noted above, decisions on housing and council tax benefit are taken by local authority officers; and decisions on tax credits, statutory sick pay and statutory maternity pay, and child benefit, are taken by the Inland Revenue.

Decisions are taken on the papers without an interview with the claimant. A claimant with a right of appeal against any such decision must be given a written decision which contains information about the right to appeal to a tribunal. If the written decision does not include reasons, the claimant has a period of one month within which to seek reasons, and the Secretary of State is obliged to respond to a request for written reasons within 14 days (*Social Security (Claims and Payments) Regulations 1987 (SI 1987 No 1968), Reg 28(1)* and *28(2)*).

### *Revising or superseding a decision* 2.10

A decision, once made, may be revised or superseded. A revision is a change in the original decision, and reflects situations where, for example, the original decision was incorrect for any reason. A supercession is a new decision which replaces the original decision, for example because there has been a change of circumstances.

#### *Revisions* 2.11

A decision is capable of being revised in two sets of circumstances. In each case the revised decision goes back to the date of the original decision.

## The 'any grounds' revision 2.12

The Secretary of State can revise a decision at a time of his choosing, or following an appeal or an application for a revision (*Social Security Act 1998, s 9(1)*). A decision may be revised within one month, and a substituted decision made, on any grounds (*Social Security and Child Support (Decisions and Appeals) Regulations 1999 (SI 1999 No 991), Reg 3(1)*). The one month period is extended by 14 days where a written statement of reasons has been requested. An 'any grounds' decision can be revised outside the one month period, but with an absolute time limit of 13 months. To extend the time limit, it must be reasonable to grant the application, the application for revision must have merit, and there must be special circumstances why the original time limit could not be complied with (*Social Security and Child Support (Decisions and Appeals) Regulations 1999 (SI 1999 No 991), Reg 4(3)*). Claimants are encouraged to negotiate unfavourable decisions.

## The 'any time' revision 2.13

A decision may be revised at any time where, among other situations:

- there has been an 'official error';
- the decision is based on a mistake of fact or is made in ignorance of a material fact, where the decision is thereby more favourable to the claimant;
- jobseekers allowance is not payable because of a sanction;
- a person is entitled to benefit, or more benefit, because of being awarded a qualifying benefit.

[*Social Security and Child Support (Decisions and Appeals) Regulations 1999 (SI 1999 No 991), Reg 3(5), (6), (7)*.]

The second of the above grounds for revision (which is normally used to revise a decision where there has been an overpayment) is limited in the case of incapacity and disability benefits. Effectively there cannot be a recoverable overpayment of any of these benefits where the claimant could not reasonably have known of a material fact of which the Secretary of State was ignorant, or as to which the Secretary of State made a mistake; or could not reasonably have known of its relevance (*Social Security and Child Support (Decisions and Appeals) Regulations 1999 (SI 1999 No 991), Reg 5(c)*).

A fresh decision on a revised application gives the claimant a right of appeal.

### *Supercessions* 2.14

A supercession enables a decision to be superseded by another one where there has been a mistake of fact or error of law, or there has been a relevant change of circumstances. This can be done by the Secretary of State at any time, or on application from the claimant (*Social Security Act 1998, s 10(1)(a)*). Grounds for supercession are set out in *Social Security and Child Support (Decisions and Appeals) Regulations 1999 (SI 1999 No 991), Reg 6(2)*, and include:

- The decision is based on a mistake as to a material fact or was made in ignorance of a material fact.
- The decision was wrong in law.
- There has been a relevant change of circumstances.

The powers of revision and supercession for decision makers on behalf of the Secretary of State are mirrored in the powers available to officers of the Inland Revenue or a local authority.

## Appeals 2.15

The Appeals Service was set up under the *Social Security Act 1998*. It is responsible for all judicial matters relating to social security appeals, except for those reserved to the Commissioners of Income Tax.

Appeals are heard by a tribunal consisting of one, two or three members. Every tribunal must include a legally qualified member *(Social Security Act 1998, s 7(2))*, who normally presides over the hearing, and who is also responsible for recording the decision and its reasons, and considering requests for permission to appeal to a Commissioner. Other panel members will be qualified in medicine or accountancy, or will have experience of disability. Regulations lay down the composition of tribunals to hear different types of appeal (*Social Security and Child Support (Decisions and Appeals) Regulations 1999 (SI 1999 No 991), Reg 36 TC9*). The default tribunal is a single (legally qualified) member sitting alone.

Notice of appeal must be in writing, and must be given to the relevant office within one month of the date on which notice of the decision appealed against was given, except in the case of tax credits where the period is 30 days from the date on the appeal letter (*Social Security and Child Support (Decisions and Appeals) Regulations 1999 (SI 1999 No 991), Regs 31(1)* and *33(1)*; *Tax Credits Act 2002, ss 23 (2)* and *39(1)*).

A legally qualified member can admit a late appeal, provided that it has reasonable prospects of success or that it is in the interests of justice for the application to be granted. The interests of justice are defined in regulations as follows:

- The claimant, their partner or a dependant has died or suffered serious illness.

- The claimant is not resident in the UK.
- Normal postal services have been disrupted.
- There are other circumstances which are 'wholly exceptional and relevant'.

[*Social Security and Child Support (Decisions and Appeals) Regulations 1999 (SI 1999 No 991), Reg 32*; *Tax Credits (Appeals) (No 2) Regulations 2002 (SI 2002 No 3196), Reg 6*.]

There is an absolute time limit of twelve months from expiry of the time limit for appeal.

An appellant is invited to apply for an oral hearing. If the form indicating whether an oral hearing is required is not returned within 14 days, the appeal is struck out. (*Social Security and Child Support (Decisions and Appeals) Regulations 1999 (SI 1999 No 991), Reg 39*; *Tax Credits (Appeals) (No 2) Regulations 2002 (SI 2002 No 3196), Reg 12(2)*). If the claimant does not opt for an oral hearing, the appeal will be a paper hearing.

Following a tribunal hearing, a decision with summary reasons is sent to the appellant. Full reasons may be requested within one month (*Social Security and Child Support (Decisions and Appeals) Regulations 1999 (SI 1999 No 991), Reg 53*; *Tax Credits (Appeals) (No 2) Regulations 2002 (SI 2002 No 3196), Reg 21*). There is provision for an appeal decision to be set aside (*Social Security and Child Support (Decisions and Appeals) Regulations 1999 (SI 1999 No 991), Reg 57*; *Tax Credits (Appeals) (No 2) Regulations 2002 (SI 2002 No 3196), Reg 25*) and a further right of appeal, with permission of a legal member or the Commissioner, on a point of law only, to the Social Security and Child Support Commissioners (*Social Security and Child Support (Decisions and Appeals) Regulations 1999 (SI 1999 No 991), Reg 58*; *Tax Credits (Appeals) (No 2) Regulations 2002 (SI 2002 No 3196), Reg 27*).

## Overpayments 2.16

Where benefit is overpaid due to either a misrepresentation as to, or a failure to disclose, a material fact, the Secretary of State may, in the case of most benefits, require it to be repaid *(Social Security Administration Act 1992, s 71)*. For there to be a recovery, there must be:

- a misrepresentation or failure to disclose a material fact; and
- a payment of benefit, or non-recovery, as a consequence of that overpayment.

The Adjudication Officer (on whom the burden of proof lies: *Duggan v Chief Adjudication Officer*, reported as an Appendix to *R(SB) 13/89*) must determine the amount recoverable and the period to which it relates.

Detailed information on overpayments and their recovery is outside the scope of this book. Advisers are referred to the specialist publications on social security benefits listed in **Appendix 5** for more information. However, one or two points may be noted:

- A claimant who signs an order for benefit, or a claim form, signs a declaration to the effect that they are entitled to the benefit claimed and that (where appropriate) their circumstances have not changed. If this statement is incorrect, the basis of a case for misrepresentation may be made out (see for example *R(SB) 9/85*).
- A misrepresentation may be entirely innocent (*R(SB) 21/82*) but may still amount to grounds for recovery under the Act. Mental incapacity may provide a limited exception (see for example *R(SB) 28/83*).
- The Court of Appeal has recently held that a person cannot fail to disclose something to the Secretary of State which the Secretary of State already knows *(Hinchy v Secretary of State for Work and Pensions (EWCA [2003] Civ 138, The Times 24 February 2003))*.
- It is a question for the decision maker, and for the tribunal on appeal, whether there has been a misrepresentation and/or a non-disclosure, and whether the misrepresentation or non-disclosure has led to the overpayment. If both questions are answered in the affirmative, it is then a matter for the Secretary of State to decide, in his discretion, whether to recover the overpaid benefit from the claimant.
- Tax credit overpayments are recoverable whatever the circumstances, even if they are the result of official error. However, it is a matter for the discretion of the Inland Revenue as to whether to recover an overpayment or not. Interest may be added to an overpayment where it is due to the fraud or neglect of the claimant (*Tax Credits Act 2002, s 28*).
- Housing benefit and council tax benefit overpayments are recoverable in most cases. There is an exception if the overpayment is due to an official error, provided that the claimant (or the person to whom the housing benefit was paid) did not contribute to the error, and could not reasonably be expected to realise that an overpayment was being made. *(Housing Benefit (General) Regulations 1987 (SI 1987 No 1971), Reg 99(2); Council Tax Benefits Regulations 1992 (SI 1992 No 1814), Reg 84(2).)*

## Personal injury: the benefits in outline

### *Benefits for incapacity for work* 2.17

One contributory benefit, one statutory benefit, and the income based benefits are able to provide an income for an injured person who is unable to work as a result of their injury or illness.

A person aged under 65 who is employed under a contract of employment is able to claim statutory sick pay for a maximum of 28 weeks absence from work.

A person under 65 who is absent from work for a longer period, or who is not employed under a contract of employment (for example, because they are self-employed) can claim incapacity benefit, which is a contributory benefit payable from the date incapacity begins (or statutory sick pay ends) until the incapacity for work ends, or until the person reaches 65.

A person who is incapable of work, and whose resources are insufficient to meet their requirements, can if certain conditions are fulfilled claim income support, whether or not they are receiving statutory sick pay, incapacity benefit or child tax credit. Someone who lives in an owner-occupied house can claim extra income support towards the costs. Someone who lives in rented accommodation can claim housing benefit whether or not they claim income support, provided their income is low enough. Those on income support can also claim a full rebate of council tax by way of council tax benefit, while those not on income support whose income is low enough may also be entitled to a full or partial rebate of their council tax.

Where the person is able to work, they may be entitled to the working tax credit. This makes special provision for those whose disability makes it more difficult for them to get and keep a job. A person with children (whether working or not) may be able to claim child tax credit for help with the cost of bringing up children.

### *Benefits for specific causes of disability* 2.18

Someone who is injured at work, or who contracts a prescribed disease, may be able to claim industrial disablement benefit. This is not means tested and non contributory, and is unaffected by income or capital (or indeed by capacity to work or otherwise). The benefit is assessed on a percentage basis, and the claimant must be at least 20% disabled to claim. Where disability is assessed at 100%, the person may be able to claim two additional benefits; constant attendance allowance is payable where the claimant needs care and attention, and exceptionally severe disablement allowance is payable where the need for care and attention is likely to be permanent.

Someone who is injured in the course of military service can claim a war pension. The benefits payable under the war pensions scheme are not means tested and do not depend on contributions. As well as a weekly payment, there is provision for various additional payments with a war pension, including both constant attendance allowance and exceptionally severe disablement allowance, together with other allowances for differing degrees of disability and their effects. War widows and war widowers pensions are also available to a war widow or widower if their spouse died or was killed as a result of military service.

A person who does not qualify for constant attendance allowance may also be able to claim both the benefits in the preceding section and those in the next following section.

### *Benefits for disability – general* 2.19

Where the cause of the disability is neither industrial nor military, the injured person has access to alternative benefits for disability. Where the person is so severely disabled, whether from a physical or mental cause, as to require regular attention in connection with their bodily functions, or continual supervision to avoid danger to themselves or others, they are likely to be entitled to one of the care components of disability living allowance or, if they are over 65 when the claim is made, attendance allowance. Both benefits are payable irrespective of the cause of the injury, but are not payable in addition to either constant attendance allowance or exceptionally severe disablement allowance (see above). There is a lower rate of disability living allowance for someone whose care needs are less. In addition to the care components of disability living allowance, someone who is unable or virtually unable to walk as the result of a physical condition can claim the higher mobility component of disability living allowance; where they can walk, but need help and guidance out of doors in unfamiliar situations, they may be entitled to the lower mobility component.

Where there is an award of attendance allowance, or of the middle or higher care component of disability living allowance (see above) a carer may be entitled to claim carers allowance.

A person who was entitled to claim it before April 2002 can continue to claim severe disablement allowance if they do not qualify for incapacity benefit. The benefit has been abolished for new claims.

Neither disability living allowance nor attendance allowance is affected by income or capital, and neither affects entitlement to income based benefits. Neither benefit is contributory.

The income based benefits referred to above make special provision for disability and sickness. Income support includes premiums for the extra cost of disability, and also for carers.

### Benefits on death 2.20

Where the accident or illness results in death, there are two available benefits. A surviving spouse may be entitled to the contributory bereavement benefits, based either on their continuing need to be responsible for children (widowed parents allowance) or on their age at the death of their spouse (bereavement allowance). Bereavement benefits are payable to those bereaved while under pension age. All those who qualify are entitled to a bereavement payment of £2000.

A person who is looking after a child because both its parents are dead, or because one os dead and the other is in prison or cannot be traced, is entitled to guardians allowance in addition to child benefit.

There are several different routes to claiming for help with funeral expenses. Where a funeral is arranged by someone in receipt of an income-based benefit, there may be an entitlement to a funeral expenses payment from the social fund. Funeral expenses may also be recoverable as part of a damages claim, and under the war pensions scheme.

### Other benefits 2.21

Where the claimant receives income support, there may be an entitlement to other social fund payments to help with the problems of disability. These are likely to be loans rather than grants.

Other health benefits which may be available either free of charge or at a reduced rate include free prescriptions, free dental treatment, free glasses and sight tests, and travel to hospital.

# 3 Industrial Injuries Benefits

## Introduction 3.1

Since the nineteenth century there has been a separate scheme of compensation for people injured or taken ill at work. Although subject to major cuts in the 1980s, the industrial injuries scheme survives as a separate entity, making provision for those who have suffered injury in the course of their employment, or who have contracted a disease which is attributable to that employment.

## Claiming industrial injury benefit 3.2

In order to claim under the industrial injuries scheme, the claimant must fulfil the following conditions:

- He or she must be or have been an 'employed earner'.
- He or she must have received personal injury in an industrial accident or be suffering from a prescribed disease.
- The accident or disease must have resulted in a loss of faculty.
- The earner must be disabled as a result of the loss of faculty.

The basic entitlement is to a pension paid at a rate reflecting the severity of the disability caused by the injury or disease. In cases of particularly severe disablement, the claimant may also be entitled to the supplements of constant attendance allowance and (in the most severe cases) exceptionally severe disablement allowance. Other supplements payable with the pension have been abolished for recent injuries or diseases, but it is still possible in some cases to backdate a claim where the injury or disease occurred some time ago. Particular mention may be made of reduced earnings allowance, whereby certain claimants who have suffered from loss of earnings as a result of the accident or disease may be entitled to additional benefit, and those who were previously so entitled may be entitled to a retirement allowance.

### *Employed earners* 3.3

The claimant must be in *employed earners employment*. Self-employed people may not claim, and most trainees are also excluded. Under the *Social Security Contributions and Benefits Act 1992 (SSCBA 1992), s 2(1)(a)*, an employed earner is a person 'gainfully employed in Great Britain either under a contract of service or in an office including elective office with emoluments chargeable to income tax under Schedule E.'

The determining factor for most claimants is whether they fall within the definition of employed earner for the purpose of paying national insurance contributions. However, there is no requirement that any contributions actually be paid to qualify for benefit – a worker on their first day at work is eligible under the scheme. In most cases the question is whether the worker actually paid Class 1 Contributions, but those whose earnings are too low to pay contributions are also covered.

Certain people are treated as employed earners, including:

- apprentices (although for those on government schemes discretionary payments are made);
- mine inspectors and rescue workers;
- taxi drivers;
- special constables;
- office cleaners;
- agency workers;
- ministers of religion;
- lecturers;
- aircrew; and
- mariners.

In some cases offshore oil or gas workers can be so treated.

The following people are excluded from the definition of employed earner:

- A person employed by their own spouse, unless the employment is for the purposes of the employer's business. Even if it is, the employed spouse must also be a Class 1 contributor.
- A person employed by a close relative, that is a parent, step-parent, grandparent, son, daughter, stepchild, grandchild, brother, sister, half-brother or half-sister, in a private household where they both live. The exclusion does not apply, however, if the employment is for the purposes of the employer's business which is carried on there.

- A member of visiting armed forces, or a civilian working for them, unless that person is normally resident in the UK and pays Class 1 contributions.

*(Social Security (Employed Earners' Employment for Industrial Injuries Purposes) Regulations 1975 (SI 1975 No 467), Sch 1 Part 1* & *Sch 3*.)

Self-employed people constitute the largest excluded group. There are some three million in the UK, about eight per cent of the workforce.

### *Residence* 3.4

The claimant must normally have contracted the disease, or had the accident, in Great Britain. Benefit may however be payable to someone who:

- is a mariner or aircrew member;
- works on the continental shelf;
- works in another European country;
- is working out of the country, provided their employer is paying Class 1 contributions for them;
- is paying Class 2 contributions as an overseas volunteer development worker; or
- works in a country with whom there is a reciprocal arrangement over the payment of industrial injuries benefits.

*(Social Security Contributions and Benefits Act, ss 115(2)* and *117*; *Social Security Benefit (Persons Abroad) Regulations 1975 (SI 1975 No 563), Regs 10C (5)* & *(6)* and *11*.)

## Personal injuries 3.5

To claim under the industrial injuries limb, the claimant must have suffered *personal injury by accident arising out of and in the course of . . . employment*. The terminology has been carried forward through sucessive legislative schemes for industrial injury and has been responsible for an abundance of case law.

### *Personal injury* 3.6

For all cases other than prescribed disease cases, the claimant must have suffered *personal injury*. This must be an injury to the body or mind, and can include mental and psychological injury, but not damage to non-bodily items such as an artificial leg *(R(I) 7/56)* or a pair of spectacles *(R(I) 1/82)*. Damage to an artificial hip joint, however, is sufficient on the basis that it has become part of the body *(R(I) 8/81)*, and on the same argument damage to items such as a pacemaker would be likely to be sufficient. It may be that, with replacement surgery now being substantially more advanced than in 1956, damage to an artificial limb which was permanently attached to the body would count as personal injury in spite of the decision in *R(I) 7/56*. Pain which is a symptom of an existing condition, and which does not make the condition worse, is insufficient – *R(I) 1/76*.

## By accident 3.7

The personal injury must have been caused *by accident*. The term 'industrial accident' is sometimes used, but the word 'industrial' is satisfied by the accident arising out of and in the course of employment (see below) and does not imply work in an industrial setting as opposed to, say, an office.

An accident is an unlooked-for occurrence. It is not confined to purely accidental occurrences, and can include deliberate acts by third parties such as horseplay or assaults (see, for example *Trim Joint District School Board of Management v Kelly [1914] AC 667*, in which pupils attacked and killed a schoolmaster). It need not be unforeseeable or exceptional. Everyday incidents of employment can be regarded as accidents. It is irrelevant that the employee has performed the task which leads to the injury on many previous occasions; it is the injury caused on the specific occasion in question which qualifies the particular occasion as an industrial accident. In *Chief Adjudication Officer v Faulds [2000] 2 All E.R. 961*, the House of Lords held that a firefighter's post traumatic stress disorder was capable of arising from an accident or series of accidents (the series of horrific fatalities which he had attended) although these might be regarded as ordinary elements of, or incidents in, his particular employment.

It is, however, nonetheless necessary to take an ordinary and everyday view of the meaning of the word 'accident'. In *CI 5249/95*, the Commissioner rejected the contention that someone who had suffered a nervous breakdown on being suspended from work by his employer had suffered an 'accident'. The suspension might have been unexpected, but it would fly in the face of ordinary use of the English language to regard it as an accident.

## Accident or process 3.8

An accident should be distinguished from a process. For the injury to be caused 'by accident' there must have been a specific incident or series of incidents over a period of time which caused or contributed to the origin or progress of the injury or disease (*Roberts v Dorothea Slate Quarries Ltd [1948] 2 All ER 201*). Each incident must be specific and ascertainable. It is not always necessary to identify the precise event which caused the injury, although each case is decided upon its own facts and the reported cases show some inconsistency. The concept of a series of accidents provides an interpretation of the legislation which appears to be generous to the claimant, and which seems to lack logic, or any support in medical practice.

In a process there will probably be no ascertainable incident when the injury could have occurred. For example, a claim for injury arising as a result of passive smoking is likely to be rejected as a process rather than an accident. However, by way of illustrating the difficulties in this area, in *R(I) 6/91* the claimant identified six separate incidents of her being moved into a smoky environment, so that the Commissioner was able to find a series of accidents to enable a claim based on passive smoking to succeed. In *Mullen v Social Security Commissioner (17 January 2002, unreported)*, the Court of Session heard an appeal from a nurse whose job included lifting elderly patients in the course of her employment. She could not identify which particular incident led to her back pain. Nevertheless the Court of Session held that *Roberts* (above) should be read as referring to a series of accidents, rather than to a case where a condition developed slowly and imperceptibly over time, and the claimant was not required to identify every incident.

The area of psychological injury, particularly in the area of post-traumatic stress, has proved problematic. In *Faulds* (above), the House of Lords, while holding that the series of incidents which Mr Faulds had attended were capable of constituting an accident or series of accidents, also doubted whether it could be demonstrated that the characteristics of post traumatic stress disorder, and in particular the post traumatic stress disorder suffered by Mr Faulds, could be readily identified with particular incidents such as those that occurred to him. It seems that few such claims are likely to succeed in practice.

In *CI 2414/98*, the claimant was subjected to aggressive and abusive behaviour by fellow employees who were on strike. She was informed that no disciplinary action would be taken against them. She suffered immediate shock and distress, and was diagnosed by her GP as suffering from extreme post-traumatic stress. The Commissioner agreed with the tribunal that she had suffered personal injury by accident arising out of and in the course of her employment.

Where the cause of the claimant's condition is process rather than accident, a claim to disablement benefit will fail based on the 'personal injury by accident' limb, but may succeed under the 'prescribed disease' limb.

## *Causation* 3.9

It is for the claimant to prove, on the balance of probabilities, that the accident caused the injury. The accident need not be the sole cause of the incident, and it is irrelevant that the claimant already suffered from a condition which rendered him or her more susceptible to the later event *(CI 147/50)*.

### ***Out of and in the course of employment*** 3.10

The accident must arise *out of and in the course of employment*. There are two tests here. The first ('out of the employment') requires a causal link between the accident and the job. 'In the course of the employment' looks at time, place and activity. There is a statutory presumption in the *Social Security Contributions and Benefits Act 1992, s 94(3)* that an accident in the course of employment also arises out of the employment, but the presumption can be defeated if there is evidence to the contrary. For example, in *Chief Adjudication Officer v Rhodes [1999] ICR 178*, a civil servant working for the Benefits Agency was assaulted at home by a neighbour whom she had reported as claiming benefit while working. The accident arose out of her employment but was not in the course of it, so her claim failed, although Lord Justice Schiemann said that it might be different if, for example, the assault had taken place while she was on her mobile phone reporting her neighbour's actions. An accident arises out of and in the course of employment, according to Lord Justice Roch in that case, if the claimant 'was doing something he or she was employed to do, or something reasonably incidental to those things that the applicant was employed to do' (at page 191).

To fulfil the requirement that the accident arises 'out of the employment', it is necessary to show that the employment is a cause of the accident, rather than merely the place where the injury occurred. If the employee has a heart attack while in the workplace, unconnected with the work, there is no industrial accident. If the heart attack is caused by particular exertion in connection with work (for example, by heavy lifting), the accident is an industrial one.

There may be a problem where there is a pre-existing condition which manifests itself during the course of the employment. The principle is that where, for example, the claimant suffers injury as a result of a fall, rather than as a result of the *cause* of the fall, there is an industrial accident. Thus the epileptic claimant who has a fit at work does not suffer an industrial accident by doing so, but if she strikes her head on the floor when falling, then she has suffered an industrial accident. The principle was laid down in *R(I) 11/80*, where the Commissioner said that, where someone suffers a psychological or pathological change at work which is caused by the work itself, that is an industrial accident, whereas if it is a purely internal event, it is not. However, where the change causes the employee to fall and injure him or herself, the resulting injury may be held to arise out of and in the course of employment.

'In the course of employment' raises a number of issues. The term is normally concerned with the place at which the accident occurred, the time at which it occurred, and the activity involved. Employment normally begins with arrival at the workplace and terminates with leaving it. Travel to and from work is therefore normally excluded, but will be included if travel is in transport provided by the employer (*SSCBA 1992, s 99*). The question is whether the worker is subject to greater risk than the general public by reason of his or her employment. It seems to have been generally accepted that a worker who deviates from his or her direct route to their place of work (for example, to visit a client) will be within the course of employment once he or she does so, and this view was given weight by the decision of the Court of Appeal in *Ball v Insurance Officer [1985] 1 All ER 833*. A policeman was injured while travelling from home to work. The workplace to which he was travelling was not his normal place of work, he had first telephoned to report for duty, and his travelling expenses were reimbursed. The Court held that he was in the course of his employment. However, the situation is by no means clearcut; a civil servant who was injured while travelling from home to a temporary place of work 100 miles away was not entitled *(R(I) 3/71)*.

An employee whose job involves travelling (such as an insurance agent) will be protected against accidents arising during his or her working time. However, where he or she is expected first to report to a particular workplace such as an office, travel from home to the office will not normally be covered unless it can fall within the type of exception outlined above.

Where the worker is injured during a break, factors which may affect a decision include whether the break was imposed or permitted by the employer, or merely condoned, or indeed forbidden. In *R v Industrial Injuries Commissioner [1966] 2 QB 31*, Lord Denning MR said (at p 49),

> '.. if a man, while at his place of work, during his hours of work, is injured by a risk incidental to his employment, the right conclusion generally is that it is an injury which arises out of and in the course of his employment, even though he may not be doing his actual work but chatting to a friend or smoking or doing something of that kind.'

Recreational activity which forms part of work may count as being within the course of employment, for example the worker injured playing football during the lunch break, although the cases indicate that such a claim is more likely to succeed if the recreational activity is compulsory rather than merely encouraged. In *R(I) 13/51*, a mental nurse who was injured while playing football with the patients succeeded in his claim. On the other hand, where the injury is not directly related to the work which the employee is employed to do, it must at least be reasonably incidental to it; thus the police constable who was injured while playing football for his force was not covered (*R v National Insurance Commissioner ex p Michael [1977] 2 All ER 420*).

An accident which occurs while the employee is dealing with an emergency is statutorily presumed to arise out of and in the course of employment (*SSCBA 1992, s 100*).

Work done at home may well be within the course of the employment. It will depend on the particular employment, and may well depend on the employment contract itself. For example, in *Rhodes* (above), Mrs Rhodes' contract allowed her to credit preparation time at home under a flexitime arrangement. However, Mrs Rhodes was not actually working at the time of the assault. In other cases time spent at home may be deemed to form part of the contract of employment even at a time when no work is being done, in which case a claim may well succeed.

An accident is deemed to arise out of employment if it arises in the course of employment and is caused by another person's misconduct, skylarking or negligence, or the behaviour or presence of an animal including a bird, fish or insect, or by being struck by an object or by lightning, provided that the worker did not directly or indirectly contribute to the accident by conduct outside the employment or conduct not reasonably incidental to it. (*SSCBA 1992, s 101*).

The employee's conduct is only relevant if his or her conduct created a different risk which was itself the real cause of the accident (*R(I) 2/63*).

### *Notification of an accident* 3.11

A person who has an accident at work is required to notify their employer, or a person nominated by the employer, or the person in charge of the workplace. Where the employer is required to maintain an accident book, details of the accident must be entered in it. An employer is required to maintain an accident book or an electronic equivalent if he or she owns or occupies a mine or quarry, or owns or occupies premises to which the *Factories Act 1961* applies, or normally employs ten or more people (*Social Security Administration Act 1992 (SSAA 1992), s 8*; *Social Security (Claims and Payments) Regs 1979, regs 24* and *25*).

It is possible, and may be advisable, to apply for a declaration that an accident was an industrial accident. The claimant makes an application on Form B195. The benefit office then writes to the employer to verify the circumstances, and if satisfied that the criteria for an industrial accident are fulfilled, will make the appropriate declaration. This may be of use where a claim is not immediately contemplated, but may be contemplated at a later date (*Social Security Act 1998, s 29*).

## Prescribed diseases 3.12

In order to qualify for benefit on the basis of an industrial disease, the worker must firstly be diagnosed as suffering from the prescribed disease, and secondly must be, or must have been, working in an occupation which is prescribed in respect of the disease. It is therefore not enough for someone to show that they are suffering from cadmium poisoning (prescribed disease C18); the worker must also show that he or she was employed in an occupation which involved exposure to cadmium dust or fumes.

A full list of prescribed diseases is in **Appendix 2**. Prescribed diseases are classified in four categories. Those with the prefix A have physical causes; those with the prefix B have biological causes; those with the prefix C have chemical causes, and those with the prefix D cover all other causes.

Where someone has contracted a prescribed disease, but did not work in an occupation specified for that disease, there is no entitlement to benefit on the basis of prescribed disease. There may be entitlement under the industrial accident provisions if the disease was caused by an accident, but a prospective claimant by this route will have to deal with the distinction between accident and process if the claim is to succeed. However, where the employee does work in an occupation for which that disease is prescribed, he or she may not proceed by the industrial injuries limb. There is a statutory presumption that, where the disease is a prescribed disease for that employment, the employee is not entitled to benefit though that disease being treatable as an industrial accident (*SSCBA 1992, s 108(6)*).

The date of onset of a prescribed disease must be on or after 5 July 1948, although there may be entitlement to benefit under the Pneumoconiosis, Byssinosis and Miscellaneous Diseases Benefit Scheme, or the Workmen's Compensation (Supplementation) Scheme.

The process is to ask the following questions:

- Is the disease a prescribed disease?
- Is the disease prescribed in relation to the claimant?

This is the prescription question, and includes the question whether the claimant was in employed earner's employment:

- Does the claimant have the disease, or have they done so?

This is the diagnosis question:

- Is the disease due to the nature of the claimant's employment?
- When was the date of onset of the disease?
- Has the claimant suffered a loss of faculty as a result of the disease?

There is a defeasible presumption that, where someone was working within the prescribed occupation at the date of onset of the disease, or has worked in the prescribed occupation within a month of contracting the disease, the occupation caused the disease. The onus of proof is on the decision maker to show that the disease was not due to the employment.

The presumption does not apply to carpal tunnel syndrome or to dermatitis. Different time conditions apply to industrial deafness, tuberculosis, pneumoconiosis, byssinosis, and chronic bronchitis and emphysema.

There is generally no requirement that the worker has worked in the prescribed employment for any minimum period, nor is there a time limit on making a claim, although the claimant who is unable to rely on the above presumption will have to establish a connection, which will be difficult to do if the claimant spent only small amounts of time on the activity giving rise to the disease. There are a number of exceptions:

- For occupational deafness, the worker has to have worked in a prescribed occupation for ten years, and to claim within five years of having done so. (*Social Security (Industrial Injuries) (Prescribed Diseases) Regulations 1985 (SI 1985 No 967), Regs 2(c), 25(2)* and *27*.)
- For occupational asthma, the worker has to claim within ten years of having worked in the prescribed occupation. (*SI 1985 No 967, Reg 36(1)*).
- For coal miners' chronic bronchitis or emphysema, the worker has to have worked in a prescribed occupation for 20 years (*SI 1985 No 967, Reg 2(d), Schedule 1*).
- For cataracts, the worker has to have worked in a prescribed occupation for five years or more in total (*SI 1985 No 967, Reg 2(e)*).

A claim for benefit as a result of a prescribed disease can be made at any time after the onset of the disease. There are specific claim forms for:

- Chronic bronchitis and emphysema.
- Allergic rhinitis.
- Occupational asthma.
- Occupational deafness.
- Pneumoconiosis, asbestosis, bilateral diffuse pleural thickening, byssinosis, diffuse mesothelioma, and primary cancer of the lung.

In other cases the claimant should use the general claim form for a prescribed disease.

If the claimant satisfies the prescription question, the claim is referred to the medical service and the claimant may be asked to attend an examination (*Social Security Act 1998, s 19*). All asbestos-related prescribed diseases, diffuse mesothelioma, unilateral or bilateral diffuse pleural thickening associated with asbestos, and primary lung cancer associated with work with asbestos, silica, or in a tin mine (prescribed diseases D3, D8, D9, D10 and D11) are treated as fast track and are given priority attention.

Hospital case notes and a GP's report may also be required.

The doctor carrying out the examination will advise on whether the claimant is suffering from a prescribed disease, and if so whether there has been a resultant loss of faculty, and the level of any disablement and how long it is expected to last. The doctor will also advise on the date of onset of the disease, that is the date on which the claimant first suffered a loss of faculty from the disease. (*SI 1985 No 967, Reg 6(2)(b).*)

In a claim for occupational deafness, the claimant will have a hearing test to determine whether they have an average hearing loss in both ears of 50 decibels. In claims for chronic bronchitis and emphysema, there may be a requirement for a breathing test. In claims for pneumoconiosis, there will normally be a chest X-ray.

Disablement benefit can be claimed 90 days after the accident or onset of the prescribed disease. In cases where the worker's condition fluctuates, it is important to identify an outbreak as either a fresh outbreak or a recrudescence. If it is a recrudescence, the worker is entitled to benefit immediately. If it is a fresh outbreak, there is no entitlement until a further 90 days have elapsed. There is a rebuttable presumption that, where the outbreak occurs during a period of assessment for that disease, it is a recrudescence, but where it occurs after the end of a period of assessment, it is treated as a new outbreak.

## Accidents and diseases-assessment 3.13

Entitlement to benefit depends on the injury or disease having resulted in a *loss of faculty*. This is an impairment of the proper functioning of part of the body or mind as a result of the accident or disease. Disfigurement is considered to be a loss of faculty on its own behalf, even though there is no loss of physical faculty.

The loss of faculty must result from the industrial accident or prescribed disease. It is for the claimant to prove this on a balance of probabilities. The accident does not have to be the sole cause, but must be an effective cause of the loss of faculty.

*Disablement* is the total of all disabilities which are incurred as a result of the loss of faculty during the period of assessment. Disablement is assessed as a percentage. The assessment is made without reference to the particular circumstances of the claimant other than age, sex and physical and mental condition (*SSCBA 1992, Sch 6 para 1(a)*). The effect of the disablement on the claimant's earning capacity, and his or her personal and social circumstances, are ignored.

Where the disability also results from some pre-existing cause, that cause is not counted, although the interaction between the two causes forms part of the assessment. See below for the rules on other causes of disability, the interaction between them, and successive accidents or diseases.

Disablement benefit consists of a pension which is payable depending on the percentage assessment. There is a threshold of 14 per cent disablement, except for byssinosis, diffuse mesothelioma and pneumoconiosis, for which the threshold is 1 per cent. A disablement of between 14 per cent and 19 per cent is rounded up to 20 per cent, and above 20 per cent disablement is rounded up to the next ten.

In cases of physical damage or mutilation, there are prescribed degrees of disablement contained in *Social Security (General Benefit) Regulations 1982 (SI 1982 No 1408), Sch 2* and reproduced in **Appendix 2**. For example, loss of a leg below the knee is assessed at 50 per cent. These prescribed degrees are used as starting points, and must take into account other disablement and also specific loss to the individual (for example the loss of a right hand is more disabling if the person is right handed than if they are left handed). If there is no prescribed degree of disablement, the level is assessed by reference to past cases and the specific circumstances of the individual.

Where the disablement has more than one cause, there are different rules depending on the circumstances. Where the cause of the disablement is two or more industrial accidents, the claimant is entitled to an assessment based on the aggregate of the disablement, which however may not exceed 100%.

Before 1986, assessments of between 1 and 14 per cent were compensated with a gratuity. The gratuity provisions have now been abolished, but remain relevant in a case where the disablement caused by one of the two industrial accidents has already been compensated by a gratuity. Where that is the case, the disablement covered by the gratuity will not be aggregated with any other accident as it has already been fully compensated.

Where the claimant's condition results from more than one cause, and not all causes are industrial accidents or prescribed diseases, the assessment will be calculated by reference to all the causes and there will then be an offset for any pre-existing condition. The decision maker must assess the pre-existing condition in accordance with the *Social Security (General Benefit) Regulations 1982*, and then offset that amount from the total disablement.

**EXAMPLE**

David has lost vision in one eye as the result of a childhood accident. He then loses vision in the other eye as a result of an industrial accident. His total disablement for loss of both eyes is 100%. Loss of vision in one eye only, the other being normal, is rated at 30% under the General Benefit Regulations. He receives benefit based on a disablement of 100% – 30% = 70%.

In the case of post-occurring conditions, if the disablement is more than 11 per cent, the total disablement from all causes is assessed and a deduction made for subsequent disablements. If the disablement is less than 11 per cent, no account is taken of it.

**EXAMPLE**

Joanne loses part of her middle finger in an industrial accident and is assessed as 9 per cent disabled. Following a later road accident, she loses the hand entirely. Her disablement remains at 9 per cent and the subsequent accident is ignored.

Simon loses two fingers in an industrial accident and is assessed at 20 per cent disabled. In a later road accident, he loses the remaining two fingers. His assessment is now 50%. Loss of two fingers is assessed at 20%, so his award has an offset of 20% for the two fingers lost in a non-industrial accident. Simon is now assessed at 30%. He has crossed the 11% barrier.

Where the total assessment of disablement is 100%, the Secretary of State has a discretion not to reduce the disablement for a non-industrial cause, provided he is satisfied that 100% is a reasonable assessment resulting from the loss of faculty. The rule is aimed at cases where the disablement from the industrial cause is 100% and it would be unjust to reduce it because of additional disablement resulting from a non-industrial cause. (*Social Security (General Benefit) Regulations 1982 (SI 1982 No 1408), Reg 11(6).*)

An assessment is made for a period. This is the period 'during which the claimant has suffered and may be expected to continue to suffer from the relevant loss of faculty' (*SSCBA 1992, s 103(6)*). The assessment may be for life, or for a set period such as one or two years. In any event it terminates on death.

The award will be provisional or final. A provisional award is made where there is doubt as to the likely long term outcome. The claimant is reassessed at the expiry of the period set. An award may be reopened on the basis of unforeseen circumstances when the original award was made. A final assessment is made where the disability is assessed as permanent and is unlikely to change.

Where an award was made, but later events appeared to depart from the prognosis on which the award was based, it was open to the claimant to seek to reopen the case by arguing that there had been 'unforeseen aggravation'. The provisions as to unforeseen aggravation were abolished by the *Social Security Act 1998* and the normal rules as to revisions and supercessions apply (see **Chapter 2**).

### Amount of award 3.14

In the case of pneumoconiosis, byssinosis and diffuse mesothelioma, industrial disablement benefit is awarded if disablement is at least 1%. In other cases, disablement must be at least 14%. Where there is more than one cause, the causes are aggregated. The maximum payable is 100% even if there is disablement amounting to more than 100%. Occupational deafness must be assessed at a minimum of 20%, and is awarded for five years, following which there is a re-examination. If the assessment is less than 20%, occupational deafness cannot be aggregated with any other assessment.

Disablement benefit cannot be paid for the first 15 weeks (90 days excluding Sundays) after the date of the onset of the disease (*SSCBA 1992, s 103(6)*; *Social Security (Claims and Payments) Regulations 1987 (1987 No 1968), Sch 4*). The exceptions are occupational deafness, where payment can be made from the date the claim form is received (*SI 1985 No 967, Reg 6(2)(c)*), and diffuse mesothelioma, where payment can be made from the date when the claimant was first disabled by the disease, but not for more than 3 months before the date of the claim (*SI 1985 No 967, Reg 20(4)(a)*).

### Rates of industrial disablement benefit

| *Disablement percentage* | *Claimant aged under 18 not entitled to an increase in respect of a dependant* | *Other claimants* |
|---|---|---|
| 100% | 71.55 | 116.80 |
| 90% | 64.40 | 105.12 |
| 80% | 57.24 | 93.44 |
| 70% | 50.09 | 81.76 |
| 60% | 42.93 | 70.08 |
| 50% | 35.78 | 58.40 |

| *Disablement percentage* | *Claimant aged under 18 not entitled to an increase in respect of a dependant* | *Other claimants* |
|---|---|---|
| 40% | 28.62 | 46.72 |
| 30% | 21.47 | 35.04 |
| 20% | 14.31 | 23.36 |
| 1–10% | 7.16 | 11.68 |

## Decision making and appeals 3.15

Once the questions above are decided, a decision maker will decide whether the claimant is entitled to benefit, and if so at what level. If the claimant is dissatisfied, he or she can ask for a revision or supercession of the decision, or can appeal to a tribunal. For details of revisions and supercessions, see Chapter Two.

## The effect of an award on other benefits 3.16

Industrial injuries disablement benefit counts in full as income for the income-based benefits (income support, income-based jobseekers allowance, housing benefit and council tax benefit) and for state pension credit, but is ignored as income for tax credits. The same applies to reduced earnings allowance and retirement allowance (see below). Constant attendance allowance is ignored as income altogether. For exceptionally severe disablement allowance, see below. Generally the overlapping benefits rule does not apply to industrial injuries benefits, so it is possible to receive both a disablement pension and incapacity benefit. However, constant attendance allowance overlaps with disability living allowance and with attendance allowance.

## Additions to basic benefit

### *Constant attendance allowance* 3.17

A claimant who is entitled to a 100% disablement pension is entitled to constant attendance allowance if they require constant attendance as a result of the relevant loss of faculty (*SSCBA 1992, s 104(1)*). It is also payable if the claimant has less than 100% disablement under the industrial injuries scheme, where he or she has a total of 100% disablement from that scheme and the War Pension scheme, or the Pneumoconiosis, Byssinosis and Miscellaneous Diseases Benefit scheme, or the Workmen's Compensation Act.

The medical question is the nature and amount of attendance needed, whether the claimant is dependent on attendance for the necessities of life, and whether attendance is needed as a result of the relevant loss of faculty.

It is payable at four rates. The higher rate of £92 a week is paid to someone who is 'so severely disabled as to be entirely, or almost entirely, dependant on (constant) attendance for the necessities of life, and is likely to remain so dependant for a prolonged period and the attendance required is whole-time.'

The lower rate of £46 a week is paid to someone who is 'to a substantial extent dependent on (constant) attendance for the necessities of life and is likely to remain so dependant for a prolonged period'.

There are two intermediate rates. Where 'the extent of such attendance is greater by reason of the beneficiary's exceptionally severe disablement' the lower rate is increased to £69. Where the need for attendance is part-time, the amount payable is such sum as may be reasonable in the circumstances, usually £23 a week.

In cases where disablement benefit is awarded at the 100% rate, a medical opinion is automatically sought as to the possibility of an award of constant attendance allowance. Where constant attendance allowance is not awarded at the same time as industrial disablement benefit, the claimant can claim it on Form BI104. The decision is notified in writing. There is no right of appeal, but the decision can be reconsidered and superseded.

Where a claimant goes into hospital, constant attendance allowance is payable for the first four weeks. It is resumed on leaving. It is payable for up to 6 months when the claimant goes abroad, or for a longer period if the Secretary of State allows.

There are no reported decisions on constant attendance allowance, which is governed by decisions made by the Secretary of State from which there is no appeal. Interpretation of the rules therefore tends to be governed by internal guidelines. For example, 'a prolonged period' is considered to be six months. It is suggested that advisers dealing with disputes in this area and wishing to negotiate with the Department should familiarise themselves with the provisions of disability living allowance and attendance allowance (**Chapter 5**) and employ caselaw from those areas in support of their arguments when appropriate.

### *Exceptionally severe disablement allowance* 3.18

Where someone is entitled to constant attendance allowance and the need for attendance is likely to be permanent, exceptionally severe disablement allowance (not to be confused with the grounds for the intermediate rate of constant attendance allowance above) of £46 a week is payable in addition to the constant attendance allowance (*SSCBA 1992, s 105(1)(a), (b)*.)

No separate claim is required. Entitlement to exceptionally severe disablement allowance is considered automatically at the same time as entitlement to constant attendance allowance. It is a decision of the Secretary of State (*Social Security and Child Support (Decision and Appeals) Regulations 1991 (SI 1991 No 991), Sch 2 para 14(a).*)

Where the claimant is absent abroad, exceptionally severe disablement allowance is payable for six months, or longer if the Secretary of State agrees (*Social Security Benefit (Persons Abroad) Regulations 1975 (SI 1975 No 563), Reg 9(4).*) It continues to be paid during a stay in hospital, even though the constant attendance allowance has stopped. It does not affect non income based benefits, but counts as income for income based benefits and tax credits.

## Benefits now withdrawn

### *Reduced earnings allowance* 3.19

Reduced earnings allowance replaced a similar benefit known as special hardship allowance with effect from 1 October 1986. It is intended to compensate someone who has sustained an industrial injury or contracted a prescribed disease for the consequent loss of all or part of their earning capacity.

Reduced earnings allowance can be paid together with industrial injuries disablement benefit, or (where disablement is assessed at less than 14%) on its own, as long as there is a disablement of at least 1%.

Reduced earnings allowance can now only be claimed in respect of an accident which took place before 1 October 1990 or a prescribed disease which began before 1 October 1990. Where it is claimed in respect of a prescribed disease, the disease must have been on the list of prescribed diseases before 10 October 1994.

In order to claim reduced earnings allowance, the claimant must have an assessment of disablement of at least 1%; must be incapable of following his or her regular occupation as a result of the loss of faculty; must be incapable of work of an equivalent standard which is suitable in their case; and either must be likely to be permanently incapable of following his or her regular occupation (the permanent condition) or must have been incapable at all times since the end of the 90 day period of following his or her regular occupation or suitable alternative employment (the continuous condition).

The question whether work is of an equivalent standard is mainly determined by reference to pay, but the loss of opportunity of promotion is sometimes relevant. Work of an equivalent standard must be employed earners employment, although regular occupation need not be (where the work being carried out at the time of the accident was employed earners employment, but was not the claimant's regular occupation).

An occupation may be treated as a regular occupation if the claimant gave it up because of the effects of an industrial accident or disease, and subsequently received a disablement assessment for it.

A person who has had more than one industrial accident or prescribed disease can claim a reduced earnings allowance is respect of each one.

Claims are made on Form BI 103. The medical service decides whether the claimant is incapable of following his or her regular occupation, and if so, the date from which this takes effect, and whether it is a temporary or a permanent incapacity. They will also decide whether the claimant is capable of alternative remunerative employment. Where the claimant's regular occupation no longer exists, reference is made to changes in the levels of earnings since the occupation ceased.

Reduced earnings allowance is first awarded for a limited period, following which the claimant is invited to renew his or her claim. Once entitlement ceases, the award cannot be reinstated.

The amount payable represents the difference between earnings in the claimant's regular occupation and in his or her alternative occupation. This is subject to a maximum award of 40% of the 100% rate of disablement benefit. Someone who receives more than one reduced earnings allowance award has a maximum entitlement to both reduced earnings allowance and disablement benefit of the 140% rate of disablement benefit.

If the claimant goes abroad, benefit continues to be paid if European Community regulations apply or there is a reciprocal arrangement. If neither of these is the case, benefit is paid for three months provided the stay is temporary and is not for business purposes. If payment ceases, the claimant may maintain an underlying entitlement which will ensure that payment resumes when he or she returns to the UK. Reduced earnings allowance is not payable in prison. It does not affect other non income based benefits, but counts as income for income based benefits and tax credits.

(*SSCBA 1992, s 106* and *Sch* 7.)

### Retirement allowance 3.20

Retirement allowance replaces reduced earnings allowance for people over retirement age. Like reduced earnings allowance, it can only be paid in respect of accidents occurring before 1 October 1990. Claimants must be over retirement age and must have given up regular employment, and must have been entitled to reduced earnings allowance of at least £2 a week. Where the claimant remains in regular employment, even if they are over retirement age, their entitlement to reduced earnings allowance continues until they retire. 'Regular employment' means working under a contract of service for an average of 10 hours a week over a period of five consecutive weeks or more.

No separate claim is necessary. Retirement allowance is paid for life

The amount payable is the lesser of 25% of the weekly rate of reduced earnings allowance to which they were entitled, or 10% of the 100% disablement pension rate. Only one award of retirement allowance can be made even though the claimant was receiving more than one reduced earnings allowance award.

Retirement allowance does not affect other non income based benefits, but counts as income for the income based benefits and for tax credits.

A person living abroad who retains an underlying entitlement to reduced earnings allowance, even though it is not actually in payment, is entitled to retirement allowance when they retire from regular employment. A person who goes abroad after an award of retirement allowance is entitled to continue to receive it for life (*Social Security Benefit (Persons Abroad) Regulations 1975 (SI 1975 No 563), Reg 9(7)*.) Retirement allowance ceases while the claimant is in prison (*Social Security (General Benefit) Regulations 1982 (SI 1982 No1408), Regs 2* and *3*.)

(*SSCBA 1992, s 106* and *Sch 7*.)

## Industrial death benefit 3.21

Industrial death benefit is payable to a widow or widower of someone who dies as a result of their industrial accident or prescribed disease. Death must have occurred before 11 April 1988. The deceased person must have been in employed earners employment.

A widow qualifies if at the date of her husband's death she was living with him, or if he was actually maintaining her to the extent of at least 25p per week, or if she was entitled to such payments under a court order or an agreement, provided she had taken reasonable steps to enforce the order or agreement.

There is an initial rate of benefit for the first 26 weeks after death, followed by either a higher or a lower permanent rate.

A widower is entitled to payment if at the date of his wife's death he was being wholly or mainly maintained by her, or would have been if the accident had not occurred; and if he is permanently incapable of supporting himself.

There may also be entitlement to increases for a child or children, provided the widow or widower is receiving child benefit for the child; a Christmas bonus; and an over 80 addition.

Industrial death benefit is taxable but increases for a child are not. Benefit is not payable if a widow or widower remarries, or during a period of cohabitation, or while s/he is in prison.

There were complicated rules regarding what happened to the benefit during a spell in hospital, which have been amended from 21 May 2003. Anyone who enters hospital for the first time after that date will not have their benefit reduced until they have been in hospital for 52 weeks.

(*SSCBA 1992, s 106* and *Sch* 7.)

## ***Unemployability supplement*** 3.22

Unemployability supplement was an increase of industrial injuries disablement benefit which was abolished on 6 April1987. Those who were receiving it at that date continue to be entitled provided the conditions are fulfilled, and in addition new claims can be made under the Pneumoconiosis, Byssinosis and Miscellaneous Diseases Benefit Scheme and the Workmen's Compensation (Supplementation) Scheme. The supplement can only be paid under those schemes if the claimant is incapable of any work as a result of the loss of faculty for which benefit has been awarded, and likely to remain so.

A claimant can continue to earn an income, provided he or she does not earn more than a prescribed amount.

As well as the basic supplement, the claimant can also receive allowances for dependants, an age of onset allowance, and an age addition. An allowance for a dependant is reduced by any amount paid for a dependant with unemployability supplement with a war pension, or by any guardians allowance.

The age of onset allowance is similar to the age addition to incapacity benefit, with which it overlaps. The age addition is payable where the claimant is over 80 and not receiving the addition with any other benefit.

Normally the supplement is awarded for a period between 6 months and 2 years. It overlaps with incapacity benefit, carers allowance, retirement pension, severe disablement allowance, and bereavement benefits.

(*SSCBA 1992, s 106* and *Sch* 7.)

### ***Hospital Treatment Allowance*** 3.23

This benefit was paid to encourage those injured at work to seek in-patient treatment in hospital. It provided for the pension payable to be increased to 100 per cent while the claimant was undergoing treatment in hospital. It was abolished except for those who began to receive in-patient treatment before 6 April 1987.

(*SSCBA 1992, s 106* and *Sch* 7.)

### ***The Pneumoconiosis, Byssinosis and Miscellaneous Diseases Benefit Scheme*** 3.24

A person who was employed in Great Britain at some time before 5 July 1948 may be able to claim under the above scheme if they were wholly or partially disabled by a specified disease and if their employment was in a job specified for that disease. They must have finished working in the job before 5 July 1948, and must normally live in the United Kingdom, another European country, or a country with whom there is a reciprocal arrangement. There is no right to an allowance if the person has had at any time a right to benefit under the main industrial injuries scheme or the Workmen's Compensation Acts (see below) or if they have received damages through the courts.

### ***The Workmen's Compensation Scheme*** 3.25

There may be an entitlement to benefit under this scheme in respect of work done before 5 July 1948. The Workmen's Compensation Scheme provided for payments to be made to the employee by the employer on a statutory basis, with the right to redress from arbitration and then the courts. The benefit payable is known as Workmen's Compensation (Supplementation), and is only payable to those receiving Workmen's Compensation.

# 4 War Pensions

## Introduction 4.1

Where disability is caused by military service, a war pension may be payable. War pensions were originally paid under the Royal Prerogative, and have only comparatively recently come under legislative control. The relevant legislation is the *Naval, Military and Air Forces etc. (Disablement and Death) Service Pensions Order 1983 (SI 1983 No 883)*, known as the *Service Pensions Order* (*SPO*), which provides that an award may be made 'where the disablement or death of a member of the armed forces is due to service' (*SPO, Art 3*).

War pensions are not payable to serving servicemen and women. War pensions are payable to those who were injured or disabled in the following circumstances:

- Through service in HM Armed Forces, including the Ulster Defence Regiment, the Royal Irish Regiment, the Home Guard, and nursing and auxiliary services.
- In the course of their duties as civilian defence volunteers.
- Civilians who were disabled by enemy action in World War II.
- Merchant seafarers, members of the naval auxiliary services, and coastguards, who were disabled through injury or disease caused in wartime, or through being a prisoner of war.
- Members of the Polish forces under British command in World War II, and members of the Polish Resettlement Forces.

There must be a causal connection between the military service and the death or disablement. The mere fact of the death or disablement having occurred during service is not enough; there is no comparison with the regulation of prescribed diseases, where the contraction of a disease in prescribed employment can lead to a presumption that the employment caused the disease.

*Article 4* of the *SPO* sets out the basic conditions for entitlement. Provided that:

- the claim is made within a period of seven years after the ending of service (for disablement); or
- a claim is made at any time in respect of a death that occurred within that time;

the disablement or death is accepted as due to service, provided:

- in the case of disablement, that the disablement is attributable to service, or existed before service and was aggravated by service; or
- in the case of death, that it was due to or hastened by an injury which was attributable to service, or the aggravation by service of a pre-existing injury.

The onus of proof is on the Secretary of State to adduce evidence which will rebut this causal link. The standard of proof is the criminal standard; the onus is on the Secretary of State to prove beyond a reasonable doubt that the injury was not attributable to, nor aggravated by, service.

Where a serviceman or woman is discharged, or dies, as the result of an injury, and there is no note of that condition in the medical report which was made on him or her at the start of service, *Article 4(3)* of the *SPO* contains a 'compelling presumption' that the pension will be awarded unless it is shown beyond reasonable doubt that the injury was not attributable to, or aggravated by, service.

Where a claim for disablement is brought, or where death occurs, more than seven years after termination of service, the onus of proof shifts to the serviceman or woman. In the case of a death, it must be certified that the death was due to or substantially hastened by an injury attributable to or aggravated by service. *Article 5, para 5(2)* of the *SPO* provides that where there is a reasonable doubt on the evidence whether the conditions set out in the article are fulfilled, the benefit of the doubt should be given to the claimant.

War pensions are determined by reference to the extent of the person's disablement, including physical or mental injury or damage, or the loss of physical or mental capacity *(SPO, Sch 4 item 22)*. Disablement is ascertained by reference to the conditions for which a person claims, namely wounds, injury or disease.

No payment is made for deafness where disablement is assessed at less than 20%. Since 1996, pensions are no longer increased as a result of increasing overall hearing loss which comes with age. Awards can no longer be made for injury resulting from the use of tobacco or the consumption of alcohol, unless as a consequence of a mental condition resulting in at least a 50% disablement.

## Attributable to or aggravated by service 4.2

The question whether an injury is attributable to service is a question for the adjudicating authorities in each case, and the fact that a previous decision held that a particular injury or disease was not attributable to service does not prevent the authorities finding in favour of the serviceman or woman in a later case. For example, in *XY v Minister of Pensions [1947] 2 All ER 501*, a serviceman committed suicide after his fiancée had written to him calling off their engagement. Mr Justice Denning, as he then was, the nominated judge hearing appeals (see below), held that the tribunal was right not to attribute the death to service. On the other hand, in a case where suicide followed pain and anxiety which resulted from a disability which was itself attributable to service, Mr Justice Edmund Davies, as he then was, held that death was attributable to service. He emphasised that each case should be decided on its own facts.

Where the serviceman or woman has a predisposition to a particular type of illness (commonly a mental condition such as neurosis), the courts have taken a view which is similar to the principles established in industrial injuries cases (see **Chapter 3**) to the effect that, where service has brought on a condition which did not exist before, it is attributable to service. Only if the claimant's pre-existing condition amounted to the condition itself, including in a latent form, can it be said merely to have been aggravated by service.

Where a claimant is killed or injured while on leave, or temporarily away from camp, the indication from the then Ministry of Pensions in a White Paper in 1943 was to the effect that accidents sustained in a soldier's spare time, or while travelling to and from home for short periods of leave, or when travelling between camp and private accommodation where he or she was allowed to live outside the camp, would be considered to be attributable to duty *(Changes in War Pensions, Cmd 6459)*. However, the nominated judge has pointed out that each case falls to be decided on its own facts in any event.

Where an injury is found not to be attributable to service, it may be held to be aggravated by service. Where the condition is attributable to service, a pension is paid for as long as the disability continues; where it is merely aggravated by service, the pension is payable only for as long as the disablement is due to an injury which 'has been and remains aggravated' by service. (*SPO, Art 4(1)(a)(ii)*). In other words, the pension ends when the aggravating factors end, even though the disability continues. Where a claim is made under *Article 4*, it may be in respect of a currently existing aggravation, or one which has passed (*Shipp v Minister of Pensions [1946] KB 386*); where the claim is made under *Article 5*, however (more than seven years after the end of service), the aggravation must be still subsisting for the claim to succeed (*Ansell v Minister of Pensions (1948) 2 WPAR 2237*).

Once an award has terminated on the ground that the aggravating condition no longer applies, it cannot be revived. The nominated judge has therefore held that the Secretary of State and the tribunal should be reluctant to rule that the aggravating factors have ended unless the evidence is clear (*Sanders v Minister of Pensions (1948) 4 WPAR 31*).

*SPO, Art 6* provides that the Secretary of State may withhold, cancel or reduce an award where the injury or death 'was caused, or contributed to, by the serious negligence or misconduct' of the claimant.

## Benefits payable 4.3

Basic benefit is paid according to a percentage calculation of disability. The principles involved in the calculation are in most respects identical with those applying to the industrial injuries scheme. Total disablement is assessed at 100%. *SPO, Sch 1 parts III and V* sets out assessments for certain injuries in a similar way to those for industrial injuries.

For those assessed as 20% or more disabled, a pension is payable, while for those whose disability is less than 20%, a gratuity is payable.

Certain supplementary allowances are also payable. These are as follows.

- *Allowance for a lowered standard of occupation*. This is broadly similar to the reduced earnings allowance formerly paid with industrial injuries benefits. It is available where disablement makes the claimant permanently unable to do their regular occupation or work of a similar standard. They must be entitled to a war pension of 40% and be under 65 when making the claim. The allowance combined with the pension may not exceed the 100% disablement rate.
- *Age allowance*. This is payable to someone aged 65 or over with a pension of 40% or more. It is payable at four different rates depending on the assessment of disablement – 40 to 50 per cent, 50 to 70 per cent, 70 to 90 per cent, and 90 to 100 per cent.
- *Clothing allowance*. This is available to someone who gets a war pension at the rate of 20% or higher and who is an amputee, or whose clothes wear out quickly because of the conditions for which the pension is paid.
- *Comforts allowance* is payable to those getting constant attendance allowance and either unemployability supplement or a 100% basic award. A lower rate is paid to those receiving either constant attendance allowance or unemployability supplement.
- *Constant attendance allowance* is payable to those in receipt of a pension of 80% or more and who need personal help as a result of the conditions. There are four rates of payment.
- *Exceptionally severe disablement allowance*. This is paid in addition to either of the two highest rates of constant attendance allowance where either is payable and is likely to remain payable. There is apparently no requirement that the claimant receive a 100% basic award.

- *Invalidity allowance* is payable to someone who is under 60 and who receives an unemployability supplement. It is similar to the age related allowance payable with incapacity benefit.
- *Mobility supplement* is payable to someone with at least a 40% assessment who is unable or almost unable to walk because of their conditions.
- *Severe disablement occupational allowance* is payable where someone who gets constant attendance allowance also has a job. In the year 2000 just 13 such awards were in payment.
- *Unemployability supplement* is payable where the claimant has an assessment of at least 60%, is under 65 when they claim, and cannot work because of the seriousness of their condition. Increases may also be paid for one adult dependant and any child dependants.

## Awards for death 4.4

A person may be entitled to a war widow's or widower's pension if any of the following applies:

- their spouse's death was due to service in the Armed Forces;
- their spouse was in the merchant navy or the naval auxiliary services, or a coastguard, and their death was due to injury or disease sustained during wartime or because they were a prisoner of war;
- their spouse's death was a result of their service in the Polish forces under British command during the 1939–45 war, or in the Polish Resettlement Forces;
- their spouse was getting constant attendance allowance or unemployability supplement at their death, or, though eligible for unemployability supplement, was in fact receiving the lowered standard of occupation allowance instead, or would have been receiving constant attendance allowance if they had not been in hospital, or would have been entitled for 26 weeks had they claimed; or
- their spouse had received an assessment of 80% and was getting unemployability supplement.

In the latter two cases, a temporary allowance is paid for 26 weeks, and then a pension or gratuity is paid. A person who is eligible for the unemployability supplement may choose instead to claim the lowered standard of occupation allowance because it does not overlap with social security benefits.

Since April 2002 widowers and widows have been treated in the same way and both are entitled to the range of benefits.

If death occurs not more than seven years after the end of service, it is accepted as due to service, provided that it was 'due to or hastened by either an injury attributable to service, or the aggravation by service of an injury which existed before or arose during service.' (*SPO, Art 4(1)(b)*). If the death occurs more than seven years after service ends, benefit is payable if it is certified that death was due to, or substantially hastened by, an injury attributable to, or aggravated by, service (*SPO, Art 5(1)(b)*).

War widow's and widower's pensions are payable to cohabitees as well as to spouses, provided the cohabitee looked after the pensioner's children.

A person who claims a war widow's or widower's pension will not be entitled at the same time to a social security bereavement benefit.

There are two rates of war widows/widowers pensions. The higher rate is payable to:

- the widow or widower of an officer above the rank of Major, or its equivalents in the other services;
- someone aged 40 or over;
- someone under 40 and getting an allowance for a child; or
- someone under 40 who cannot support themselves financially.

The lower rate is payable to anyone else until they reach 40, when they become entitled to the higher rate.

Allowances are also payable for children, and a rent allowance is paid where the household includes a child.

If the deceased spouse was discharged from the forces on or before 31 March 1973, a supplementary pension is payable.

Older widows and widowers get age allowances at 65, 70 and 80. A temporary allowance is paid if the spouse was getting constant attendance allowance or unemployability supplement at their death. This is paid for the first 26 weeks after death, following which the widow or widower receives a war widows or widowers pension.

Remarriage or cohabitation affects entitlement. Benefit for the widow or widower is effectively suspended, although allowances for children can sometimes continue. Payment resumes if the war widow or widower again becomes widowed, or is divorced, or ceases to cohabit. This is a different rule from that covering social security bereavement benefits, where the benefit is lost altogether on remarriage.

The Secretary of State also has power to defray funeral expenses. These are payable where death is due to military service, and either constant attendance allowance was being paid (or would have been paid if the person was not in hospital when they died); or there is an assessment of 80% or more and an unemployability supplement is in payment at the time of death; or the person died while they were receiving hospital treatment for a disablement for which they received a war disablement pension. Claims must be made within three months of the funeral.

The War Widows Association exists to improve the conditions of war widows and their dependants in Great Britain. They can be contacted c/o 48 Pall Mall, London SW1Y 3JY, by phoning 0870 2411 305, or by visiting the website at www.warwidowsassociation.org.uk. The association deals with war widowers as well as war widows.

## Making a claim 4.5

Claims are made on prescribed forms, obtainable from the Veterans Agency whose address is Norcross, Blackpool FY5 3WP (tel 0800 169 2277) or through their website (http://www.veteransagency.mod.uk/). In the case of a claim for a war disablement pension, the claimant's service records are obtained and medical evidence is obtained where necessary, including reports from doctors or hospitals, and a hearing test in appropriate cases. If necessary a medical examination is arranged. A decision is then taken based on the evidence supplied and obtained. The Veterans Agency aims to clear cases within an average of 82 working days. War widows and widowers pension cases follow a similar procedure but are expected to be cleared in an average of 34 days.

The obtaining of medical evidence involves the Veterans Agency Medical Services. They do not themselves make decisions, but supply evidence and information to enable a decision to be made. The examining doctor will diagnose the condition which causes the disablement, and will also certify where appropriate that the condition is attributable to service. If the condition was not caused by service, but was aggravated by it, the examining doctor will so certify, provided that the military service is still making the condition worse at the time of the claim.

If the condition is accepted as a qualifying condition, the examining doctor will make an assessment of the appropriate percentage by comparing the claimant with a healthy individual of the same age and sex. If the condition is not presently causing a problem, the assessment will be 0%. If there is more than one condition a combined assessment is made. The combined assessment cannot exceed 100%.

Certain disablements have assessments laid down in regulations (for example, amputation cases). These assessments are known as scheduled assessments.

Payment is made through a bank account or through an account at the Post Office.

The Secretary of State may order that a pension be withheld or forfeited on the ground that the claimant is serving a term of imprisonment or detention, or is deported or required to leave the UK (*SPO, Art 62*). If the claimant unreasonably refuses to undergo medical, surgical or rehabilitative treatment, the Secretary of State may reduce the pension by not more than half (*SPO, Art 63*).

An award is payable from the date of termination of service, or the date of death, or the date of claim, whichever is the later. There is limited provision for backdating an award. Where a claim is made within three months of the date of termination of service or the date of death, the award is backdated to the earlier date. Where the Secretary of State is satisfied that the claimant was incapable of pursuing a claim because of illness or disability, the claim can be backdated by up to three years.

Where medical evidence has developed, or where additional evidence becomes available, or where the decision is revised following a test case, the award may be backdated for up to three years. If an award is made following a successful appeal to the High Court, payment can be made for a period not exceeding six years back to the date of the application for permission to appeal. Finally, in the case of administrative error by the authorities, which continues to be the dominant reason for the delay, backdating is unlimited (*SPO, Sch 3*).

## Overlapping provisions **4.6**

*SPO, Art 55* entitles the Secretary of State to take into account any other compensation which is, or which may be, awarded to a claimant, and to reduce any pension or gratuity accordingly. The purpose is to prevent over-compensation from public funds, or from a combination of public funds and a damages award. 'Compensation' is defined as including any periodical or lump sum payment in respect of death or disability for which provision is made under any form of legislation, or damages awarded at common law.

## Appeals **4.7**

There is a right of appeal against a decision. Appeals are heard by the Pensions Appeal Tribunal (PAT). The Royal British Legion and the Royal Air Forces Association can help and represent at appeals. Contact details are as follows.

The Royal British Legion
48 Pall Mall
London
SW1Y 5JY
Tel: 0207 973 7200
Website: www.britishlegion.org.uk

The Royal British Legion Scotland
The Earl Haig Fund Scotland and the Officers' Association Scotland
New Haig House
Logie Green Road
Edinburgh
EH7 4HR
Tel: 0131 557 2782
Fax: 0131 557 5819
Website: www.rblscotland.org.uk

The Royal Air Forces Association
43 Grove Park Road
London
W4 3RX.
Tel: 0208 994 8504
Fax: 0208 742 1927
Website: www.rafa.org.uk

Issues which may be addressed by the PAT include the following:

- Entitlements to benefit. Here the main question is whether the disablement or death is the result of service in the armed forces.
- Assessment of pension. In these cases, the tribunal assess the percentage disablement appropriate in a particular case.
- Supplementary Allowance. In these cases the tribunal assesses whether the conditions for a Supplementary Allowance have been met.

Appeals should be made by using the appeal form sent by the War Pensions Agency. The form is then returned to the War Pensions Agency, who will notify the Pensions Appeal Officer of the appeal.

The time limit for appeals is three months for an interim decision and six months for any other type of decision. Time runs from the date of the letter notifying the decision. An appeal can be made out of time where there has been death or serious illness of the claimant or their partner or dependants, or where the Secretary of State has failed to notify the claimant about the appeal, or where normal postal services are disrupted, or where there are exceptional circumstances applying to the claimant. It is a matter for the PAT whether they will accept a late appeal. In no case can an appeal be made more than 15 months (for an interim assessment) or 18 months (for any other assessment) after the decision.

A Statement of Case is prepared and the appellant is invited to comment. The Statement of Case will include documents such as the appellant's claim form and appeal form, a note of the reasons for the decision which has been taken, medical records both before and after service, copies of any supporting documents submitted by the appellant and a medical opinion about the disablement. The appellant is invited to send an answer, including any additional evidence which he or she may wish to adduce.

If the matter is not resolved, a hearing is arranged before the PAT. The claimant may attend the appeal, and may be represented if he or she so chooses. The appellant is entitled to call witnesses in support of their case. The tribunal has the power to pay witness expenses. Appellants are asked to notify the pensions appeal office at least seven days in advance if a medical witness will be attending.

The appellant will usually receive a Notice of Hearing from the Pensions Appeal Office at least ten days before the date fixed for the Hearing. The hearing will take place in London or in another city within the UK. An appellant who is unable to attend the hearing should notify the Pensions Appeal Office as soon as possible.

The appeal hearing is informal and is in the style of similar tribunals. The members of the tribunal will discuss their decision after the conclusion of the hearing, and will notify the appellant of the outcome as soon as possible. The appellant will in any event by notified of the decision in writing.

An appellant may withdraw an appeal at any time. If an appellant does not respond to correspondence from the Pensions Appeal Office, the matter may be placed on the 'deferred list' for a period of twelve months. If no further action is taken, the appeal may then be struck out.

With permission the claimant may make a further appeal to the High Court against the decision of the tribunal. Permission can be granted at the hearing of the appeal, or in response to a request in writing made within six weeks of the decision. The right of appeal is confined to a point of law which must be set out in the notice applying for permission to appeal. If permission is refused by the tribunal, the appellant may apply directly to the High Court. A High Court judge is nominated to hear appeals.

The tribunal will pay travelling and other expenses for a tribunal. If necessary a railway warrant can be sent in advance, both for the claimant and any travelling companion. Other travelling expenses may be reimbursed in cash on the day of the hearing.

The Pensions Appeal Office is at 48/49 Chancery Lane, London, WC2A 1JF (Telephone: 020 7947 7032). In Scotland the office is at 20 Walker Street, Edinburgh, EH3 7HS (Telephone: 0131 220 1404) and in Northern Ireland at 6th Floor, Lancashire House, 5 Linen Hall Street, Belfast, BT2 8AA (Telephone: 028 9033 2344). The War Pensions Agency is at Norcross, Blackpool, FY5 3WP (Telephone: 0800 169 2277).

## Medical treatment and care for war pensioners

### *Appliances* 4.8

Someone who has been prescribed an aid or appliance for their condition will get it free from either their local hospital or from their local authority social services department.

Someone who needs an artificial limb is sent to a limb-fitting centre by the hospital. The Veterans Agency will only pay for artificial limbs in certain defined circumstances. The National Health Service is responsible for supplying hearing aids to war pensioners.

### *Convalescence* 4.9

Where the accepted conditions prevent the pensioner from taking a normal holiday in a hotel or boarding house with their usual carer, convalescent holidays can be arranged. These normally consist of no more than two 2-week breaks in a period of twelve months.

### *Home nursing equipment* 4.10

Home nursing equipment is normally the responsibility of the Health Authority. The Veterans Agency will only pay for necessary, medically approved items if the pensioner would otherwise have to pay themselves.

### *Hospital travelling expenses* 4.11

The Veterans Agency can pay travel expenses to and from hospital for treatment for accepted conditions.

### *House adaptation grants* 4.12

Where it is necessary to adapt the pensioner's home as a result of the accepted condition, there is a one off grant of up to £750 available.

### Treatment allowance 4.13

Where a war pension is awarded, and the pensioner receives medical, surgical or rehabilitative treatment in a hospital or at home, treatment allowance consisting of the 100% war pension rate is payable provided the treatment will help the pensioner to get better, where they lose some of their earnings as the result of the treatment, and where it is the treatment and not the conditions that stops them working for eight days or more.

Where the treatment stops the pensioner working for less than eight days but they still lose money as a result of their inability to work, part time treatment allowance is paid in addition to the basic pension. There is a daily maximum, and it is also limited to the actual loss incurred.

### Free prescriptions 4.14

Where the pensioner is under 65, they are normally issued with a prescription exemption certificate. Where they are over 65, they will be entitled to free prescriptions in any case.

### Priority treatment 4.15

A war pensioner normally gets priority in NHS hospitals or NHS Trust hospitals if they need treatment for the disablement for which the pension is paid. This is subject to the needs of emergency cases in the hospital.

### Private treatment 4.16

Private treatment is only payable where the need cannot be met under the NHS.

### Skilled nursing care 4.17

Long term nursing care may be available, but only if the pensioner has not been assessed for community care services. The care is that obtainable from trained nursing staff in a nursing home.

# 5 Benefits for Disability

## Disability living allowance 5.1

Disability living allowance is a non-contributory, non-income based benefit for those who need care or supervision, or who have difficulties with mobility. It must be claimed before the claimant reaches 65. It is not affected by the claimant's income or by capital, and is tax-free. There are five 'components' for disability living allowance, three resulting from a person's care needs and two resulting from their mobility needs.

The five components are as follows:

- the higher care component is payable where the claimant needs attention or supervision both by day and at night;
- the middle care component is payable where the claimant needs attention or supervision either by day or at night;
- the lower care component is payable where the claimant needs help with bodily functions for a significant portion (around an hour) of the (24-hour) day, or help with preparing a cooked meal;
- the higher mobility component is payable where because of a physical disability the claimant is unable or virtually unable to walk; or where because of a combination of blindness and deafness the claimant is unable to walk out of doors without help from another person; or where the claimant is unable to walk because of severe behavioural problems which qualify for the higher rate care component;
- the lower mobility component is payable where the claimant can walk, but needs help and guidance in getting around.

The qualifying conditions are as follows.

### *Age* 5.2

The claimant must claim before their 65th birthday. The benefit can be paid after that age, but must be claimed before it. (*SSCBA 1992, s 75*.)

For the care components, the claimant must be aged at least three months (because of the qualifying condition of a three month qualifying period) unless the child is terminally ill (in which case there is no qualifying period). For the higher mobility component, the child must be aged at least three, and for the lower mobility component must be aged at least five (*SSCBA 1992, s 73(1A)*).

## Residence 5.3

The claimant must be ordinarily resident in Great Britain (*Social Security (Disability Living Allowance) Regulations 1991 (SI 1991 No 2890), Reg 2(1)*). At the time of making the claim, the claimant must also be present in Great Britain, and have been in the United Kingdom, the Isle of Man, Jersey or Guernsey for at least 26 weeks in the last 12 months. Time spent in another country of the EEA may count towards the 26 week period.

Certain people can qualify even though they do not fulfil the above conditions, namely those who:

- have been serving abroad in the forces (including their families);
- are mariners and aircrew working abroad;
- are working on the UK sector of the continental shelf;
- are abroad temporarily (during the first six months of their absence);
- are temporarily abroad for some form of medical treatment.

(*SI 1991 No 2890, Reg 2(2)*.)

The 26 week rule does not apply to those who are terminally ill (who can claim at once) nor to those who receive earnings on which they do not pay UK tax, who must have been in Great Britain for three out of the last four years before they started getting those earnings. For a child under 6 months old, the qualifying period is reduced to 13 weeks.

## Immigration status 5.4

A person who is subject to immigration control may not claim (*Immigration and Asylum Act 1999, s 115*). People who are European Economic Area nationals, or members of the family of an EEA national, may claim, as may:

- nationals of Algeria, Morocco, Slovenia, Tunisia or Turkey who are lawfully working here, or members of their families;
- people who are nationals of a state which has a reciprocal agreement with the UK;
- refugees;
- people who have been given exceptional leave to enter and remain in the UK; and

- people who have been given indefinite leave to remain, subject to a formal sponsorship undertaking.

## Qualifying period 5.5

In order to claim disability living allowance, the claimant must have satisfied the relevant qualifying condition below for a period of at least three months immediately preceding the claim. He or she must also be likely to continue to satisfy it or them for a further period of six months (*SSCBA 1992, s 72(2)(a), (b)*; *s 73(9)(a), (b)*).

## Qualifying conditions – care components 5.6

Details of the benefit are found in *SSCBA 1992, s 72(1)*, as follows:

> 'Subject to the provisions of this Act, a person shall be entitled to the care component of a disability living allowance for any period throughout which:
>
> a) he is so severely disabled physically or mentally that:
>
> i) he requires in connection with his bodily functions attention from another person for a significant period of the day (whether during a single period or a number of periods); or
>
> ii) he cannot prepare a cooked main meal for himself if he has the ingredients; or
>
> b) he is so severely disabled physically or mentally that, by day, he requires from another person:
>
> i) frequent attention throughout the day in connection with his bodily functions; or
>
> ii) continual supervision throughout the day in order to avoid substantial danger to himself or others; or
>
> c) he is so severely disabled physically or mentally that, at night:
>
> i) he requires from another person prolonged or repeated attention in connection with his bodily functions; or
>
> ii) in order to avoid substantial danger to himself or others he requires another person to be awake for a prolonged period or at frequent intervals for the purpose of watching over him.'

The Act thus provides for three care components. The lower care component is payable to a person who satisfies the conditions at *section 72(1)(a)* above. The middle rate care component is payable to a person who satisfies one or both conditions in either *section 72(1)(b)* or *section 72 (1)(c),* but not in both of them – that is, they require attention by day or at night, but not both. The higher rate care component is payable to a person who satisfies one or both of the conditions in both *sections 72 (1)(b)* and *72 (1)(c)* – that is, they require attention both by day and at night.

It follows from the wording above that a claim does not depend on whether the claimant lives alone or on whether the help required is actually being provided. The attention must have been needed for at least three months, and the need for it must be expected to continue for at least six months.

The claimant must be 'severely disabled physically or mentally'. This means that there must be a condition which can be medically defined, even though there has been no specific diagnosis; there is no requirement for a separate finding of 'severe disablement'.

### *Requiring attention* **5.7**

The attention which is required to comply with the sub-section does not have to be medically required. It is sufficient if it is 'reasonably' required. In the case of *Secretary of State for Social Security v Fairey [1997] 1 WLR 799,* the claimant was a profoundly deaf young woman whose first language was not English. She found communication with people who did not know sign language difficult. One of the arguments mounted against her entitlement to the benefit was that attention in connection with the bodily function of hearing and communication was not 'required', because for adults, communication was more a matter of choice than necessity.

This argument was rejected by the House of Lords. Lord Slynn said:

> '. . . on the question of principle I reject the contention that the relevant attention must be essential or necessary for life and that attention must not be taken into account if it is merely desirable. The test, in my view, is whether the attention is reasonably required to enable the severely disabled person as far as reasonably possible to live a normal life.
>
> He is not to be confined to doing only the things which totally deaf (or blind) people can do and provided with only such attention as keeps him alive in such a community . . . In my opinion the yardstick of a normal life is important; it is a better approach than adopting the test as to whether than something is essential or desirable'.

Note once more that the test is whether the attention is required, not whether it is provided. It is not essential that frequent attention is being provided to the claimant throughout the day, nor indeed that it be provided on every day. The test is whether the attention is required. It follows from this that the test of frequency (see below) may be met where the only care and attention actually provided to the disabled person is at either end of the day, or morning or evening, because that suits the convenience of the carer; but there is unmet need at other times.

What is required is attention 'in connection with . . . bodily functions'. Attention has been held to indicate something more than personal service, such as something which involves care, consideration and vigilance for the person being attended (Lord Justice Dunn in *Packer*, below). Service need not involve physical contact, but could include (for example) spoken guidance for a blind person, or reassurance for someone who is mentally ill. The attention must be carried out in the presence of the disabled person; see *Cockburn* (below), and also (for disability living allowance) the statutory provisions of the *Social Security (Disability Living Allowance) Regulations 1991 (SI 1991 No 2890), Reg 10C*, and the (*Social Security (Attendance Allowance) Regulations 1991 (SI 1991 No 2740), Reg 8BA* for attendance allowance.

### *Bodily functions* **5.8**

The classic definition of 'bodily functions' is that of Lord Denning in the case of *R v National Insurance Commissioner ex parte Secretary of State for Social Services [1981] 1WLR 1017 (the Packer Case)* in the Court of Appeal. Lord Denning held that the term 'bodily functions' included:

> 'bathing, hearing, seeing, eating, drinking, sitting, sleeping, getting in or out of bed, dressing, undressing, eliminating waste products and the like'.

These are activities which a ordinary fit person who does not have a disability can do for themselves. The term 'bodily functions' is intended to exclude domestic duties such as shopping or cooking.

The attention must be 'in connection with' the bodily functions. The case of *Cockburn v Secretary of State of Social Security [1997] WLR 799* (which was heard together with the *Fairey* case – see above) concerned a lady who was incontinent and had arthritis. Her incontinence generated extra laundry which she was unable to do herself because of the arthritis. The laundry was therefore done by her daughter who collected it, took it home and washed it, and returned it.

The issue for the House of Lords was whether the actions of Mrs Cockburn's daughter amounted to 'attention in connection with bodily functions'. The House of Lords held that it did not. The assistance with laundry amounted to a domestic duty.

This is not to say that activities such as laundering can never constitute attention in connection with bodily functions. It would be possible for them to do so where they formed part of a continuing operation. For example, Lord Mustill in the House of Lords proposed the following line of reasoning:

- The emptying of the bladder, whether voluntary or involuntary, is a bodily function.
- Accompanying a disabled person to or from the toilet due to their incontinence constitutes attention in connection with a bodily function.
- Changing the clothes or bedclothes of a person who cannot get to the toilet in time constitutes attention in connection with a bodily function.
- If the carer also strips the disabled person's bed and stays to rinse the linen and hang it up to dry, that also qualifies as attention in connection with a bodily function.
- Because the process of laundering forms part of the continuous operation of dealing with the bodily function, it is acceptable to say that it satisfies the test of being in connection with the bodily function. Where it fails, however, is on the word 'attention'. It is not possible to escape the conclusion that for an activity to qualify, it must be performed whilst the other person is in attendance on the disabled person, that is in his or her actual presence. It may be noted that in the *Packer* case (see above), the Court of Appeal had also expressed the view that attention would have to be in the presence of the disabled person.

## *Continual supervision* **5.9**

The term 'continual supervision' has also been subjected to widespread interpretation. The Commissioner in *R(A) 6/72* held that:

> 'supervision denotes a more passive concept than attention, such as being in the same room with a disabled person so as to be prepared to intervene if necessary, but not actually intervening save in emergencies'.

A Tribunal of Commissioners has held that there are four elements to this route to qualification. Firstly, the claimant's medical condition must be such as to give rise to substantial danger to the claimant or someone else. Secondly, the substantial danger must not be too remote a possibility. Thirdly, supervision by a third party must be necessary to effect a real reduction in the risk of harm, and fourthly that supervision must be continual *(R(A) 1/83)*.

The case of *Moran v Secretary of State for Social Services (1987)* Court of Appeal (reported as an appendix to *R(A) 1/88*) confirms that supervision may be precautionary and anticipatory. A person who stands by to intervene in the event of danger can be said to be exercising supervision between periods during which danger arises. The likely frequency of a dangerous event is immaterial to the question of whether the supervision itself is continual, so long as the risk of substantial danger arising is not to remote a possibility.

The requirement for the night condition that a person be awake at frequent intervals has been interpreted by the NI Commissioner as requiring such intervals to be 'more than twice at least' (*R 2/99 (DLA)*, obiter).

### *The lower care component* **5.10**

For those who are unable to qualify for either the middle or higher rate care component, there is the possibility of qualifying for the lower component. For a claim to be successful, attention in connection with the bodily functions will have to be for a significant portion of the day. A day in this context means 24 hours. A government spokesperson in the House of Lords (Hansard, 25 March 1991 col. 884) said that the term 'significant portion of the day' could amount to 'an hour or thereabouts.' In *CGLA 58/93 (*94/94)* the Commissioner dismissed the argument that the question of significance could be determined by reference to the quality or nature of the care provided. The Commission held that the wording of the provision was such that the only question at issue the amount of care provided, rather than its quality. The Commissioner said that he would not dissent from the view that the term could be considered as a minimum of one hour.

The alternative route to the lower care component is by way of the cooking test. In *Moyna v Secretary of State [2002] EWCA Civ 408*, the Court of Appeal took the view that a regular pattern of inability to cook on at least one day a week was sufficient to meet the test, but the House of Lords disagreed and reinstated the decision of the appeal tribunal that the apellant, who could prepare a cooked main meal on most of the days of the week, did not qualify on this ground.

It will be observed that the route to qualification for disability living allowance is to demonstrate that the claimant requires assistance with the tasks of everyday life. The actual medical diagnosis is irrelevant, as is the question of whether the disability should be regarded as mental or physical. Indeed, there is no strict necessity for a medical diagnosis at all. The issue for the decision maker is rather the effects of the claimant's disabilities.

## Rules for special groups

### *Children and young people* **5.11**

A person who is under the age of sixteen is not eligible for an award under *SSCBA 1992, s 72(1)(a)(ii)* (the cooking test). There is otherwise no lower age limit on qualification for the benefit, but for a person under the age of sixteen to qualify, they must show that their attention or supervision requirements are either 'substantially in excess of the normal requirements of persons of his age' or of 'such description which younger persons in normal physical and mental health may also have but which a person of his age and in normal physical and mental health would not have'.

### *People receiving renal dialysis* 5.12

A person who is receiving renal dialysis on two or more occasions a week, who normally requires attendance or supervision from another person during that time, is entitled to the middle rate care component, provided that, if the claimant undergoes dialysis at an NHS hospital, supervision is not provided by the staff of that hospital (*SSCBA 1992, s 72(7)*; *Social Security (Disability Living Allowance) Regulations 1991 (SI 1991 No 2890), Reg 7*).

### *People who are terminally ill* 5.13

Special rules provide for people whose condition may be described as a 'terminal illness.' *Section 66 (2)* of the *SSCBA 1992* provides 'a person is terminally ill at any time if at that time he suffers from a progressive disease and his death in consequence of that disease can reasonably be expected within 6 months.' Where this applies, the person concerned is treated as being able automatically to satisfy *section 72 (1)(b)* and *section 72 (1)(c)*, which means that they qualify for the higher rate care component, which is normally awarded for life *(SSCBA 1992, s 72(5))*. The claiming process is also made simpler for a person to whom this applies. There is no need to fulfil the 13 week qualifying period. A claim can be made on behalf of a person with a terminal illness without their knowledge or consent.

## ***Qualifying conditions – mobility components*** 5.14

The higher rate of the mobility component is governed by *section 73* of the *Social Security Contributions and Benefits Act 1992*. *Section 73(1)* provides that the higher mobility component is payable to anyone over the age of three in any of the following circumstances:

(*a*) The person is either unable or virtually unable to walk as the result of a physical disablement, or has no legs or feet, whether from birth or through amputation.

(*b*) The person is both blind and deaf, and satisfies other prescribed conditions.

(*c*) The person is severely mentally impaired, has severe behavioural problems, and qualifies for the higher rate care component.

(*d*) The effort of walking would endanger their life or cause deterioration to their health.

The mobility component is only payable provided that the claimant is able to benefit from enhanced facilities for locomotion (*section 73(8)*.) There is a qualifying period of three months, and the person must expect to remain in the same condition for a further six months (*section 73(9)(a), (b)*). Persons suffering from terminal illness are exempt from the time limits (*section 73(12)*).

Additional criteria are laid down in subsidiary legislation. *Regulation 12* of the *Social Security (Disability Living Allowance) Regulations 1991 (SI 1991 No 2890)* provides for circumstances in which a person is to be taken as being unable or virtually unable to walk, specifies the prescribed conditions for those who are blind and deaf, and provides for the definition of 'severely mentally impaired' and 'severe behavioural problems.' No account is taken of the personal circumstances of the claimant (for example, where they live) in determining entitlement.

*Sub-paragraph (1)* of *Regulation 12* provides that a person will be treated as being unable or virtually unable to walk only if their physical condition as a whole is such that, without having regard to circumstances peculiar to them as to the place of residence or the place of, of the nature of, their employment:

- they are unable to walk; or
- their ability to walk out of doors is so limited as regards the distance over which or the speed at which or the length of time for which or the manner in which they can make progress on foot without severe discomfort, that they are virtually unable to walk; or
- the exertion required to walk would constitute a danger to life or be likely to lead to a serious deterioration in health.

The sub-paragraph further provides that a double amputee, or a person in similar circumstances, is also to be regarded as unable or virtually unable to walk.

Walking where severe discomfort is caused is disregarded in determining the claimant's ability to walk. However, the discomfort must be as a result of walking, and not because of some extraneous cause. Thus a claimant with porphyria, who could walk but who suffered severe discomfort by being exposed to daylight, was not entitled to claim the mobility component (*Hewitt v Chief Adjudication Officer; Diment v Chief Adjudication Officer reported as R(M) 6/99, Court of Appeal*).

In order to qualify under *section 73(1)(b)* of the *SSCBA 1992* (blind and deaf), the degree of disablement resulting in the loss of vision must be 100% and the degree of disablement resulting from loss of hearing must be not less than 80% on a scale where 100% represents absolute deafness. The use of percentage disablements is further discussed above (**Chapter 3**). The regulations give no guidance as to how 100% loss of vision is to be determined, and the Commissioners have given support to decision makers applying similar rules to those used under the industrial injuries scheme (*R(DLA) 3/95*). In addition, the combined result of the blindness and deafness must be such that the person is unable to walk to any intended or required destination out of doors without the assistance of another person.

For the purposes of the severe mental impairment criterion, a person is treated as severely mentally impaired if they suffer from 'a state of arrested development or incomplete physical development of the brain, which results in severe impairment of intelligence and social functioning'. (*Regulation 12(5)*). The Court of Appeal has held that impairment of both intelligence and social functioning is required; (*M (a child) v Chief Adjudication Officer*, reported as *R(DLA) 1/00*).

A person is treated as having severe behavioural problems if they exhibit disruptive behaviour which is extreme, and which regularly requires another person to intervene and physically to restrain them in order to prevent them causing physical injury to themselves or to others or damage to property, and their behaviour is so unpredictable that they require another person to be present and watching over them whenever they are awake.

Finally, *Regulation 12* provides *(paragraph 4)* that the determination of the question as to whether or not a person is unable or virtually unable to walk is determined taking into account the use of any prosthesis or artificial aid which they habitually use, or which would be suitable in their case.

The word 'walk' is an ordinary English word and means to move by means of a person's legs and feet or a combination of both *(R(M) 3/78)*. In *R(M) 1/90*, the Commissioner said 'clearly not all progress that is made constitutes walking; for instance I should not regard hopping on one foot as walking; and I would venture to suggest that not every form of movement on crutches amounts to walking. There are several kinds of crutches; some placed under the arms to enable a person to propel himself forwards placing not more than one foot on the ground; while others are little more than elaborate walking sticks with clips at the forearms'. The Commissioner went on to say that, if the best progress that can be made does not amount to walking, the claimant should be found to be unable to walk.

If it does amount to walking, then the decision maker should go on to consider the question of virtual inability to walk. The test is whether a person is able to walk out of doors.

The four tests contained in the Regulations must each be considered, although it is not necessarily an error of law if the tribunal fails to make a finding of fact on each one. The adjudicating authorities have consistently set their faces against designating a particular distance for which a person can walk as being decisive of the question whether or not a person is, or is not, virtually unable to walk. In several decisions, the Commissioners have made it clear that even someone who can walk no more than 50 yards may, in certain circumstances, be described as not being virtually unable to walk (*eg CSDLA/252/1994*).

Where the claimant is only able to walk with severe discomfort, time spent walking while experiencing such discomfort should be disregarded in determining whether or not the claimant passes the test.

### *Lower rate mobility component* 5.15

The lower rate mobility component is available to people aged over 5 who are able to walk, but who need someone with them to provide them with guidance or supervision for most of the time they are out of doors. A person does not qualify if his or her failure to take advantage of the facility of walking out of doors is due to fear or anxiety (*Social Security (Disability Living Allowance) Regulations, Reg 12(7)*) as amended), unless the fear or anxiety is itself a symptom of a mental disability.

In both cases, where an artificial walking aid such as a walking stick is used, the ability to walk is assessed using the aid.

### *Good and bad days* 5.16

For both care and mobility components, it is likely that the condition of the claimant will fluctuate from one day to another. As a general rule, the assessment of entitlement to the benefit will take into account the pattern of the disability, and will adopt a normative rather than an arithmetical approach. Advisers should be warned that full disclosure should be made where a condition fluctuates, and this should be made known to decision makers at all stages.

### *Effect on other benefits* 5.17

Disability living allowance is not treated as income in assessing means tested benefits or tax credits. Its receipt may qualify the claimant for further payments on account of disability. It is a qualifying benefit for both the disability premium and the disabled child premium in income support, income based jobseekers allowance, housing benefit and council tax benefit. Furthermore, the severe disability premium is included in the calculation of income based benefits for a person who lives alone, provided that nobody claims carer's allowance for looking after them. In the case of a couple, both of whom receive disability living allowance or attendance allowance, there is an entitlement to a double severe disability premium provided no other non-dependant lives with them. Where someone is in receipt of the higher care component, the enhanced disability premium is payable with income-based benefits. Receipt of disability living allowance also provides qualification for extra tax credits with the child tax credit and the working tax credit schemes.

It is not affected by income or capital. The only overlap with other benefits is with constant attendance allowance under the industrial injuries scheme, or mobility supplement under the war pensions scheme. If the claimant is entitled to either, that benefit will normally be paid in place of disability living allowance.

A person who lives in the household of another person who is claiming housing benefit is exempt from paying a non-dependant's contribution towards that person's housing benefit if they get disability living allowance.

A person who claims the higher rate of mobility component can apply for exemption from vehicle excise duty.

Both disability living allowance care component and mobility component cease after 28 days in hospital. The care component also ceases after 28 days in a residential care home where the claimant is funded by the local authority, but the mobility component continues.

## Claims 5.18

A claim pack is obtainable from local offices of the Department, or from the Benefit Enquiry Line on 0800 882200. Leaflet DS704 contains a postage-paid coupon to send for a claim pack. If the coupon is used, the claim is dated from the date of receipt of the coupon. If the claim pack is used, it is date stamped with the date of the telephone call or visit, and the claim will run from that date provided the claim form is completed within six weeks. Where a special version of the claim pack, used for Citizens Advice Bureaux and other agencies, is used, the date of claim is the date the completed form is received.

Where a claim is being made by or on behalf of a person with a terminal illness, the claim form should be accompanied by a form DS1500 medical report.

A decision maker first considers whether the non-medical conditions such as age are complied with. If they are not, the claim is rejected. If they are, the medical evidence is considered. There may be a request for further information, or a request that the claimant attend a medical examination.

Benefit can be awarded for a fixed period, or for an open-ended period. Where it is for a fixed period, the claimant needs to make a renewal claim before the award expires.

Awards are subject to review if circumstances change, and a claimant is obliged to inform the Department of any relevant changes.

The rules on the payment of disability living allowance for someone in hospital or a residential care home are the same as for attendance allowance (see below).

### *Motability* **5.19**

Where the claimant receives the higher mobility component, he or she can use the money to pay for a car through the Motability scheme. The scheme can also pay for an electric scooter or wheelchair. The Disability Benefits Unit pays the benefit direct to Motability, which is a charity. The same rules apply to those receiving war pensioners mobility supplement. The car may be available on contract hire or can be bought on hire purchase. The award must be of a length to cover the period of the contract hire or HP repayment period. For a new car on HP the minimum period is four or five years; for a used car it is two or three years; and for an electric wheelchair or scooter it is two or three years.

The claimant must agree to their benefit being paid to Motability, and must agree to pay any balance. Any excess benefit is paid to the claimant. Repairs and maintenance are provided free under the hire agreement, but it is the responsibility of the claimant to arrange for servicing and repairs, and to look after the car. A charge is made if average mileage exceeds 45,000 over three years.

## Attendance allowance **5.20**

Attendance allowance is the equivalent of disability living allowance for those aged 65 or over.

It is not a contributory benefit and it is payable irrespective of the income and capital of the claimant or of members of the claimant's family.

The special rules for terminally ill people apply in the same way as they do for disability living allowance (*SSCBA 1992, s 66*).

### *Residence* **5.21**

The claimant must normally live in Great Britain. (*Social Security (Attendance Allowance) Regulations 1991 (SI 1991 No 2740), Reg 2(1)*). At the date of the claim, the claimant must be in Great Britain, and must have been in the United Kingdom, or the Isle of Man or the Channel Isles, for at least 26 weeks in the last twelve months.

Certain people can qualify even though they do not fulfil the above conditions, namely those who:

- have been serving abroad in the forces (including their families);
- are mariners and aircrew working abroad;
- are working on the UK sector of the continental shelf;
- are abroad temporarily (during the first six months of absence);
- are temporarily abroad for some form of medical treatment.

(*SI 1991 No 2740, Reg 2(2)*.)

People who live or have lived in another European Economic Area country may in some circumstances be treated as resident in Great Britain.

The 26 week rule does not apply to those who are terminally ill (who can claim at once) nor to those who receive earnings on which they do not pay UK tax, who must have been in Great Britain for three out of the last four years before they started getting those earnings.

### *Immigration status* 5.22

A person who is subject to immigration control may not claim (*Immigration and Asylum Act 1999, s 115*). People who are EEA nationals, or members of the family of an EEA national, may claim, as may:

- nationals of Algeria, Morocco, Slovenia, Tunisia or Turkey who are lawfully working here, or members of their families;
- people who are nationals of a state which has a reciprocal agreement with the UK;
- refugees;
- people who have been given exceptional leave to enter and remain in the UK; and
- people who have been given indefinite leave to remain, subject to a formal sponsorship undertaking.

### *Qualifying conditions* 5.23

It is payable to someone who is aged 65 or over when they claim, who is so disabled physically or mentally as to fulfil the conditions for either the higher or the middle rate care component of disability living allowance, namely that they are so severely disabled as to require:

- frequent attention throughout the day in connection with his or her bodily functions; or

- continual supervision throughout the day in order to avoid substantial danger to him or herself or others; or
- prolonged or repeated attention at night in connection with his or her bodily functions; or
- in order to avoid substantial danger to him or herself or others, another person to be awake for a prolonged period or at frequent intervals for the purpose of watching over him or her.

(*SSCBA 1992, s 64.*)

The lower rate is payable to someone who fulfils either or both of the daytime conditions, or either or both of the night-time conditions; the higher rate to someone who fulfils both at least one of the day conditions and at least one of the night conditions.

A person aged over 65 cannot claim for either of the mobility components, or for the lower rate care component. Like disability living allowance, attendance allowance is based on the help that the disabled person needs, and not on the help that they actually receive. A person who undergoes kidney dialysis at least twice a week, and who needs attendance or supervision from another person to do so, also qualifies (*SSCBA 1992, s 64(4); SI 1991 No 2740, Reg 5*). A person in a voluntary hospice is normally entitled to the higher rate.

The qualifying period for attendance allowance is that the claimant has satisfied the relevant qualifying condition for six months (not three) unless the claimant is terminally ill. He or she must also be likely to continue to satisfy it or them for a further period of six months (*SSCBA 1992, s 65(1)*). A person who is terminally ill qualifies immediately for the higher rate of attendance allowance without a qualifying period, and is deemed to fulfil the requirement that he or she is likely to fulfil the qualifying conditions for a further six months (*SSCBA 1992, s 66*). For further information about the treatment of those who are terminally ill, see above.

### *Claims* 5.24

A claim is made on the self-assessment claim form available from local social security offices, or from the Benefit Enquiry Line on 0800 882200. Leaflet DS702, *Attendance Allowance*, is available from advice centres and welfare rights agencies, and contains a coupon to send for a claim pack. Provided the claim form is completed promptly (a period of six weeks is allowed), the claim will be dated from the date of the first enquiry. A claim cannot under any circumstances be backdated.

Where a person has received attendance allowance within the last two years, they will not necessarily have to wait a further six months for a claim (*Social Security (Attendance Allowance) Regulations 1991 (SI 1991 No 2740), Reg 3*).

The claim is considered by a decision maker in the Disability Benefits Unit. If the claimant does not fulfil non-medical conditions (for example, about age), the claim will be rejected. If these conditions are fulfilled, then benefit will be awarded if the medical conditions are met. Further information or evidence may be requested, or a medical examination may be sought.

Benefit may be awarded for a fixed period, or for an open ended period. All awards are subject to review and may be affected by a change in circumstances. There is a duty on the claimant to tell the Disability Benefits Unit of any change in their condition. If the condition worsens, there may be an entitlement to the higher rate.

## *Attendance allowance for people in hospital or a care home* 5.25

Because of the rule that a person should not be paid twice for the same set of circumstances, a claimant who goes into hospital or residential care will lose their attendance allowance in many cases. Benefit continues to be paid for 28 days after admission to hospital. Where a person spends a series of short periods in hospital, they are treated as cumulative for the purposes of the 28-day rule unless separated by another period of 28 days.

**EXAMPLE**

David is spending time in and out of hospital. He gets attendance allowance. His attendance allowance will continue to be paid for the first 28 days of any spell in hospital, and will then be suspended.

He spends six days in hospital and then comes home. Three days later he is readmitted. He is then in hospital for a further fourteen days. This is added to the earlier six to make 20. He comes home again and a week later is readmitted for a further ten days. His total of days is now 30 and his attendance allowance therefore stops after 28 days.

He then comes home again. He is immediately entitled to his attendance allowance back, but it will stop again when he next goes into hospital, until a period of 28 days has elapsed since his last admission. At this stage his slate is wiped clean and the 28 day period starts again.

The same rule applies to permanent (not temporary) admission to a residential care home which is funded by the local authority (*Social Security(Disability Living Allowance) Regulations 1991 (SI 1991 No 2890), Reg 8(1)*).

Someone who funds themselves in a care home, or is in a private hospital or other private institution (for example, a hospice) is entitled to keep their attendance allowance throughout, as is a person who is terminally ill.

Where a person goes into residential care who owns their own home, which is to be sold to pay for the care home fees, they will continue to be entitled to their attendance allowance during a period while the house is being sold, even though the local authority is paying for their care on a temporary basis (*Chief Adjudication Officer v Creighton [2000] NI 222 (Northern Ireland Court of Appeal) and CA/2937/1999 and CA/2604/1998*).

### *Effect on other benefits* 5.26

The only benefit which affects the amount of attendance allowance is constant attendance allowance under the industrial injuries or war pensions scheme. Any constant attendance allowance which is in payment reduces the amount of attendance allowance payable.

## Carers allowance 5.27

Where the injured party makes a successful claim either for attendance allowance or for the middle or higher rate care components of disability living allowance, it may be possible for a person who cares for them to make a claim for carer's allowance. Carer's allowance is not a contributory benefit and is not affected by the level of a claimant's capital, although other income may affect entitlement. A successful claim will normally lead to credits of national insurance contributions while benefit it is in payment, and the claimant may also be able to build up a State Second Pension for every complete tax year from 6 April 2002.

In order to make a claim, the following conditions apply.

### *Residence* 5.28

The residence conditions for carer's allowance are the same as for attendance allowance and disability living allowance. The carer must be ordinarily resident in Great Britain and also be present in Great Britain (*Social Security (Invalid Care Allowance) Regulations 1976 (SI 1976 No 409), Reg 9(1)*), and must have been present in the United Kingdom (including the Isle of Man and the Channel Isles) for a total of 26 weeks in the past 12 months.

Certain people can qualify even though they do not fulfil the above conditions, namely those who:

- have been serving abroad in the forces (including their families);
- are mariners and aircrew working abroad;
- are working on the UK sector of the continental shelf;
- are abroad for up to four weeks;
- are temporarily abroad with the disabled person to care for them, so long as that person continues to receive attendance allowance, constant attendance allowance, or the higher or middle care components of disability living allowance.

(*Social Security (Invalid Care Allowance) Regulations 1976 (SI 1976 No 409), Regs 9(2), 9(3)*.)

## *Immigration status* 5.29

The carer must not be subject to immigration control. A person is subject to immigration control if they are not a national of the European Economic Area and either:

- they require leave to enter the UK or to remain but do not have it;
- they have leave to enter or remain, but this is subject to a restriction on their claiming from public funds;
- they have leave to enter or remain and are the subject of a special undertaking from a sponsor;
- they are appealing to gain a decision about their immigration status.

(*Immigration and Asylum Act 1999, s 115*.)

Certain people who are entitled include:

- people who are EEA nationals, or members of the family of an EEA national;
- nationals of Algeria, Morocco, Slovenia, Tunisia or Turkey who are lawfully working here, or members of their families;
- refugees;
- people who have been given exceptional leave to enter and remain in the UK; and
- people who have been given indefinite leave to remain, subject to a formal sponsorship undertaking.

### *Person cared for* 5.30

The carer must be caring for a person receiving either the higher or middle care components of disability living allowance, or attendance allowance or constant attendance allowance following either an industrial injury or disease or the award of a war disablement pension.

(*SSCBA 1992, s 70.*)

### *Extent of care* 5.31

The care given must be regular and substantial.

Regular and substantial care is defined as care of 35 hours a week or more (*Social Security (Invalid Care Allowance) Regulations 1976 (SI 1976 No 409), Reg 4(1)*). The test is applied separately in each week, so it is not possible to take an average number of qualifying hours as meeting the condition. Care must be for a single disabled person, and caring for more than one disabled person for a total of 35 hours does not count.

### *Not in employment* 5.32

The claimant must not be gainfully employed. The claimant is considered to be gainfully employed if earning more than the lower earnings limit, that is £77 per week (2003/4). This rule does not apply during any period when the claimant is entitled to the benefit but is not actually engaged in caring for the disabled person, for example, during the first 28 days when the claimant is in hospital, or during a claimant's break from caring (see below) (*SSCBA 1992, s 70(1)*).

### *Not in full-time education* 5.33

Full time education is defined as 21 hours a week or more of 'supervised study'. Supervised study is work which is undertaken to meet the reasonable requirements of the course, and does not necessarily require the presence of a supervisor.

The carer must not be in full-time education (*SSCBA 1992, s 70(3)*). This is defined as supervised study at a university, college or school for at least 21 hours a week. 'Supervised study' includes not only lectures, seminars and tutorials, but work in preparation for them (*Flemming v Secretary of State, [2002] EWCA Civ 641*).

### *Age* 5.34

The claimant must be aged 16 or over on the date when they begin to qualify for carer's allowance (*SSCBA 1992, s 70(3)*).

Before 28 October 2002, there was an upper age limit for claiming carer's allowance (or invalid care allowance as it was then known) of 65. The benefit could continue to be paid to those over 65, but only if they made a claim before reaching that age. This upper age limit was abolished from that date. Those carers who claimed benefit from before that date are entitled to continue to receive carer's allowance provided that they claimed before reaching the age of 65 (*Regulatory Reform (Carer's Allowance) Order 2002 (SI 2002 No 1457)*), which also removed the anomaly that previously existed whereby a person aged 65 or over whose entitlement to invalid care allowance ceased continued to be entitled to the benefit.)

## *Breaks from caring* 5.35

The claimant is able to have a four weeks break from caring in any period of 26 weeks.

If either the disabled person or carer is in hospital for at least 8 weeks, then a break of up to 12 weeks does not effect entitlement. However, entitlement to the benefit stops when payment of the attendance allowance, disability living allowance or constant attendance allowance ceases (*Social Security (Invalid Care Allowance) Regulations 1976 (SI 1976 No 409), Reg 4(2)*).

## *Claims and payments* 5.36

Carers Allowance is claimed on form DS700. A completed claim for is sent to the Carers Allowance Unit, Palatine House, Lancaster Road, Preston, PR1 1NS. The claimant must provide their National Insurance number and also the National Insurance number of any adults for whom they are claiming. Benefit increases are payable for a spouse who is living with them and not earning more than the amount of the increase. Where the spouse is receiving a contributory or statutory benefit in their own right, other than disability living allowance, attendance allowance, industrial disablement benefit or a war pension, the increase is reduced by the amount of the benefit.

Claims may be backdated for up to three months provided that the qualifying conditions were satisfied throughout that period.

A claim for income support, in the course of which the claimant told the Department that they could not work because they were caring for a disabled person, counts in certain circumstances as a claim for carer's allowance.

The benefit is payable with increases for adult dependants. To claim for a spouse, the claimant must actually reside with them; it is not enough simply to be maintaining them. A carer with dependent children should claim child tax credit (**Chapter 7**).

Carer's allowance cannot be paid in full if the claimant is receiving any of the following benefits:

- incapacity benefit;
- severe disablement allowance;
- contributory jobseekers allowance;
- unemployability supplement paid with an industrial injuries disablement benefit or a war pension;
- maternity allowance;
- state retirement pension;
- bereavement benefits;
- industrial death benefit or war widows pension;
- certain training allowances.

(*Social Security (Overlapping Benefits) Regulations 1979 (SI 1979 No 597).*)

However, the claimant retains an underlying entitlement to carer's allowance which qualifies them for the carer's premium as part of their income support, income based jobseekers allowance, housing or council tax benefits.

If the person being cared for receives income support, income based jobseekers allowance, housing or council tax benefit, they may be entitled to the severe disability premium. A successful claim for carer's allowance will remove entitlement to this premium, and this should therefore be considered before a claim is made.

## Severe disablement allowance 5.37

Severe disablement allowance (SDA) was a non-contributory version of incapacity benefit which was abolished in April 2001. It continues to be paid to those who were in receipt of it on 5 April 2001, or who are able to use the linking rules to make another claim.

In order to make a claim, the claimant had to be incapable of work for at least 196 days (28 weeks) and also, unless their incapacity began before the age of 20, had to be at least 80% disabled (*SSCBA 1992, s 68*). The section was repealed by the *Welfare Reform and Pensions Act 1999*, but *sections 68–69* remain in force for existing claimants under *Article 4* of the *Welfare Reform and Pensions Act 1999 (Commencement No 9, and Transitional and Savings Provisions) Order 2000 (SI 2000 No 2958).*

For the incapacity for work qualification, reference should be made to **Chapter 6** (Incapacity Benefit), which applies to everyone except those who were in receipt of SDA on 12 April 1995, who are exempt from the current test for incapacity unless there is reason to doubt capacity. For the assessment of percentage disability, see **Chapter 3**.

Someone who gets the highest rate of care component of disability living allowance, or has or has had an invalid tricycle, invalid car or private car from the former Invalid Vehicle scheme, or was assessed as 80% disabled (whether for SDA, or for the industrial injuries scheme or war pensions scheme) for a period which covered the claim, or has received a payment under the vaccine damage scheme, is treated as 80% disabled without having to undergo further tests. The listed disabilities in Appendix 1 cover certain disabilities and the appropriate degree of disability in an assessment.

Once benefit was awarded to a claimant, he or she continued to be able to receive it during that period of incapacity for work.

A person can make a renewed claim for SDA if they:

- were getting SDA eight weeks ago or less;
- were getting SDA 52 weeks ago or less, and went into work or training within seven days of ceasing to receive it and notified the Jobcentre Plus or social security office within 4 weeks that they had done so;
- gave up SDA to start work and qualify for a disability element of working tax credit, or want on a training course; had to give up the job or training; and made a fresh claim for SDA within two years.

There was another route to SDA, which was that it was available to those whose incapacity for work began before the age of 20. People in this position are now able to claim incapacity benefit without having paid any contributions.

In addition to flat rate benefit for the claimant, additions to SDA may be paid for a spouse or for a person looking after the claimant's children. Benefit for a spouse, where there are no children, is only payable for a spouse over 60. Where a spouse has earnings of their own, and earn more than the weekly earnings limit, SDA is not payable for that spouse. This also applies to a person living with the claimant who looks after the claimant's children, but where the carer does not live with the claimant, but is employed by them to look after children, their earnings do not count.

SDA is not payable with the following benefits:

- Incapacity benefit.

- Maternity allowance.
- Retirement pension.
- Unemployability supplement with a war or industrial disablement pension.
- Bereavement benefits including industrial widows benefit or war widows pension.
- Carers allowance.
- Certain training allowances.

(*Social Security (Overlapping Benefts) Regulations 1979 (SI 1979 No 597).*)

Where the claimant qualifies for both, the higher of the two benefits is paid.

### *Claims* 5.38

Claims are made on claim pack SDA1 which is available from local Jobcentre Plus or social security offices.

# 6 Benefits for Incapacity

## Statutory sick pay

### *Who can claim?* 6.1

Broadly the statutory sick pay scheme covers those who are treated as employed earners for social security purposes, and so are liable to pay Class 1 National Insurance Contributions. In order to qualify:

- The person must be employed under a contract of service (*SSCBA 1992, s 151*).
- They must be earning enough to pay national insurance (£77 a week 2003/4) (*SSCBA 1992, s 163(2)*.)
- They must be incapable of work (*SSCBA 1992, s 151(4)*.)
- They must be aged between 16 and 65 (*SSCBA 1992, s 153(3)* and *Sch 11*).
- The employer must be resident in or present in Great Britain, or have a place of business there, and must not be exempt from the legislation under an international treaty (*Statutory Sick Pay (General) Regulations 1982 (SI 1982 No 894), Reg 16(2)*).

The provisions also cover married women who pay the reduced rate of contribution.

The following are not covered:

- Those employed for less than three months, unless their contract is one for a longer period, or was preceded within the eight weeks before its commencement with another contract with the same employer (*SSCBA 1992, Sch 11 para 4*).
- Those who have not yet started work under their contract of employment.

(*SSCBA 1992, Sch 11 para 2*; *Statutory Sick Pay (General) Regulations 1982 (SI 1982 No 894), Reg 16*.)

Employers cannot exclude the right to statutory sick pay, and are liable to pay it after the ending of the contract if the employee is dismissed solely or mainly to avoid paying it. An employee is entitled to statutory sick pay for every job which he or she has and which qualifies.

### *Incapable of work* 6.2

A person is incapable of work where:

- because of a specific disease, or bodily or mental disablement, they are incapable of doing work which they could reasonably be expected to do under the terms of their contract; or
- they are treated as incapable of work (*SSCBA 1992, s 151(4)*).

The employer can treat a person as incapable of work where:

- they are under medical observation as the possible carrier of an infectious disease; or
- they are under medical care in connection with a specific illness or bodily or mental disablement and their doctor has stated that they should not work as a precaution or in order to convalesce. The employee must do no actual work for their normal employer (*Statutory Sick Pay (General) Regulations 1982 (SI 1982 No 894), Reg 2*).

In addition, a person who is sick for part of a day, and who does no work on that day, is treated as incapable of work for the whole day.

An employer can seek the assistance of the Inland Revenue (who are responsible for the administration of statutory sick pay) in dealing with an individual SSP case. The Inland Revenue may arrange for a medical examination in case of doubt.

### *When SSP is payable* 6.3

Statutory Sick Pay is payable during a 'period of incapacity for work' during a 'period of entitlement'. A period of incapacity for work is a period of four or more consecutive days of incapacity. Every day of the week, including Sunday, counts for this purpose. Two or more periods of incapacity for work separated by less than eight weeks count as a single period (*SSCBA 1992, s 152(3)*).

A period of entitlement limits the employer's liability to 28 weeks of incapacity for work. The period of entitlement starts on the first day of incapacity for work, unless the contract starts during a period of incapacity, in which case it starts on the first day of the contract. If a contract starts between two linked periods of incapacity, the period of entitlement begins on the first day of the second period of incapacity (*SSCBA 1992, s 153(7)*).

A period of entitlement ends when the period of incapacity for work ends, or when the period of 28 weeks entitlement ends (*SSCBA 1992, s 155(4)*). It also ends when the employee becomes entitled to statutory maternity pay or maternity allowance, or is incapable of work because of pregnancy (*SSCBA 1992, s 153(2)(d)*); or on the third anniversary of the start of the period of entitlement (*Statutory Sick Pay (General) Regulations 1982 (SI 1982 No 894), Reg 3(3)*); or where the person is in prison or detained in legal custody, or leaves the European Union (*SI 1982 No 894, Reg 3*; *Statutory Sick Pay (Mariners and Persons Abroad) Regulations 1982 (SI 1982 No 1349), Reg 5*; *SSCBA 1992, s 162*).

If a period of entitlement ends, the person cannot again be entitled to statutory sick pay until a period of eight weeks has elapsed. The person may be entitled to incapacity benefit during any intervening period. An employer who ceases to pay statutory sick pay because they consider that a period of entitlement has ended is required to notify the employee accordingly on form SSP1.

There can be no period of entitlement where:

- the employee is aged 65 or over, unless it began before they reached 65 and has not yet ended;
- the employee qualified for and claimed incapacity benefit or severe disablement allowance during the 57 days before the day on which the period of entitlement would have begun (including a case where there was no entitlement to incapacity benefit because the contribution conditions were not satisfied);
- the employee is a 'welfare to work' beneficiary who has moved from incapacity benefit or severe disablement allowance into work, but who has stopped work again because of incapacity within 52 weeks of receiving either benefit (in which case they are likely to be entitled to reclaim the earlier benefit);
- there is a stoppage of work at the employee's place of work on the day when the period of entitlement should have begun, unless the employee did not have a 'prior direct interest' in the dispute. This does not disqualify the employee for incapacity benefit or income support (see below);
- the employee is within a maternity pay period, or is incapable of work due to pregnancy;
- the employee is in prison or other legal custody.

(*SSCBA 1992,s 153(3), Sch 11*; *SI 1982 No 894, Reg 3*.)

In order for the employee to qualify for statutory sick pay, their 'normal weekly earnings' must be of at least the lower earnings limit for that year (£77 per week 2003/4). This is determined by reference to gross earnings, and is calculated by averaging gross earnings over a period ending with the last normal pay day before the period of entitlement, and beginning with the day after the last normal pay day which falls at least eight weeks before the end date (*SI 1982 No 894, Reg 19*).

Benefit is payable for qualifying days (*SSCBA 1992, s 154*). A 'qualifying day' is usually a day on which the employee would normally work. SSP is paid only for days when the employee would normally work, so that for example someone who works on a regular three days in the week will only be paid SSP for those days. It is possible to agree qualifying days where working arrangements are complex (*SSCBA 1992, s 154(2)*). Otherwise, qualifying days are:

- the days on which the employee is required to work; or
- if the employee is required to work no days in that week, Wednesday; or
- in the absence of agreement, every day in the week, unless employer and employee can agree on days on which nobody works.

(*SI 1982 No 894, Regs 5(2), 5(3).*)

It is not permissible to define qualifying days retrospectively so as to consist of, or entirely to exclude, days of incapacity.

Benefit is not payable for the first three qualifying days (sometimes described as waiting days) (*SSCBA 1992, s 155(1)*).

## ***How SSP is paid*** 6.4

The employee is required to notify the employer of their incapacity. The method of notification is a matter for agreement (*Social Security Administration Act (SSAA) 1992, s 14(1)*), but the employer cannot insist on notification:

- earlier than the first qualifying day, or by a specific time on the first qualifying day (*SI 1982 No 894, Reg 7(1)*);
- personally; (*SI 1982 No 894, Reg 7(4), (5)*);
- by providing medical evidence (*Statutory Sick Pay (Medical Evidence) Regulations 1985 (SI 1985 No 1604), Reg 2(2)*; *SI 1982 No 894, Reg 7(4), (5)*);
- more than once a week (*SI 1982 No 894, Reg 7(4) (5)*); or
- on a document or printed form provided by the employer (*SI 1982 No 894, Reg 7(4), (5)*).

For the first seven days the employer is not entitled to medical evidence. It is sufficient for the employee to self-certify. Thereafter the employer can ask for medical evidence in support of the claim (*Statutory Sick Pay (Medical Evidence) Regulations 1985 (SI 1985 No 1604), Reg 2(2)*).

A claim must be made within the agreed time. A third party can claim on the employee's behalf. If no time limit is agreed, notification must be within seven days of the first qualifying day. If a claim is not made immediately, but is made within a month, and there is good reason for the delay, statutory sick pay can be backdated as if the claim was made on the first qualifying day. If it is not practicable to notify the employer immediately, but notification is made within 91 days of the first qualifying day, the claim will be likewise backdated (*SSP Regs 7(1), 7(2)*).

### *Challenging an SSP decision* 6.5

If the claimant is dissatisfied with the employer's decision, the Inland Revenue can be asked to make a decision on the claim (*Social Security Contributions (Transfer of Functions, etc) Act 1999, s 8*).

The employer should provide a form SSP1 which is both an application to the Inland Revenue for a decision, and a claim form for incapacity benefit. The employee should complete the form and send it, not direct to the Inland Revenue, but to the local office of the Department of Work and Pensions. (However, it may be advisable to send a copy to the local national insurance contributions office.) Where applicable the DWP forwards a copy to the Inland Revenue so that they can be asked to make a decision on the claim.

An application to the Inland Revenue can be made in writing if no Form SSP1 is provided (*SSP & SMP (Decisions) Regs 1999, Reg 3*).

An application for a decision must be made within six months of the earliest date in respect of which entitlement to statutory sick pay is in dispute (*Statutory Sick Pay and Statutory Maternity Pay (Decisions) Regulations 1999 (SI 1999 No 776), Reg* 3).

Where the Inland Revenue make a decision on a claim, both the employer and the employee have the right to appeal to the Commissioners of Income Tax (*Social Security Contributions (Transfer of Functions, etc.) Act 1999, s 11(2)(a)*). The appeal must be lodged within thirty days of the decision complained about.

Where the employer does not pay statutory sick pay to which the employee is entitled, the Inland Revenue is required to pay it (*SSCBA 1992, s 151(6)*; *SI 1982 No 894, Reg 9A*).

## Incapacity benefit

### *Who can claim?* 6.6

A person must have enough contributions to qualify, or must qualify for benefit without contributions, either because their incapacity began in youth, or because they were receiving sickness or invalidity benefit on 12 April 1995 and their incapacity results from an industrial accident or prescribed disease.

They must be incapable of work (*SSCBA 1992, s 30a, 30C*).

They must not be entitled to statutory sick pay (*SSCBA 1992, Sch 12 para 1*).

They must be aged less than 65 (for long term incapacity benefit) or no more than 5 years above pension age (for short term incapacity benefit) (*SSCBA 1992, s 30A*).

## Contributions 6.7

A detailed explanation of contribution rules is outside the scope of this book. Briefly, in order to qualify for incapacity benefit, a person must fulfil two contribution conditions (*SSCBA 1992, s 21, Sch 3 para 2*).

*The first condition* is that the contributor has actually paid contributions (Class 1 or Class 2) in one tax year producing an earnings factor of 25 times that year's lower earnings limit, or 25 flat rate contributions if paid before 6 April 1975. They must have been paid in one of the last three complete tax years ending before the calendar year in which the benefit claim is made. In other words, for a claim made at any time during benefit (calendar) year 2004, the contributions must have been paid in 2000/01, 2001/02 or 2002/03.

'Earnings factors' are the amounts of earnings on which the contributions are paid. For example, in tax year 2002/3, the lower earnings limit was £75 a week. For that year to count, the contributor must have paid contributions on earnings of 25 times £75, ie £1875.

The first condition is relaxed for those who were:

- receiving invalid care allowance during the last complete tax year before the benefit year in which the claim is made, or entitled to it but not receiving it because of the overlapping benefit rules;
- working and entitled to disability working allowance or disabled persons tax credit for at least two years immediately before their incapacity began;
- working for more than two years and entitled to the disability or severe disability element of working tax credit immediately before their incapacity began;
- receiving incapacity benefit in the last complete tax year before the benefit year of the new claim;

- entitled to credited contributions because they had been in prison or detention, and their conviction was subsequently quashed.

The effect of the relaxation is that the claimant can satisfy the first contribution condition in any tax year, and not necessarily one of the last three.

*The second condition* is that the contributor has paid or been credited with contributions producing an earnings factor of 50 times the lower earnings limit in each of the last two complete tax years ending before the benefit year in which the claim is made. For a claim made during benefit year 2004, this condition will have to have been fulfilled during tax years 2001/02 and 2002/03.

In practice these conditions mean that the claimant must have been in work at some time during the preceding three tax years (to have fulfilled the first condition) and must have maintained contact with the job market during the past two tax years (by paying contributions, or by obtaining credits by signing on or receiving a benefit such as incapacity benefit for which credits are provided, in order to have fulfilled the second condition).

There is one exception to the rules on contributions. This is where incapacity began in youth. A person qualifies for incapacity benefit irrespective of their contribution record if they are aged 16 or over and have been incapable of work for at least 196 days, where the period of incapacity began before the person's 20th birthday. If under 19, they may not be in full time education. For certain groups of people who have been in education or training, the rule is relaxed to include those whose incapacity began before age 25.

## Incapacity for work 6.8

There are two tests of incapacity for work; the 'own occupation' test and the 'personal capability assessment' (PCA) test. The former applies to someone who has a regular occupation when their period of incapacity begins. This applies for the first 28 weeks of the claim. The PCA applies to all other claimants. The tests apply in respect of all benefits except statutory sick pay (see above) and industrial injuries benefits. The tests will apply to anyone who is not deemed incapable of work.

The following are deemed incapable of work:

- those who are under medical observation as a possible carrier of an infectious disease, and who hold a certificate from a medical officer of environmental health excluding them from work; (*Social Security (Incapacity for Work) Regulations 1995 (SI 1995 No 311), Reg 11*).
- those receiving in-patient treatment at a hospital or similar institution; (*SI 1995 No 311, Reg 12*).

- those receiving regular treatments such as kidney dialysis or radio-therapy, on the days when they are receiving that treatment (*SI 1995 No 311, Reg 13*);
- those who are pregnant, where there would be a risk to the baby's health if the person were to work in their own occupation or any occupation, as appropriate (*SI 1995 No 311, Reg 14(a)*);
- women who are pregnant or have recently had a baby, who are not entitled to either maternity allowance nor statutory maternity pay but who are within the period beginning six weeks before week in which the baby is due and ending fourteen days after the baby is born (*SI 1995 No 311, Reg 14(b)*);
- 'welfare to work' beneficiaries who can link their incapacity to a period of incapacity before they moved from benefit and into work (*SI 1995 No 311, Reg 13A*).

The own occupation test determines whether the claimant is incapable by reason of some specific disease or bodily or mental disablement of doing work which they could reasonably be expected to do in the course of the occupation in which they are engaged (*SSCBA 1992, s 171B (2)*). The test applies to someone who, in the 21 weeks immediately before the start of the period of incapacity, has done paid work for at least 16 hours a week for at least eight weeks. Where a person has, on this definition, more than one regular occupation, the test applies to the last one before the period of incapacity. A person who has worked in two jobs during the last week in which they worked must satisfy the test in respect of both occupations. 'Paid work' includes work done in expectation of payment, and periods of paid or unpaid leave where a person normally works in that occupation (*SSCBA 1992, s 171B (1)* and *(3)*; *SI 1995 No 311, Reg 5*).

The claimant may be self-employed or may have worked for more than one employer.

For the first seven days of sickness, self-certification is required. Thereafter, a medical certificate is required, or (if it is unreasonable for the claimant to obtain one) other suitable evidence (*Social Security (Medical Evidence) Regulations 1976 (SI 1976 No 615), Reg 2(1)(a)*). The onus of proof is on the claimant *(R(S) 13/52)*.

After 196 days (28 weeks) of the own occupation test, or immediately on claiming for someone who has no 'own occupation', the PCA determines capacity or otherwise for work. Unlike the own occupation test, the test is one of ability to perform certain tasks, and not of ability to carry out the claimant's own job.

The PCA requires the claimant to carry out certain activities described in the regulations (*Social Security (Incapacity for Work) (General) Regulations*). For physical disabilities, these activities are within a total of 14 areas, namely:

- walking on level ground;
- walking up and down stairs;
- sitting in an upright chair;
- standing;
- rising from sitting;
- bending and kneeling;
- manual dexterity;
- lifting and carrying;
- reaching;
- speech;
- hearing;
- vision;
- continence;
- remaining conscious;

and for mental incapacity within four broad areas, namely:

- completion of tasks;
- daily living;
- coping with pressure;
- interaction with other people.

For each activity there are a number of 'descriptors' which describe the task the claimant is expected to perform. The claimant's ability or otherwise to carry out the specified activities results in the award of a certain number of points (between 0 and 15 points for physical disabilities, and 1 or 2 points for mental disabilities). To fail the all work test, and to be considered incapable of work, the claimant must score fifteen points if their disability is purely physical, or is both physical and mental, and ten points if it is mental only. Certain people (notably those with life-threatening diseases or who are about to undergo a major operation) are treated as satisfying the test.

The test for vision is set out below as an example of the factors to be considered in determining physical abilities. The full set of descriptors appears in Appendix 3. Note that the descriptors below relate purely to vision, and not to comprehension or the ability to read and write. Only one score will be allocated to the claimant for each activity.

| **Activity** | **Descriptor** | **Score** |
|---|---|---|
| Vision in normal daylight or bright electric light with glasses or other aid to vision if such aid is normally worn | Cannot tell light from dark | 15 |
| | Cannot see the shape of furniture in the room | 15 |
| | Cannot see well enough to read a large print book | 15 |
| | Cannot see well enough to recognise a friend across the room | 12 |
| | Cannot see well enough to recognise a friend across the road | 8 |
| | No problem with vision | 0 |

In the case of mental disabilities, the claimant will receive all the scores to which he or she is entitled, irrespective of the headings under which they appear. An example of the test for mental disability appears below.

| **Daily living** | | |
|---|---|---|
| 16(a) | Needs encouragement to get up and dress | 2 |
| (b) | Needs alcohol before midday | 2 |
| (c) | Is frequently distressed at some time of day due to fluctuation of mood | 1 |
| (d) | Does not care about his appearance and living conditions | 1 |
| (e) | Sleep problems interfere with his daytime activities | 1 |

It will be noted that, for someone with their own occupation, the test for the first 28 weeks is related to their ability to do their own job, whereas the PCA is more of a test of disability. A person may qualify for 15 points on the above scale, and yet be capable of doing a job.

A person can only receive points in one category under each physical activity (the highest for which they qualify) but can receive points for each mental descriptor they satisfy.

Points from both the physical and the mental list can be aggregated. A score of 10 from the list of mental descriptors means that the person is incapable of work. A score of between 6 and 9 is taken as a score of 9. A score of fewer than 6 is disregarded.

Where a person's ability to perform the various tasks fluctuates, the decision maker and the tribunal should take a broad view rather than a literal one. The descriptor should apply if the person is unable to perform the activity most of the time.

Some people are exempt from all tests because of their condition, including people who:

- are terminally ill;
- are nearing retirement age and have been sick for a long time;
- were receiving severe disablement allowance (SDA) on 12 April 1995 and have continued to send in medical certificates;
- are assessed as being at least 80 per cent disabled for SDA or industrial disablement benefit;
- are receiving the highest care component of disability living allowance, or constant attendance allowance at a rate higher than the lower weekly rate;
- are registered blind;
- are tetraplegic, paraplegic, dementing or are in a persistent vegetative state; or
- can produce medical evidence of a progressive or wasting disease, severe mental illness or learning difficulties.

(*SI 1995 No 311, Reg 10.*)

Certain people are also treated as incapable of work in 'exceptional circumstances', even though they pass the PCA. This includes those who have:

- a severe life-threatening disease that is uncontrollable by recognised therapeutic treatment, or which is uncontrolled for a reasonable cause;
- a previously undiagnosed and potentially life-threatening condition discovered in the course of the examination;
- medical evidence that the claimant is likely to undergo a major operation or other major therapeutic procedure within three months of the date of the examination carried out as part of the PCA.

(*SI 1995 No 311, Reg 27.*)

The question of incapacity for work is one which is frequently contested and consideration should always be given to an appeal in the case of benefit disqualification.

## *Personal capability assessment procedure* 6.9

The claimant is sent a Form IB50, which is a questionnaire on capacity for work. The claimant is asked to assess their own ability to perform the various tasks comprised in the PCA. When the test is first applied, the claimant is also asked to produce a medical certificate from their GP at the same time as they return the questionnaire (*SI 1995 No 311, Reg 6(1)(a)* and *(b)*). This will be sent unless the claimant is exempt from the PCA, or is deemed to be incapable of work, or has severe mental health problems.

Where there is evidence of possible mental health issues, the Department will make enquiries of the claimant's doctor to determine whether he or she might be exempt from the test.

The claimant has six weeks in which to return the questionnaire. If it is not returned, the claimant is treated as capable of work unless he or she can show good cause for not having returned it (*SI 1995 No 311, Regs 7(1)* and *9*). If the claimant does not appear to be exempt from the answers given, their score is assessed by a decision maker. If the result is that the claimant does not appear to be incapable of work, or if any of the mental health descriptors apply, the case is referred for a medical examination.

If the claimant appears to be incapable of work, the case is referred for medical scrutiny. Where the scrutineer is dissatisfied that the claimant is incapable, they will be asked to attend an examination (*SI 1995 No 311, Reg 8*).

The doctor carrying out the examination prepares two reports, one for the decision maker who will determine whether or not the claimant is capable of work, and one for the claimant's Personal Adviser which is intended to place emphasis on what the claimant can do, rather than on what they cannot do (*SSCBA 1992, s 171A(2A)*).

The report of the doctor carrying out an examination is advisory only (*Social Security and Child Support (Decisions and Appeals) Regulations 1999 (SI 1999 No 991), Reg 11*). Following the examination, the case is referred back to the decision maker who must then decide on the basis of the information given (including the results of the medical examination) whether the claimant is incapable of work. There is a right of appeal against a decision. Claimants will be called back for periodic reassessments. (*SSCBA 1992, s 171C (5)*).

## *Permitted work* 6.10

A person who is found to be incapable of work is nevertheless treated as capable of work for any week in which they actually do any work, with certain exceptions. A person is treated as capable of work only on the days that they actually do work (rather than for the whole week) if work is undertaken during the first week of the claim, or the last week during which they were found to be incapable, or during a week when they are receiving plasmapheresis, parenteral chemotherapy, radiotherapy, renal dialysis or total parenteral nutritional treatment.

Certain types of work are allowed. This includes:

- minimal amounts of work (*CIB/5298/1997*);
- 'approved work' arranged with the DWP (*SI 1995 No 311, Reg 10A*);
- the care of certain specified relatives (*SI 1995 No 311, Reg 16(2)*);
- domestic work at home (*SI 1995 No 311, Reg 16(2)*);
- work in an emergency to prevent damage to people, property or livestock (*SI 1995 No 311, Reg 16(4)*);
- work as a local councillor (*SSCBA 1992, s 171F*);
- work as a 'disabled panel' member of an appeal tribunal (not exceeding one day a week) (*SI 1995 No 311, Reg 17(1)(c)*);
- voluntary work, not for a close relative, receiving no payment other than expenses (*SI 1995 No 311, Reg 17(1)(b)*).

In addition, a person in receipt of incapacity benefit may undertake permitted work without affecting their status as incapable of work. It is not necessary to have the support of a doctor, or to undertake the work on medical advice, but the Department for Work and Pensions must be informed within 42 days of the start of a period of work.

- A person can work during a treatment programme, either as a hospital in-patient or out-patient, provided they earn no more than £67.50 a week.
- A person can work for as long as they wish (both in terms of hours per week and in terms of duration), provided they earn no more than £20 a week. In practice the minimum wage will limit such work to around five hours a week.
- A person can work for a period not exceeding 26 weeks, provided they work on average for no more than 16 hours a week and earn no more than £67.50 a week net.
- A person who ceases to claim an incapacity-related benefit for at least eight weeks during a period of permitted work is entitled to a further 26 weeks of up to 16 hours a week earning no more than £67.50 a week.
- Where there is evidence that further work could help the claimant towards full-time work, there can be a further 26 weeks work for no

more than 16 hours a week and for no more than £67.50 net. This evidence can be from a New Deal Job-Broker, a Personal Adviser, or a Disability Employment Adviser. Evidence from the claimant or an employer can also be considered.

- In appropriate cases (determined by considering evidence as above) there can be a further 52 weeks work for up to 16 hours a week, earning no more than £67.50 a week, at the discretion of the Department, after a break of at least 52 weeks, during which the claimant can carry out permitted work at £20 a week.
- Someone who has continuing support from a social services or voluntary agency employment worker can work for as long as they like in supported work, provided they do not work for more than 16 hours a week nor earn more than £67.50 a week.

(*SI 1995 No 311, Reg 17*.)

## Payment of incapacity benefit 6.11

Benefit is payable for a day of incapacity for work. It is not payable for the first three days of a period of incapacity for work, which is normally a period of four or more days of incapacity, except for certain persons who receive medical treatment (such as renal dialysis) where any two days of incapacity (consecutive or not) within a period of seven days count as a period of incapacity (*SSCBA 1992, s 30C (4)(a)* and *Social Security (Incapacity Benefit) Regulations 1994 (SI 1994 No 2946), Reg 6*). Where two or more such periods are separated by periods of no more than eight weeks, the two periods are linked together and the waiting days rule does not apply (*SSCBA 1992, s 30(1)(c)*).

There are two exceptions to the rules on linking periods. A welfare to work beneficiary may link together two periods of incapacity provided they are not separated by more than 52 weeks. This is a person who has been receiving a benefit for incapacity for more than 28 weeks which has now stopped, and who started paid employment or went on a training course within a week of the cessation of his or her benefit. (*SI 1995 No 311, Reg 13A*). Secondly, people who are normally engaged in remunerative work which has stopped, and who were receiving working tax credit including a disability element in the week in which they stopped, have a two-year linking period provided they qualified for working tax credit in the first instance by being paid either the short-term higher rate or the long-term rate of incapacity benefit. (*SSCBA 1992, s 30C(5)*).

Days of absence from Great Britain or days spent in custody (not exceeding six weeks) are excluded, as are days of attendance at certain training courses for which a training allowance is paid (*SI 1994 No 2946, Reg 4*). A day falling within the maternity pay period is a day of incapacity for work unless the woman is disqualified.

Regulations permit the disqualification of an incapacity benefit claimant because their incapacity is due to their own fault, for example by becoming incapable of work through misconduct (*SSCBA 1992, s 171E (1)(a)*; *SI 1995 No 311, Reg 18(1)(a)*), refusing medical treatment (*SSCBA 1992, s 171F (1)(b)*; *SS(IFW) Regs, reg 18(1)(b)*), or acting in such a way as to slow down recovery (*Reg 18(1)(c)(i)*). A person who is absent from their residence without leaving word of where they may be found may also be disqualified (*Social Security (Unemployment, Sickness and Invalidity Benefit) Regs 1983 (SI 1983 No 1598), Reg 17(1)(d)(ii)*). In all cases there is a defence of good cause. The maximum period of disqualification is six weeks.

A person who fails to attend a medical examination of which they have had at least seven days' notice is deemed capable of work (*SI 1995 No 311, Reg 8(2)*) subject to a defence of good cause (*SI 1995 No 311, Reg 9*).

The benefit is paid at three rates. The *short-term lower rate* is payable for the first 28 weeks of incapacity. The *short-term higher rate* is payable for the next 24 weeks, and the *long-term rate* thereafter until pension age. Long-term rate incapacity benefit is not paid after retirement age. Short-term rate incapacity benefit is payable to those not more than five years over pension age who have deferred their claim to a Category A or Category B retirement pension and whose period of incapacity began before they reached pension age.

Increases in benefits are paid for dependent adults. Increases are also payable for children provided they were already in payment at 7 April 2003 (when the new child tax credit took over payment of additions for children). Someone who is under 45 on the first day of their period of incapacity is also entitled to an age addition.

| **Rates of incapacity benefit** | | |
|---|---|---|
| *Long-term rate* | *Claimant under pension age* | *Claimant over pension age* |
| Claimant | £72.15 | N/A |
| Adult dependant | £43.15 | N/A |
| Eldest dependent child | £9.55 | N/A |
| Other children | £11.35 | N/A |

| **Rates of incapacity benefit** | | |
|---|---|---|
| *Short-term higher rate* | *Claimant under pension age* | *Claimant over pension age* |
| Claimant | £64.35 | £72.15 |
| Adult dependant | £33.65 | £41.50 |
| Eldest dependent child | £9.55 | £9.55 |
| Other children | £11.35 | £11.35 |
| *Short-term lower rate* | *Claimant under pension age* | *Claimant over pension age* |
| Claimant | £54.40 | £69.20 |
| Adult dependant | £33.65 | £41.50 |
| Eldest dependent child | £9.55 | £9.55 |
| Other children | £11.35 | £11.35 |
| Age addition – aged under 35 on first day of incapacity | £15.15 | |
| Age addition – aged under 45 on first day of incapacity | £7.60 | |
| *Earnings rules for adult dependants* | | |
| Short-term rate | £33.65 | £41.50 |
| Long-term rate | | £43.15 |

# 7 Income Based Benefits and Tax Credits

## Introduction 7.1

The principal income based benefits are income support; housing benefit; and council tax benefit. Since in many cases the personal injury claimant will not be capable of work, at least in the initial stages following an injury or disease, they are unlikely, at least in the initial stages, to be looking for work; the remaining income based benefit, namely income based jobseeker's allowance, is therefore not covered in this section. For further information, see the specialist works mentioned in **Appendix 5**. Any of the other three benefits may be applicable, and all are covered below.

For those who do continue to work following an injury or illness, working tax credit may enable low earnings to be topped up. For those with dependent children, child tax credit should be claimed, whether the injured person (or their partner) is in or out of work.

Those aged over 60 are now covered by the state pension credit, introduced in October 2003. This provides not only a top-up to a low income, but additional income for those with capital or savings, or who have made provision for themselves by way of a private or occupational pension.

This chapter also covers health benefits provided free or at a reduced rate, and payments from the discretionary social fund to meet needs which cannot be met from income.

## Income support 7.2

Note: many income support rules are common to housing benefit and council tax benefit. Certain such rules which are significant are indicated below by references to the regulations for those two benefits, as well as for income support.

### *Who can claim: the family* 7.3

Income support is calculated not for individuals within a family (as incapacity benefit is), but for families as a whole. This means that a husband and wife and their children form a single unit for benefit purposes. A man and a woman who live together as husband and wife are treated as a couple, whether they are married to each other or not. Their income and capital is aggregated for the purpose of calculating benefit, which is assessed by reference to their joint needs and not their needs as individuals (*SSCBA 1992, s 136(1)*). Provided that both qualify, either can make the claim (*Social Security (Claims and Payments) Regulations 1987 (SI 1987 No 1968), Reg 4(3)*). Unlike jobseeker's allowance, there is no provision for joint claims.

Whereas the contributory benefits deal largely with spouses, and cohabitees are ignored as dependants unless there are children, the income based benefits make no distinction between couples who are married and couples who are unmarried. Where a couple are married and live together, there is a presumption that they are living together as husband and wife, and their benefits are calculated accordingly (*CIS/2900/1998*). A man and a woman who live together are treated as a couple and their income support (and other income based benefits) calculated accordingly. The question whether a couple are, or are not, living together is therefore fundamental to entitlement in many cases. Consideration of the detailed law on cohabitation is outside the scope of this book; for a discussion see *Tolley's Social Security and Family Benefits; A Practical Guide* (**Appendix 5**).

Dependent children (children for whom their parents are 'responsible') form part of the claim by their parent or parents. A person is treated as responsible for a child for whom they receive child benefit (*Income Support (General) Regulations 1987 (SI 1987 No 1967), Reg 16(1)*). A child is always treated as a dependent up to their 16th birthday, even if he or she has a child of their own (*SI 1987 No 1967, Reg 15(1A)*). Once a child has reached the age of 16, he or she continues to be treated as a dependent if he or she is in full-time non-advanced education. Once he or she leaves full-time non-advanced education, he or she continues to be treated as their parents' dependant until the 'terminal date' (effectively the end of the holiday after they leave school), unless they get a job before that date. A child always ceases to be a dependant on their nineteenth birthday.

A child normally counts as a dependant if child benefit is being paid for them. A child's earnings are usually ignored (except for maintenance), but capital possessed by a child may affect the benefit entitlement of the family. The child's capital is ignored (*SI 1987 No 1967, Reg 47*), but if it exceeds £3000, the child is not treated as a member of the family and benefit is not paid for him or her (*SI 1987 No 1967, Reg 44(5)*). In the case of housing and council tax benefits, from 6 October 2003, this same rule applies to claimants under 60, but for those over 60 (or whose partner is over 60) and not claiming income support, benefit will still be paid for a child (*Housing Benefit (General) Regulations 1987 (SI 1987 No 1971), Reg 16(1)(b) – (e)*; *Council Tax Benefit (General) Regulations 1992 (SI 1992 No 1814), Reg 8(1)(b) – (e)*).

At present the income support calculation includes amounts for children (see below). From April 2004, these allowances will be entirely replaced by child tax credit. This is so whether their parents are in or out of work.

## *Capital* 7.4

Income support has both a capital cut-off point and a tariff income rule. The term capital is not defined in the regulations, but is accepted as including money, in any form, and assets other than personal belongings. The value of a house (after deduction of any charges on it) counts as capital unless it can be disregarded. It will be disregarded if:

- the claimant lives in it; or
- it is occupied by the claimant's partner; or
- it is occupied by an aged or incapacitated relative.

*(SI 1987 No 1967, Sch 10 paras 1, 4.)*

Its value is disregarded for six months following the breakdown of marriage or cohabitation; and for six months, or longer if reasonable, if it is:

- being sold; or
- being repaired in order to be lived in; or
- subject to legal action to recover possession.

*(SI 1987 No 1967, Sch 10 paras 26 – 28.)*

### *Capital cut-off* 7.5

A claimant who has more than a certain amount of capital is disqualified for income support (*SSCBA s 134(1)*). Where the claimant is one of a couple, the capital cut-off point applies to the aggregate of the capital of the two partners. The cut-off points are:

| | |
|---|---|
| Claimant permanently in residential care | £16,000 |
| Claimant or partner 60 or over | £12,000 |
| Claimant and partner both under 60 | £8,000 |

Where the claimant or their partner is over 60, income support payable to them is usually known as minimum income guarantee. When the state pension credit replaces minimum income guarantee in October 2003, the capital cut-off rule will be abolished but the tariff income rule (see below) will still apply.

## *Tariff income* 7.6

Income is deemed to be received from capital at the rate of £1 a week for every £250 or part £250 above a certain level, which is £6000 for those claimants who are, or whose partner is, over 60, and £3000 for everyone else. Actual income received is ignored. Claimants living permanently in residential accommodation have the first £10,000 ignored, and the tariff income rule applied to capital between £10,000 and £16,000 (*Income Support (General) Regulations 1987 (SI 1987 No 1967), Reg 53*).

When the state pension credit is introduced in October 2003 for those over 60, the rate of tariff income will be £1 for every £500 or part £500 above £6000 (*State Pension Credit Act 2002, s 15(2)*; *State Pension Credit Regulations 2002 (SI 2002 No 1792), Reg 15(6)*).

## *Valuing capital* 7.7

Capital is valued at the figure which it would fetch from a willing purchaser in the open market. Selling expenses of 10 per cent, where appropriate, may be deducted (*Income Support (General) Regulations 1987 (SI 1987 No 1967), Reg 49*). Where only one of joint owners of a capital asset is claiming benefit, their share should be valued according to its open market value, and not by dividing the value of the whole asset by the number of co-owners (*SI 1987 No 1967, Reg 52; Chief Adjudication Officer v Palfrey (R(IS) 26/95)*; *Secretary of State for Work & Pensions v Hourigan [2002] EWCA Civ 1890*).

## *The notional capital rule* 7.8

A person disposing of capital for the purpose of obtaining benefit is treated as if they still possessed it (*SI 1987 No 1967, Reg 51(1)*). If its possession takes the claimant's capital above the capital cut-off, he or she will be disqualified for benefit. Note that there is no time limit on the notional capital rule. Where the rule applies, the claimant will be deemed to live on his or her capital until such time as its value is reduced to below the capital cut-off. This is done under a formula known as the diminishing notional capital rule (*SI 1987 No 1967, Reg 51A*).

**EXAMPLE**

Roger is claiming income support. He inherits a house from his uncle. A house is only disregarded where the claimant lives in it. If Roger moves into the house, it will not affect his benefit claim. If, however, he gives the house away in order to retain his entitlement to income support, he will be treated as if he had capital amounting to the value of the house. If this exceeds £8,000, he will not be entitled to income support.

If he has actually parted with the house, he will be disqualified for benefit. He is deemed to live on his capital, and his disqualification will last until his notional capital is deemed to have been reduced below £8,000. This is determined according to the notional capital rule.

### *The effect of damages on capital* **7.9**

It will be appreciated that, where a person receives a capital sum as damages for a personal injury, that capital sum is likely to disqualify them for benefit; and furthermore that the notional capital rule prevents their disposing of the capital.

It would therefore appear that an award of damages for personal injury which brings the claimant's capital to more than £8,000 or £12,000 (as appropriate) would have the effect of terminating entitlement to benefit. However, *SI 1987 No 1967, Sch 10* provide for certain items of capital to be disregarded. Where the claimant is awarded damages in respect of a personal injury, this may be caught by either *paragraph 12* or *paragraph 44* of *Schedule 10*.

*Schedule 10* states that the following capital is to be disregarded:

> '12. Where the funds of a Trust are derived from a payment made in consequence of any personal injury to the claimant, the value of the trust fund and the value of the right to receive any payment under that trust.
>
> [ . . .]
>
> 44. Any sum of capital administered on behalf of a person by the High Court under the provisions of Order 80 of the Rules of the Supreme Court, the County Court under Order 10 of the County Court Rules 1981, or the Court of Protection, where such sum derives from:
>
> (a) an award of damages for a personal injury to that person; or
>
> (b) compensation for the death or one or both parents where the person concerned is under the age of 18.'

In order for *paragraph 12* to apply, there must be a trust of the compensation. If there is no such trust, then the amount of compensation counts as the claimant's capital, even though it is not in the claimant's own hands but in the hands of the claimant's solicitor (*Thomas v Chief Adjudication Officer,* reported as *R (SB) 17/87*). (This does not apply in circumstances where the solicitor is holding the money while it is ascertained whether any part of it is payable to the Legal Services Commission under the statutory charge provisions of the *Access to Justice Act 1999*.)

The exception for capital in trust applies as soon as the claimant transfers the capital into the hands of trustees, even though it was previously taken into account as his or her capital, and he or she will not be treated as having deprived him or herself of the capital by placing it into the hands of trustees. It is not necessary for the trust to be set up before the compensation is received, although during the interim period the claimant will be caught by the capital cut off rule.

A personal injury apparently includes personal injury to the claimant's partner or dependent children. A personal injury includes a disease and injuries suffered as the result of a disease (*R (SB) 2/89*).

For the treatment of income from the capital, see below.

*Paragraph 44* covers funds which are held in court for damages for personal injury. The provision is no longer (as formerly) limited to under 18 year olds, but, since October 1997, applies to everyone without age limit. However, where the compensation is awarded in respect to the death of a parent, the claimants must be under 18.

The provision does not apply to death benefits paid under a pension or insurance policy. These do not represent compensation, but rather the payment under a contract between the insurer and the injured or deceased person (*McAuley v Department for Social Development, Court of Appeal of Northern Ireland, reported as R 3/01 (IS)*). The exception in *paragraph 44* applies to awards for personal injury to the claimant and apparently does not apply to awards for the claimant's partner or dependent children, unlike *paragraph 12*.

For the purposes of pension credit, and of housing benefit and council tax benefit where the claimant or their partner is over 60 and is not claiming income support or income based jobseekers allowance, the trust must be set up for the benefit of the claimant or their partner. The trust does not have to be set up by a formal Deed of Trust.

Note that the notional income and capital rules cannot apply to trusts or funds administered by the Court which have been set up following personal injury.

## *Prescribed categories of people who can claim* 7.10

In order to claim income support, a claimant must be in a prescribed category (*SSCBA 1992, s 124(1)(e)*). The following categories are those which are most likely to be relevant to those who have suffered personal injury and their carers. However, presence in any prescribed category (for example, every lone parent of a child under 16 is in a prescribed category) will potentially give entitlement to income support even though the claimant cannot fulfil any of the criteria listed below:

- a person who is incapable of work because of illness or disability;
- a disabled person with limited earning capacity;
- a disabled student (within certain limitations);
- a blind person;
- a person who is appealing a decision refusing them incapacity benefit on the ground that they are not incapable of work;
- a carer who is receiving carers allowance;
- a carer who is caring for someone who receives either attendance allowance, or the middle or higher rate care component of disability living allowance;
- a carer who is caring for someone who has claimed either attendance allowance or disability living allowance within the last six months;
- a person who is caring for a family member who is ill;

A carer continues to be within a prescribed category for eight weeks after ceasing to fulfil the condition.

(*SI 1987 No 1967, Reg 4ZA, Sch 1B.*)

Others who may be in a prescribed category include those over 60, and those with child care responsibilities.

## ***Conditions of entitlement to income support*** 7.11

In addition to being in a prescribed category, the claimant must fulfil the following conditions.

### *Presence and residence* 7.12

The claimant must be present in Great Britain, and habitually resident in the United Kingdom, the Channel Islands, the Isle of Man, or the Republic of Ireland (known as the common travel area) (*SI 1987 No 1967, Sch 7 para 17*). The habitual residence test requires the claimant to have been resident in the common travel area for 'an appreciable period of time', along with a settled intention to remain (*R(IS) 6/96*). The following people are treated as habitually resident, and are therefore exempt from the test:

- Nationals of European Economic Area countries who are classed as workers under European law.
- Refugees and people granted exceptional leave to remain in the UK.
- People who left Montserrat after 1 November 1995 because of the volcanic eruption.

- People who have been deported to the UK from another country, unless they are subject to immigration control.

(*SI 1987 No 1967, Reg 21(3)* and *(3F)*; *Housing Benefit (General) Regulations 1987 (SI 1987 No 1971), Reg 7A(4)(e)* and *(5)*.)

There is no clear definition of habitual residence, which will be determined according to individual circumstances, and is a question of fact and degree (*Nessa v Chief Adjudication Officer [1999] 4 All ER 677*). The appreciable period of time is likely to be at least three weeks. Former residents returning to the UK may be treated as habitually resident immediately (*Swaddling v Adjudication Officer [1999] All ER (EC) 217*).

A claimant who is temporarily absent from the UK may have that temporary absence ignored for up to four weeks, provided they fulfil one of the following conditions (*SI 1987 No 1967, Reg 4(1)–(2)*):

- The claimant is in Northern Ireland.
- The claimant is not excluded from this concession by *Schedule 1B* – largely those who are incapable of work (other than those mentioned below) or appealing against a decision that they are not incapable of work, or in full-time education, or affected by a trade dispute, or a person from abroad.
- The claimant is incapable of work and has gone abroad for the sole purpose of receiving treatment.
- The claimant has been incapable of work for a continuous period of 52 weeks (28 weeks if terminally ill, or on the highest care component of DLA).
- The claimant has a partner who is also abroad, and who is entitled to a pensioner premium, a higher pensioner premium, a disability premium, or a severe disability premium.

Income support can be paid for up to eight weeks where the claimant is accompanying a child or young person for treatment abroad, provided the child or young person is a member of their family.

### *Immigration control* **7.13**

The claimant must not be subject to immigration control (*Immigration and Asylum Act 1999, s 115*).

### *Remunerative work* **7.14**

Neither the claimant nor their partner (if any) may be in remunerative work, ie work of 16 hours a week or more for the claimant, or 24 hours a week or more for the claimant's partner (*SI 1987 No 1967, Reg 5(1)*). The work must be done in expectation of payment. Where working hours fluctuate, an average is taken (*SI 1987 No 1967, Reg 5(2)(a)*). A person who is off work because of sickness will normally be able to claim income support if other conditions are fulfilled.

Certain people are deemed not to be engaged in remunerative work even if they work for more than 16 hours a week, including those who:

- Have their earning capacity reduced by 25 per cent or more as a result of mental or physical disablement.
- Are regularly and substantially engaged in caring for another who is entitled to disability living allowance or attendance allowance.
- Are carers.

(*SI 1987 No 1967, Reg 6(1)* and *(4)*.)

The person must be in a prescribed category.

### *Education* **7.15**

If the claimant is under 19, he or she must not be receiving 'relevant' (non-advanced) education (*SSCBA 1992, s 124 (1)(d)*). There are several exceptions to this rule, which include claimants who:

- Have no parent and nobody acting in their place.
- Are the parent of a child for whom they are responsible.
- Are so severely disabled that they are unlikely to get a job in the next 12 months.
- Have left local authority care, and have to live away from home.
- Have to live away from their parents because they are estranged from them, or because they are in physical or moral danger, or because there is a serious risk to their physical or mental health
- Live apart from their parents who cannot support them, where the parents are in prison, or are unable to come to the UK because they do not have leave to enter under UK immigration law, or are chronically sick or mentally or physically disabled.
- Are refugees learning English.

(*SI 1987 No 1967, Reg 13*.)

If the claimant is in full-time advanced education, he or she is classified as a student and is also excluded from income support from the beginning of the course until its end (*SI 1987 No 1967, Reg 4ZA(2)*). To this rule there are the following exceptions:

- A lone parent, including a foster parent, of a child under 16.
- A student from abroad who is temporarily without funds and is entitled to an urgent cases payment.
- A disabled student who satisfies certain conditions.
- One of a couple who are both full-time students, provided they are in a prescribed category and are responsible for a child. This only applies during the summer vacation.
- A pensioner (until 6 October 2003).
- A refugee learning English.

(*SI 1987 No 1967, Reg 4ZA (3).*)

A claimant in part-time education can claim income support provided they fulfil all the necessary qualifying conditions.

### *Age* **7.16**

The claimant must be at least 16 (*SSCBA 1992, s 124(1)(a)*). Most young people leaving local authority care are excluded from income support and are the responsibility of the local authority (*Children (Leaving Care) Act 2000, s 6*).

From 6 October 2003 a claimant must also be less than 60.

### *Relationship with other benefits* **7.17**

The claimant must not be receiving jobseeker's allowance, either contributory or income based; the claimant's partner, if any, must not be receiving income based jobseeker's allowance. From 6 October 2003 the claimant's partner must not be getting pension credit (*SSCBA 1992, s 124*).

## ***Calculating income support*** **7.18**

Income support consists of the amount by which a person's income falls short of their applicable amount. The applicable amount consists of a personal allowance for every member of the family, plus premiums as appropriate, plus any qualifying housing costs.

## *Personal allowances* **7.19**

Rates of personal allowances are as follows.

| | |
|---|---|
| **Single people** | |
| Aged 16–17, including a lone parent, normal rate | 32.90* |
| Aged 16–17, including a lone parent, higher rate | 43.25* |
| Aged 18–24 | 43.25 |
| Aged 25 or over | 54.65 |
| * – see below | |
| **Couples** | |
| Both aged under 18 (maximum) | 65.30 |
| Both 18 or over | 85.75 |
| **Dependent children** | |
| Aged under 19 | 38.50 |

The higher rate of personal allowance for a 16–17 year old is payable where the claimant:

- qualifies for the disability premium; or
- is an orphan and nobody is acting in place of their parents; or
- is living away from their parents, and was in custody or being looked after by a local authority immediately before reaching 16; or
- is living away from their parents as part of a resettlement programme, or to avoid physical or sexual abuse, or to live in special accommodation because of a mental or physical condition; or
- is living away from their parents who are unable to support them financially, and who are in custody, or unable to enter Great Britain, or are chronically sick or disabled; or
- is living away from their parents because they are estranged from them, or because they are in physical or moral danger, or there is a serious risk to their health.

(*SI 1987 No 1967, Sch 2 para 1A.*)

## *Premiums* **7.20**

The following premiums are those directly relevant to disability and incapacity for work. There is no restriction on any of the premiums listed being paid with any others which are also listed. Other premiums (not directly relevant to incapacity or disability) are listed below.

### Carer's premium – £25.10

Where the claimant or their partner receives carers allowance, or would do so but for the overlapping benefit rules. The person cared for need not be a family member. Entitlement continues for eight weeks after caring responsibilities end. Where both the claimant and their partner receive carers allowance, a double carer premium is paid.

### Severe Disability premium – £42.95

This is applicable to a claimant who is on attendance allowance or the middle or higher care component of disability living allowance, **and** there is no non-dependant over 18 residing with them, **and** no-one is receiving carers allowance for looking after them. Where someone comes to the household to care for the disabled person, the premium continues for twelve weeks. Note that a person who is themselves claiming attendance allowance or the middle or higher care component of disability living allowance does not count as a non-dependant. It is therefore possible for both members of a couple to qualify for the severe disability premium, which is then worth £85.90.

### Disability premium – £23.30 (single claimant) £33.25 (claimant with a partner)

Applicable where the claimant or their partner are both under 60, and either of them:

- is in receipt of disability living allowance or constant attendance allowance; or
- is in receipt of mobility supplement (war pensions); or
- is in receipt of severe disablement allowance; or
- is in receipt of the disability or severe disability element of working tax credit; or
- is in receipt of long-term incapacity benefit; or
- is registered blind or has recovered their sight in the last 28 weeks; or
- has an invalid tricycle;

or where the claimant (but not their partner):

- has been incapable of work for 196 days and is terminally ill; or

- has been incapable of work for 364 days.

## Disabled child premium – £41.30

Payable where a child in the family claims the middle or higher rate care component of disability living allowance, or is blind or has regained their sight within the last 28 weeks. This premium is not applicable if the child has more than £3,000 capital.

## Enhanced Disability premium – £11.40 (single claimant, or disabled child), £16.45 (claimant who is one of a couple) £16.60 (in respect of a child)

Applicable where the claimant or their partner, both of whom are under 60, or a dependent child, receives the highest rate care component of disability living allowance. It is payable with both the disability and with the severe disability premium. The child rate is not applicable where the child has more than £3,000 capital.

| **Other premiums** | |
|---|---|
| Family premium – normal rate | 15.75 |
| Family premium – lone parent rate | 15.90 |
| Bereavement premium | 22.80 |
| Pensioner/enhanced/higher pensioner premium | 47.45 (single claimant) |
| | 70.05 (couple) |

A disability premium may not be paid with a pensioner premium. The lone parent rate of family premium is not payable where a disability premium is also payable. With the introduction of the state pension credit in October 2003, the pensioner premiums will effectively disappear, and since pensioners with dependent children will have income for their child or children paid through the child tax credit system from that date, the family premium will also disappear. It will still be possible to qualify for the higher pensioner premium, which may be important as it gives a right to a £20 disregard on earnings, but only if both partners are over 60.

*(SI 1987 No 1967, Sch 2.)*

### *Housing costs* **7.21**

The eligible housing costs of a house-owner are included as part of their applicable amount. 'Eligible housing costs' consist primarily of the interest (but not capital) payments on a mortgage, and other prescribed housing costs such as ground rent. Costs are worked out on a weekly basis. Note that an income support claimant who lives in a rented property will be entitled to housing benefit for his or her maximum eligible rent, instead of housing costs paid by income support.

Mortgage interest is included, up to a maximum loan of £100,000. Benefit is paid at a standard rate of interest, unless the actual rate is less than 5%, in which case it is paid according to the actual rate. The amount allowed may therefore be less than the claimant actually pays. Insurance premiums for an endowment mortgage are not paid. Payments are limited where the loan is 'excessive'.

Even after these restrictions, the full amount of mortgage interest may not be payable. The full amount (calculated as above) is payable as soon as the claim is made if the claimant or their partner is over 60. For anyone else who is a new claimant, the amount payable will depend on when they took out the mortgage.

For those who took out their mortgage before 2 October 1995, no housing costs at all are included in the applicable amount for the first eight weeks of the claim. For the next eighteen weeks, 50% of housing costs are included. Thereafter the full amount is payable. There is a standard twelve-week linking period (*Sch 3, para 14*). For those taking out a loan after that date, no housing costs at all are included in the applicable amount for the first 39 weeks, with the full amount being paid thereafter. Certain claimants (including carers, and those refused payment under a mortgage protection policy because of a pre-existing condition or who have been infected by HIV) are always treated as if they had taken out the mortgage before 2 October 1995, irrespective of when they actually did so.

(*SI 1987 No 1967, Sch 3.*)

### ***Calculating the applicable amount*** **7.22**

The income support applicable amount may therefore be calculated by adding together personal allowances for every member of the family, together with any applicable premiums, together with any qualifying housing costs.

**EXAMPLE**

Dennis and Heather have two children aged eight and four. The younger child is in receipt of disability living allowance. Dennis has been on incapacity benefit for eighteen months since being injured in an accident at work.

Their applicable amount will be:

| | |
|---|---|
| Personal allowance for Dennis and Heather | 85.75 |
| Personal allowance for the elder child | 38.50 |
| Personal allowance for the younger child | 38.50 |
| Family premium (for any family with at least one child) | 15.75 |
| Disabled child premium | 41.30 |
| Disability premium (couple) for Dennis' incapacity | 33.25 |
| Total | 253.05 |

Note that, if Heather is the principal carer for the child, she may qualify for carer's allowance, and hence for the carer's premium.

### *Income* 7.23

Income support entitlement is determined by deducting income from the applicable amount. Not all income is taken into account. Some income is taken into account in full; some is partially disregarded; and some is wholly disregarded.

### *Income which is completely disregarded* 7.24

The following items of income are entirely ignored when working out income for income support purposes:

- charitable or voluntary payments for items not covered by benefit;
- payments in kind (but note the notional income rule);
- disability living allowance, attendance allowance, housing benefit, council tax benefit;
- actual interest on capital.

(*SI 1987 No 1967, Reg 48, Sch 9.*)

### *Income which is partly disregarded* 7.25

A number of items of income are partially disregarded when working out income. The most common is part-time earnings, the rules for which are set out below. (Full-time earnings would disqualify the claimant for income support.) There are also special rules for income payments from an award of damages for personal injury, which are also set out below. Other items which are partially disregarded include:

- widowed mothers allowance and bereaved parents allowance (£10);
- war disablement pension (£10);
- war widows or widowers pension (£10);
- widows or widowers pension payable to a spouse of someone who died as a result of service in the armed forces (£10);
- extra-statutory payments made in place of any of the above pensions (£10);
- child support maintenance paid under the new child support rules (£10).

(*SI 1987 No 1967, Sch 9*.)

## *Part-time earnings* **7.26**

The disregards available on part-time earnings are based on net earnings. To calculate net earnings take gross earnings and deduct tax actually paid, national insurance contributions paid, and half of any contributions to an occupational pension scheme. Everything else is included, even if deducted at source (*SI 1987 No 1967, Sch 8*).

Then apply the disregard. Ignore the first £20 where:

- the claimant qualifies for the lone parent premium;
- the claimant or their partner qualifies for the disability or carers premium;
- one or both partners is over 60 and disabled.

Otherwise disregard £10 for a couple and £5 for a single person (*SI 1987 No 1967, Sch 8 paras 6, 9*).

## *Income from awards for personal injury compensation* **7.27**

The rules allowing capital payments to be disregarded discriminated against claimants who were receiving income under a structured settlement or a Trust, who where not subject to similar disregards. The rules have therefore been amended to provide for certain disregards in respect of payments made from personal injury capital sums.

This disregard applies to the following types of payment:

- Payments from a trust fund set up out of personal injury compensation.

- Payments under an annuity purchased under an agreement or court order following a personal injury.
- Payments under an agreement or court order because of a personal injury.

*(SI 1987 No 1967, Sch 9 para 15 (5)(a); SI 1987 No1971, sch 4 para 13(6); Council Tax Benefit (General) Regulations 1992 (SI 1992 No 1814), Sch 4 para 13(6).)*

Payments made from any of the above sources are disregarded if they are intended and used for anything other than items which are intended to be covered by benefits. This includes food, ordinary clothing or footwear, household fuel, council tax, water charges and rent for which housing benefit could be payable. If such payments are intended for any of these purposes, then they are subject to a disregard of the first £20 although the disregard may overlap with other disregards for those war pensions listed above for which a £20 disregard is allowed, or student loans, when a combined maximum of £20 is allowed.

### *Income which is taken into account in full* **7.28**

Items of income which are fully taken into account include:

- benefits except disability living allowance, attendance allowance, housing and council tax benefits, and those partial disregards listed above;
- maintenance, other than disregarded child support maintenance;
- tariff income from capital.

### *The calculation* **7.29**

Income support consists of the amount by which the claimant's assessed income falls short of his or her applicable amount.

#### EXAMPLE

See the example of Dennis and Heather, above. Dennis and Heather have two children aged eight and four.The younger child is in receipt of disability living allowance. Dennis has been on incapacity benefit for eighteen months since being injured in an accident at work. Their applicable amount is £253.05.

Their income consists of Dennis' incapacity benefit, which consists of benefit for himself (£72.15), Heather (£43.15), the younger child (£11.35) and the elder child (£9.55); child benefit for the elder child (£16.05) and the younger child (£10.75); and disability living allowance for the younger child (£38.30).

All are taken fully into account except the disability living allowance for the younger child which is ignored. This gives a total income of £163.00. Their income support is £253.05 minus £163 which equals £90.05.

Note that this assumes that they are existing claimants as at 6 April 2003. Families with children making a new claim for incapacity benefit after that date will not receive additions for children, and will instead claim the child tax credit (see below). With effect from April 2004, the amounts allowed in their applicable amount for children will also be removed and the support of children will, apart from child benefit, be entirely a matter for the child tax credit.

## Tax credits 7.30

A new system of Tax Credits was introduced from 6 April 2003. Child Tax Credit provides a means of supporting all those who are responsible for children, whether they are in or out work. Allowances for children payable with a claim for non-means tested benefits, allowances for children previously paid with working families tax credit or disabled persons tax credit, and the child tax allowance have all been abolished from that date. Claimants of income support and income based jobseeker's allowance will move on to child tax credit with effect from April 2004.

This part outlines the new tax credit system, but does not set out to explain it in detail, for which reference should be made to the guides published by the Inland Revenue or specialist welfare rights works referred to in Appendix 5.

### *Working tax credit* 7.31

Working tax credit is a benefit for people who are engaged in remunerative full-time work. In order to claim, a person must be in full-time paid work, must be present and ordinarily resident in Great Britain, and must not be subject to immigration control.

There are particular provisions for claimants who are disabled. Where the claimant has a physical or mental disability that puts them at a disadvantage in getting a job, they qualify for a disability element as part of their working tax credit. The full-time work requirement is that they should work for at least 16 hours a week. They must be aged at least 16. A person who does not fit into this category, but who is nevertheless responsible for a child so as to qualify for child tax credit, can claim working tax credit on the basis of the same definition of full-time work. However, a person who does not fall into either of these categories must be aged at least 25 and must work for at least 30 hours per week (*Working Tax Credits (Entitlement and Maximum Rate) Regulations 2002 (SI 2002 No 2005), Reg 4*).

In order to claim with the benefit of the disability element, the claimant must meet one of the requirements listed in *SI 2002 No 2005, Sch 1*. These are as follows:

- When standing he or she cannot keep their balance unless continually holding on to something.
- He or she cannot (with the assistance of a stick or other aid normally used) walk a continuous distance of 100 metres along level ground without stopping or without suffering severe pain.
- He or she can use neither of their hands behind their back as in the process of putting on a jacket or of tucking a shirt into trousers.
- He or she can extend neither of their arms in front of them so as to shake hands with another person without difficulty.
- He or she can put neither of their hands up to their head without difficulty so as to put on a hat.
- Due to lack of manual dexterity he or she cannot, with one hand, pick up a coin which is not more than two and a half centimetres in diameter.
- He or she is not able to use hands or arms to pick up a full jug of one litre capacity and pour from it into a cup, without difficulty.
- He or she can turn neither hand sideways through 180 degrees.
- He or she is registered either as blind or as partially sighted.
- He or she cannot see to read 16 point print at a distance greater than 20 centimetres, if appropriate wearing glasses.
- He or she cannot hear a telephone ring in the same room, if appropriate using their usual hearing aid.
- In a quiet room he or she has difficulty hearing what someone talking in a loud voice at a distance of 2 metres says, if appropriate using their usual hearing aid.
- People who know the claimant well have difficulty in understanding what he or she says.
- When a person the claimant knows well speaks to him or her, he or she has difficulty in understanding what that person says.
- At least once a year during waking hours, he or she is in a coma or has a fit in which he or she loses consciousness.
- He or she has a mental illness which is being regularly treated under the supervision of a medically qualified person.
- Due to mental disability he or she is often confused or forgetful.
- He or she cannot do the simplest addition and subtraction.

- Due to mental disability he or she strikes people or damages property or is unable to form normal social relationships.
- He or she cannot normally sustain a normal eight hour working day or a five day working week due to a medical condition or intermittent or continuous severe pain.
- As a result of an illness or accident he or she is undergoing a period of habilitation or rehabilitation.

In addition, the claimant must:

- be receiving (or on at least one day in the one hundred and eighty two days immediately preceding the claim have been in receipt of) the higher rate of short-term incapacity benefit, long-term incapacity benefit, severe disablement allowance, or a higher pensioner premium or disability premium paid with income support, income based jobseeker's allowance, housing benefit or council tax benefit; or
- on the date of the claim they must receive disability living allowance, attendance allowance or a mobility supplement or constant attendance allowance payable with a war pension or industrial injuries disablement benefit; or
- have an invalid carriage or similar vehicle; or
- have received for at least one hundred and forty days forming a single period of incapacity for work (the last of which must have fallen within 56 days of the date of the claim), statutory sick pay, occupational sick pay, short-term incapacity benefit at the lower rate, or income support on account of incapacity, or credits for Incapacity for a period of twenty weeks; and
- have a disability at the date of the claim which is likely to last for at least six months, or for the rest of the claimant's life if that is likely to be shorter; and
- have gross earnings which are less than they were before the disability began by at least the greater of 20% and £15 per week; or
- have undertaken training for work' for at least one day in the 56 days immediately preceding the claim, and be receiving long-term incapacity benefit, severe disablement allowance or the higher rate of short-term incapacity benefit within the 56 days before that training started.

Provided the claimant can pass these tests, then he or she will be entitled to claim working tax credit with a disability element. If he or she receives the highest rate of the care component of disability living allowance or the higher rate of attendance allowance, he or she will also be entitled to a severe disability element as part of their entitlement (*SI 2002 No 2005, Reg 17*). A severe disability element can also be included for the claimant's partner if he or she meets the conditions (*SI 2002 No 2005, Reg 3(3)*).

Working tax credit contains an element for essential childcare costs, where either both partners are working or the claimant is a lone parent. Childcare costs may also be claimed where the principal carer is disabled and his or her partner is in remunerative work (*SI 2002 No 2005, Regs 3 & 13*).

The calculation of working tax credit is outside the scope of this book.

### *Child tax credit* 7.32

To claim child tax credit, a person must be responsible for a child or young person (*Child Tax Credits Regulations 2002 (SI 2002 No 2007), Regs 3–5*).

A person is a child until 1 September following his or her 16th birthday. A young person under 19 counts as a child during any period between 1 September following their 16th birthday and their 19th birthday, provided they were in full-time non-advanced education, or provided they are under 18 and have ceased such education in the last 20 weeks.

A person is responsible for a child who lives with them, or for whom they have the main responsibility. There is no provision for child tax credit to be split between partners.

### *Claiming tax credits* 7.33

The claimant must be present and ordinarily resident in Great Britain, and must not be subject to immigration control (*Immigration and Asylum Act 1999, s 115*).

The claimant must be at least 16 (*Tax Credits Act 2002 (TCA 2002), s 3(3)*).

Tax credits are claimed together on form TC600. Claim forms are obtainable from Inland Revenue Enquiry Centres or direct from the Inland Revenue by phone or letter. Claims can be backdated by up to three months. A claim must include necessary supporting information. In the case of a couple, a joint claim is made (*TCA 2002, s 3(3)(a), 3(8)*).

For someone who has recently become sick or disabled, there is a fast track procedure to enable them to claim the working tax credit. To qualify, the claimant must:

- have recently become sick or disabled;
- have been receiving a qualifying benefit, or national insurance credits because of incapacity for work, within the eight weeks before the claim.

The qualifying benefits are statutory sick pay, occupational sick pay, short-term lower rate incapacity benefit, or income support because of the incapacity. The benefit must have been in payment for at least 20 weeks, which can be in more than one period separated by no more than eight weeks;

- have a disability which puts them at a disadvantage in getting a job (see above);
- have gross earnings that are at least 20% less than before the sickness or disability; and
- have their earnings reduced by at least £15 a week.

The tax credit is assessed on a provisional basis and an award is made which lasts for a tax year. During the year enquiries are made of the claimant as to their circumstances, and where these have changed or are different from those estimated at the start of the tax year, the award is revised. Increases of income of up to £2,500 are ignored.

Overpayments are recoverable. Where there has been an overpayment as a result of a change of circumstances during the tax year (for example, as the result of an increase in income), the overpayment will usually be recovered from the following year's tax credit.

Working tax credit is paid direct by the employer of the working partner. Child tax credit, and the childcare element of working tax credit, is paid direct to the main carer, normally into a bank account.

There is an obligation to report when a single claimant becomes a member of a couple, or when a couple breaks up. There is also an obligation to report significant changes to childcare costs (i.e. when they stop, or when they change by at least £10 a week for four weeks or more). In such circumstances there will be a new award of tax credit. There is no obligation to report other changes of circumstances (including the birth of a child), but a failure to do so can lead to an overpayment, and it is frequently good advice to a claimant to report significant changes (*TCA 2002, s 6(3), 32(3)*; *Tax Credits (Claims and Notification) Regulations 2002 (SI 2002 No 2014), Reg 21*).

## Housing benefit 7.34

Housing benefit is payable to help with the cost of rent. A person on income support or income based jobseeker's allowance is automatically entitled to maximum housing benefit. Others may qualify on the ground of their income.

Housing benefit is administered by the local authority.

## *Conditions of entitlement* 7.35

For practical purposes, the claimant must be at least 16, although there is no specific legal requirement to that effect. If the claimant is aged 16 or 17 and is caught by the *Children (Leaving Care) Act 2000*, they will be unable to claim benefit and the responsibility for looking after them is that of the local authority.

The claimant must be liable to make payments in respect of a dwelling normally occupied as their home, or be the partner of such a person. Benefit may also be paid to someone who is not legally liable to pay the rent (eg a deserted wife) *(Housing Benefit (General) Regulations 1987 (SI 1987 No 1971), Reg 6(1))*.

The claimant (and their partner, if applicable) must have no more than £16,000 capital. The tariff income rule outlined above under Income Support applies to capital of between £3,000 and £16,000 (*SI 1987 No 1971, Reg 37*).

## *Liability to make payments* 7.36

Certain people are treated as not liable to make payments in respect of rent. These are as follows:

- Those whose tenancy is not on a commercial basis.
- Those whose landlord also resides in the dwelling and is a close relative.
- Those whose liability is to a former partner in respect of a former shared home, or to their partner's former partner in respect of their former matrimonial home.
- Those who are, or whose partner is, responsible for a child of the landlord.
- Those whose liability is to a company, or to a trustee of a trust, and the claimant, the claimant's partner, the claimant's former partner, or a close relative of the claimant who resides with them, is a director or employee of the company or a trustee or beneficiary of the trust.
- Those who were a non-dependant of someone who lived in the house and continues to do so.
- Those whose liability is to a trust of which their child is a beneficiary.
- Those who owned the house within the last five years, unless they can show that they could not have remained in occupation without relinquishing ownership.
- Those who occupy the house as an employee of the landlord, and as a condition of their employment.

- Those who are members of and are fully maintained by a religious order.
- Those who are in residential accommodation.
- Those living in a tenancy which the local authority is satisfied was created to take advantage of the scheme.

(*SI 1987 No 1971, Reg* 7.)

In certain limited circumstances it is permissible for a person to be absent from the dwelling. This includes cases where the claimant is a hospital in-patient, provided the period of absence is not expected substantially to exceed 52 weeks (*SI 1987 No 1971, Regs 5(8), 5(8B)*).

There are also certain situations where a claimant can be paid benefit for two homes at one time. Where a claimant is delayed in moving into a house while it is being adapted for their occupation as a disabled person, and as a result is incurring liability on both the old and the new home, housing benefit for both may be paid for up to four weeks (*SI 1987 No 1971, Reg 5(5)(e)*).

### *Eligible rent* — 7.37

Housing benefit is based on eligible rent. This is restricted to the actual accommodation, and excludes, for example:

- other payments which the rent may be expressed to include, such as water rates;
- charges for fuel;
- charges for food.

The rules on service charges are complex. Some service charges are eligible and are included in eligible rent, while others are specifically excluded.

### *Restrictions on eligible rent* — 7.38

A local authority may in certain circumstances restrict the rent on which housing benefit is based.

Where the tenancy began after 2nd January 1996, the rent officer is asked to set a rent for the property as part of the assessment of the tenant's claim (*SI 1987 No 1971, Reg 12A(1), (8)*). The rent officer's determination is binding. The rent must itself be reasonable, and also be no more than the average of rents in the locality. The local authority will base their calculation of housing benefit on the amount assessed as eligible.

The Government has announced that it intends to run a series of pilot schemes which will operate on the basis of a standard rent. The intention is to reduce complexity in the system. Benefit will be calculated on the basis of the standard rent, and this will provide an incentive for the claimant to find a cheaper property. The pilot schemes will operate from late 2003.

Single people under the age of 25 without children are restricted to a 'single room rent', that is, a rent for a single bedroom with shared sitting, kitchen and bathroom facilities. The rent officer will set an appropriate rent. Accommodation provided by a housing association, charity or voluntary association where care or support is provided is exempt from these rules (*SI 1987 No 1971, Reg 11(3A)*).

It is possible to apply for a pre-tenancy determination to find out what rent will be considered appropriate for housing benefit.

Where a tenancy began before 2 January 1996, there was greater discretion as to the rent payable. A rent fixed by the Rent Officer was not binding on the authority.

## ***Working out housing benefit*** **7.39**

Housing benefit is calculated by comparing the claimant's income with their applicable amount. The same rules outlined under income support apply with regard to the family; a man and a woman who live together as husband and wife are treated as a couple, and their needs and their means are aggregated. Dependent children form part of the family for the purpose of the calculation.

### *Step One: calculate eligible rent and Step Two: calculate applicable amount* **7.40**

The calculation of the applicable amount is very similar to the calculation carried out for income support (see above). The principal differences are that the personal allowance for all 16–24 year olds is £43.25, and the lone parent rate of family premium is £22.20. There is an addition for a child aged under one of £10.45 a week, to reflect the former child tax allowance which is now absorbed into the child tax credit.

With the introduction of state pension credit in October 2003, the applicable amounts for pensioners are amended to reflect the new calculation. The amounts are:

| | |
|---|---|
| Single, aged 60–64 | £102.10 |
| Single, aged 65 or over | £116.90 |

| | |
|---|---|
| Single, aged 60–64 | £102.10 |
| Couple, aged 60–64 | £155.80 |
| Couple, aged 65 or over | £175.00 |

(*State Pension Credit Regulations 2002 (SI 2002 No 1792), Reg 6.*)

### *Step Three: calculate income* **7.41**

Again the procedure is similar to that for calculating income support. Income is calculated in the same way, but there are different disregards for earnings. These are:

- £15 disregard on widowed mothers allowance and bereaved parents allowance (£10 for income support);
- £25 earnings disregard (£15 for income support) for lone parents not on income support;
- £15 disregard for maintenance received, where both partners are under 60 or are claiming income support or income based jobseeker's allowance, provided the claimant is a lone parent or are a couple with a child (for income support, £10 of any child support maintenance is disregarded;
- other types of maintenance are taken fully into account;
- up to £94.50 (one child) or £140 (two or more children) child care costs may be disregarded.

(*SI 1987 No 1971, Sch 3.*)

Tariff income starts at £6,000 for over 60s.

If income exceeds applicable amount, calculate excess income.

### *Step Four: calculate housing benefit* **7.42**

If income is less than or equal to applicable amount, housing benefit is the same as the eligible rent.

If income is greater than applicable amount, housing benefit equals 100% of eligible rent less 65% of excess income.

### *Step Five: deduct for any non-dependants in household* **7.43**

There may be a deduction from housing benefit where there is a non-dependant in the house. There is no deduction where the non-dependant is aged 16–17, or aged 18–24 and on income support or income-based jobseeker's allowance, or on a youth training scheme, or a full-time student, or a boarder; or where the claimant or partner is blind or is on attendance allowance or disability living allowance. Other deductions are determined by gross income, as follows.

| Aged 18+ and in full time work, gross income | Deduction |
|---|---|
| £293 or more | £47.75 |
| £235–£292.99 | £43.50 |
| £177–£234.99 | £38.20 |
| £137–£176.99 | £23.35 |
| £92–£136.99 | £17.00 |
| All others for whom a deduction is made | £7.40 |

The rate of £7.40 a week applies where the non-dependant is aged 18+ and neither in remunerative work nor on income support or income-based jobseeker's allowance, or is aged 25 or more and is receiving income support or income-based jobseeker's allowance, or is in remunerative work and earns less than £81 a week.

### *Claiming and being paid housing benefit* 7.44

Housing benefit must be claimed in writing on the local authority form. A person who is also claiming income support or income based jobseeker's allowance receives a housing benefit claim form with their claim pack.

From 6 October 2003, claimants who are 60 or over will receive a separate claim form sent to them direct after they claim pension credit.

If the claimant is also claiming income support, incapacity benefit or income based jobseeker's allowance, the claim form can be sent to either the local authority's housing benefit office or to the Department for Work and Pensions with the claim for the other benefit. In all other cases, the form must be returned to the local authority.

Claims can be backdated by up to 52 weeks where there is 'good cause for late claim' (*SI 1987 No 1971, Reg 72(15)*).

Benefit is paid for a fixed period. At the end of the period it is necessary to make a renewal claim. The government has announced that renewal claims for housing benefit are shortly to be abolished for all claimants. They are abolished for pensioners with effect from 6 October 2003.

Where the landlord is the local authority, benefit is paid by way of a reduction in rent due. Where the landlord is private, rent is normally paid direct to the tenant, but may be paid to the landlord.

### *Discretionary housing payments* 7.45

Local authorities have a discretion to pay extra amounts of housing benefit. The amount is a matter for them. A claim is made separately from the claim for housing benefit (*Child Support Pensions & Social Security Act 2000, s 69; Discretionary Financial Assistance Regs 2001 (SI 2001 No 1167), Reg 2(1)*).

## Council tax benefit 7.46

The payment of council tax benefit is governed by the *Council Tax Benefit (General) Regulations 1992 (SI 1992 No 1814)*. They are closely modelled on the housing benefit regulations.

Benefit is received by way of a rebate of council tax.

### *Conditions of entitlement* 7.47

The claimant is liable to pay council tax (*SSCBA 1992, s 131(1)(a), (3)–(5)*).

The claimant must be habitually resident in Great Britain and must not be subject to immigration control (*Immigration and Asylum Act 1999, s 115*).

The claimant must not have capital in excess of £16,000 (*Council Tax Benefit (General) Regulations 1992 (SI 1992 No 1814), Reg 28*).

### *Working out council tax rebate* 7.48

The calculation is identical to that for housing benefit, except that:

- There is no calculation of 'eligible council tax'. All council tax paid is eligible.
- The taper (the rate at which benefit is withdrawn) is 20%, not 65%.
- The calculation of non-dependent deductions is different. Anyone aged 18 or over who shares the house, unless they are jointly liable for council tax or they pay rent, is a non-dependant; a close relative is always a non-dependant, even if paying rent (*SI 1992 No 1814, Reg 3(1), 51(1)*).

All non-dependants on income support or jobseeker's allowance are ignored. Certain other people (children for whom child benefit is payable, severely mentally impaired people, certain carers) are also ignored. Deductions are made for other non-dependants on the basis of their weekly income, on a sliding scale between £2.30 and £6.95.

Where a couple have joint liability, there is a single calculation. Where the claimant or couple share liability with another person or persons, the liability is apportioned on the basis of the number of liable people.

### *Second adult rebates* 7.49

Where the household contains at least one non-dependant, someone claiming council tax benefit must be assessed for a second adult rebate. This is a fixed deduction from council tax according to the income of the second adult. If the other resident(s) are in receipt of income support or income based jobseeker's allowance, the rebate is 25% of the liability; where this does not apply, the reduction is of 15% or 7.5% depending on the income of the second adult.

## State pension credit 7.50

The state pension credit comes into effect on 6 October 2003. It introduces a benefit known as guarantee credit to replace the system of income support (usually known as minimum income guarantee or MIG), and adds an additional factor in the form of a savings credit. Despite its name, it is a benefit, not a tax credit, and is dealt with by the Department for Work and Pensions instead of the Inland Revenue.

A person can claim guarantee credit if they are:

- aged 60 or over (*State Pension Credit Act 2002 (SPCA 2002), s 1(2)(a)*; *State Pension Credit Regulations 2002 (SI 2002 No 1792), Regs 2–4*);
- in Great Britain (*SPCA 2002, s 2(2)*; *SI 2002 No 1792, Reg 6*);
- habitually resident in Great Britain (*SPCA 2002, s 2(2)*; *SI 2002 No 1792, Reg 6*); and
- not subject to immigration control (*SPCA 2002, s 3*).

The claimant must have no income, or income below the minimum guarantee level.

A person can claim savings credit if:

- they (or their partner if they have one) are aged at least 65 (*SPCA 2002, s 1(2)(a)*; *SI 2002 No 1792, Regs 2–4*);
- they are in Great Britain (*SPCA 2002, s 4(2)*);
- they are habitually resident in Great Britain (*SPCA 2002, s 4(2)*); and

- they are not subject to immigration control (*SPCA 2002, s 3(2)*).

The person must have a qualifying income to claim. 'Qualifying income' excludes working tax credit, incapacity benefit, contributory jobseeker's allowance, severe disablement allowance, maternity allowance, and maintenance from their former spouse.

The lower age for claiming guarantee credit increases as womens pension ages increase.

The benefit includes provision for claiming for a partner. If the claimant or their partner has dependent children, they will be able to claim child tax credit (see above).

### Guarantee credit 7.51

The maximum credit is the total of the standard minimum guarantee together with additional amounts as appropriate. The Standard Minimum guarantee for 2003/4 is as follows.

| | |
|---|---|
| Single person | £102.10 |
| Couple | £155.80 |
| In a polygamous marriage, each additional spouse | £53.70 |

The additional amounts are as follows.

| | |
|---|---|
| Severe disability (qualifying conditions as for income support) | £42.95 (single claimant) |
| | £85.90 (couple) |
| Carer | £25.10 per qualifying carer |
| Housing costs | as for income support |

In addition, transitional protection is provided to those moving to guarantee credit from income support or income based jobseeker's allowance, so that their income does not fall as a result of the change.

Income for the purposes of guarantee credit ignores disability living allowance, attendance allowance and child benefit (*SI 2002 No 1792, Reg 15(1)*). There is no capital cut-off point, but tariff income is applied to capital in excess of £6,000 (£10,000 if the claimant is permanently resident in a care home) at a rate of £1 for every £500 above the threshold (*SPCA 2002, s 15(2)*; *SI 2002 No 1792, Reg 15(6)*).

Also disregarded are income from an annuity which is equal to the interest payable on the loan with which the annuity was purchased, provided that at least 90% of the loan was used to buy the annuity, and the claimant or their partner pay interest on the loan, and the claimant or their partner was at least 65 when the loan was made, and the loan is secured on the claimant's owner-occupied home, or that of their partner (*SI 2002 No 1792, Sch 4 para 10*).

Periodic payments made to a claimant or their partner under an agreement settling a claim for injury to the claimant or their partner, or ordered to be made by a court for a personal injury to the claimant, their partner, or their child, is also disregarded (*SI 2002 No 1792, Sch 4 para 13,14*).

Discretionary payments made by trustees under a discretionary trust (whether of personal injury compensation or not) for items other than food, fuel, clothes, footwear, rent, council tax or water charges are also ignored (*SI 2002 No 1792, Sch 4 para 11*). If they are made for those items, they carry a disregard of £20 per week.

Where a claimant is claiming housing or council tax benefit along with the guarantee credit, the £16,000 capital cut-off for housing and council tax benefits will not apply. Where the claim is for either of those two benefits with the savings credit alone, then it will.

Guarantee credit is the amount by which the claimant's income falls short of their maximum credit.

## Savings credit 7.52

Savings credit provides additional income on top of the guarantee credit for those with qualifying income. Qualifying income is as follows.

| | |
|---|---|
| Single person | £77.45 |
| Couple | £123.80 |

Maximum savings credit consists of 60% of the difference between the savings credit threshold and the standard minimum guarantee, namely as follows.

| | | |
|---|---|---|
| Single person | £24.65 x 60% | £14.79 |
| Couple | £32.00 x 60% | £19.20 |

Qualifying income above the standard minimum guarantee also entitles to savings credit, but at a decreasing rate.

### *Going into hospital* 7.53

After 4 weeks in hospital, disability living allowance or attendance allowance ceases (see **Chapter 6**) so that any severe disability premium paid as part of the guarantee credit will cease unless the claimant is one of a couple who both receive the severe disability premium and one or both is in hospital, in which case it continues to be paid at a single rate. (*SI 2002 No 1792, Sch 1 para 1(2)(b)*).

A carer's addition continues for eight weeks after carers allowance stops (*SI 2002 No 1792, Reg 4(3)(b)*).

Pension credit is covered by the announcement in the 2003 budget that benefits in hospital will now not be downrated until after the person has spent a total of 52 weeks in hospital.

### *Making a claim* 7.54

Claims may be in writing, or by telephone, or personally. Telephone claims lead to an application form being completed over the phone and sent for signature. Claims may be made to the Department for Work and Pensions or a local authority housing benefit office. A national insurance number is required. In the case of a couple, either may make a claim. Provided the qualifying conditions were met, a claim can be backdated for up to three months. During the initial stages of the benefit, claims will be backdated to 6 October 2003 if made by 5 October 2004. Benefit is paid in advance on Mondays (or on another day if retirement pension is paid on another day) unless paid by credit transfer into a bank account.

The intention is that awards should be made for five years where possible. To assist this process, income assessments will be made over a five year 'assessed income period'. Where someone is transferred from income support, this period will be seven years to prevent large numbers of claims requiring reassessment in 2008. To qualify, the claimant or their partner must be 65 or over. The assessment covers 'relevant provision', which is a retirement pension not payable under the *SSCBA 1992*, an annuity, or capital. The claimant does not have to report changes. At the renewal date, the figure is reassessed and adjusted for future claims (*SPCA 2002, ss 6–10*; *SI 2002 No 1792, Regs 10–12*)).

An assessed income period ends when the claimant:

- becomes one of a couple; or
- ceases to be one of a couple; or
- ceases to be entitled to pension credit; or

- goes permanently into a residential care home; or
- has a temporary stop placed on their retirement pension, which in turn leads to a supersession of their pension credit entitlement.

*(SPCA 2002, s 9(4); SI 2002 No 1792, Reg 12.)*

Pension credit is not taxable.

## The social fund

### *Discretionary grants and loans* 7.55

The Social Fund provides both discretionary grants and loans, and mandatory grants for certain specified purposes. Discretionary grants and loans are met from a fixed budget, and are allocated according to local and national priorities. The scheme is governed by Directions issued by the Secretary of State, which are legally binding on the social fund officer who makes the decision. The procedure for making an application, however, is covered in regulations. The Social Fund Guide contains Directions (which are mandatory) and guidance (which is not).

Claimants of community care grants and budgeting loans must be on income support or income based jobseeker's allowance *(Direction 8)*. Crisis loan claimants need not be on benefit at all, but a crisis loan is only payable if it is the only means of avoiding serious damage or serious risk to the health or safety of a family member. Someone not on benefit may have other sources of income.

There is a binding capital limit applying to community care grants and budgeting loans (and by implication crisis loans as well). Capital of up to £500 (£1,000 if the applicant is over 60) is ignored; excess capital is deducted from any payment, pound for pound.

### *Budgeting loans* 7.56

Budgeting loans are to meet intermittent expenses which cannot be met from the applicant's normal weekly benefit. Loans can be made for anything within the following categories:

- furniture and household equipment;
- clothing and footwear;
- rent in advance and/or removal expenses;
- improvement, maintenance and security of the home;
- travelling expenses;

- expenses of entering or re-entering work;
- HP and other debts for the above items.

It is not necessary to specify the precise item. The official making the decision does not exercise individual discretion. The official is required to follow the Secretary of State's Directions in deciding whether to make a payment, and also to have regard to the criteria set out in the act, although the criteria which apply to both other types of payment from the discretionary fund (in particular, having regard to the nature, extent and urgency of the need) no longer apply to budgeting loans.

*Directions 50 to 53* set out the detailed requirements for making an award. The first question is whether a payment can be made under the 'initial test'; if it cannot, then wider criteria (eg amount of time on tax credit) are applied to determine whether a payment should be made.

The amount payable is determined by a weighting system which attaches weight to two factors; the size of the claimant's family, and the time they have spent on benefit.

The maximum that can be awarded is £1,000, and the minimum is £30. The local office sets a standard figure for a payment, to which the weighting criteria are applied to determine the amount payable. This will also be affected by any existing loans and the amount outstanding.

### *Crisis loans* **7.57**

Crisis loans are payable 'in circumstances so specified for the purpose of meeting an immediate short term need'. (*SSCBA 1992, s 138(5)*). *Direction 3* says that the object of any loan is 'to assist an eligible person to meet expenses . . . in an emergency, or as the consequence of a disaster'.

With the exception of a payment of rent in advance, a payment must be 'the only means by which serious damage or serious risk to the health or safety of [the claimant], or to a member of his family, may be prevented'. A rent in advance payment is made to someone leaving institutional or residential care and who receives a community care grant.

Certain items for which a payment might be requested are specifically excluded, eg school items, rehousing costs following a compulsory purchase order, medical needs, etc. (These are also excluded from community care grants.) Most housing costs are also excluded. The maximum amount allowed for a crisis loan is £1,000.

Under *Direction 14* the claimant must be 'without sufficient resources to meet the immediate short-term needs of himself or his family, or both himself and his family.' In assessing resources, the mobility component of disability living allowance is ignored (*SSCBA 1992, s 73(14)*). Most other resources are liable to be taken into account. It is not necessary for a crisis loan claimant to be on income support or income based jobseeker's allowance.

Both budgeting and crisis loans are repaid (*Direction 5*) by deduction from benefit at one of three rates – 5%, 10% and 15%, depending on other commitments. The maximum period of repayment is 78 weeks or (for crisis loans only, and in exceptional cases) 104 weeks. The terms and conditions of an award are not appealable. (*Social Security and Child Support (Decisions and Appeals) Regulations 1991 (SI 1991 No 991), Sch 2 para 23*). A crisis loan for someone not on benefit is repayable at the same rate. Loans are not made unless the social fund officer is satisfied that they will be repaid. No interest is charged.

## *Community Care Grants* **7.58**

Community Care Grants are intended to promote community care (*SSCBA 1992, s 138(5)*) by enabling someone to move out of residential accommodation, or to prevent someone having to enter residential accommodation, or to relieve exceptional pressure on families (*Direction 4*).

Guidance contained in the Social Fund Guide (which is not mandatory) suggests that applications should be prioritised according both to the significance of their impact on the client's circumstances, and their relative importance in fulfilling the purposes of community care.

Payments will normally be made for:

- a person moving into the community from residential or institutional care;
- a person staying in the community rather than entering such care;
- a family under exceptional pressure;
- urgent travel expenses.

Any item can be claimed as long as it does not appear on the list of exclusions. Examples of what might be claimed include:

- furniture, household equipment, bedding, etc.
- removal charges to a new home;
- necessary clothes, etc.;
- travel expenses.

### *Mandatory grants from the social fund* 7.59

In these cases a payment must be made if conditions are met. There is no capital rule. Three categories of payment are included, namely funeral expenses payments, sure start maternity grants, and cold weather payments. The only one considered in this book is the payment of funeral expenses, which is considered in **Chapter 11**.

## Health benefits 7.60

The following are exempt from charges for health care. In addition to those listed, certain people are exempt from charges for specific benefits and are listed under the individual benefits:

- someone who is entitled to income support;
- someone who is entitled to the guarantee credit of state pension credit;
- someone who is receiving child tax credit, or child tax credit and working tax credit, or working tax credit which includes a disability element, provided their total income for tax credit purposes does not exceed £14,200 per annum;
- someone permanently resident in a care home whose place is wholly or partly funded by a local authority;
- a hospital in-patient;
- an asylum seeker who is receiving support from the National Asylum Support Service;
- a war disablement pensioner who needs the particular benefit for that disability;
- a person aged 16 or 17 who was formerly in local authority care and is now being maintained by them;
- a person who qualifies on low income grounds. People who do not qualify for free benefits under this scheme may, depending on income, be able to get items at a reduced rate. This does not apply to prescriptions.

In the case of war pensioners, note also the services listed in **Chapter 4**.

### *Free prescriptions* 7.61

The following are entitled to free prescriptions:

- people over 60;
- people under 16, or under 19 if still in full-time education;

- people in Wales aged under 25;
- pregnant women, and women who have given birth in the last 12 months (even if the child has died);
- someone with one of the specified medical conditions. These are:
  - a continuing physical disability which prevents their leaving home without help from another;
  - epilepsy which requires continuous anti-convulsive therapy;
  - a permanent fistula, including a caecostomy, ileostomy, laryngostomy or colostomy, which needs continuous surgical dressing or an appliance;
  - diabetes mellitus (except where treatment is by diet alone);
  - diabetes insipidus and other forms of hypopituitarism;
  - myxoedema;
  - hypoparathyroidism;
  - forms of hypoadrenalism (including Addison's disease) for which specific substitution therapy is essential; or
  - myasthenia gravis.

Those who do not qualify under any of the above may be entitled to a 'season ticket' or prepayment certificate which can be bought for four months or a year.

*(National Health Service (Travelling Expenses and Remission of Charges) Regs 1988 (SI 1988 No 551); National Health Service (Charges for Drugs and Appliances) Amendment Regulations 2000 (SI 2000 No 620); National Health Service (Charges for Drugs and Appliances) (Wales) Regulations 2001.)*

## Free dental treatment, and dentures 7.62

The following can claim free dental treatment and appliances (including dentures) if, when the treatment is arranged or the charges are made, the person is:

- aged under 18, or 19 if still in full-time education;
- a pregnant woman, or a woman who has given birth in the last 12 months (even if the child has died);
- aged under 25 or over 60, for an examination (Wales only);

- a patient of the Community Dental Service.

*(National Health Service (Travelling Expenses and Remission of Charges) Regulations 1988 (SI 1988 No 551); National Health Service (Dental Charges) Regulations 1989 (SI 1989 No 394); National Health Service Act 1977, Sch 12.)*

### Free glasses 7.63

Free glasses and lenses are available by way of a voucher to the exempt groups listed above, and also to the following:

- someone under 16, or 19 if still in full-time education;
- someone who is a Hospital Eye Service patient with constantly changing eyesight;
- someone who has been prescribed complex lenses.

Vouchers are issued by opticians and hospitals, and are exchangeable for the particular glasses or repairs required.

*(National Health Service (Optical Charges and Payments) Regulations 1997 (SI 1997 No 818).)*

### Free sight tests 7.64

Those in the exempt groups listed above are entitled to free sight tests, as are those who:

- are under 16, or 19 if still in full-time education;
- are registered blind or partially sighted;
- have been prescribed complex or powerful lenses;
- are diabetic or have glaucoma; or
- are over 40 and have a parent, brother, sister or child with glaucoma; or
- are a patient of the Hospital Eye Service.

*(NHS (General Ophthalmic Services) Regulations 1986 (SI 1986 No 975); National Health Service (Optical Charges and Payments) Regulations 1997 (SI 1987 No 818).)*

### Wigs and fabric supports 7.65

These are subject to a special prescription charge. They are provided free of charge to those who

- are in one of the exempt groups; or
- are on a low income; or

- are under 16, or under 19 and in full-time education; or
- are an in-patient in a hospital when the wig or fabric support is supplied.

*(SI 1988 No 551; National Health Service (Charges for Drugs and Appliances) Regulations 2000 (SI 2000 No 620); National Health Service (Charges for Drugs and Appliances) (Wales) Regulations 2001.)*

## Fares to hospital **7.66**

Help with fares to attend a hospital or other establishment for NHS treatment is available to those in the exempt groups, and also to those who are:

- a patient at a genito-urinary medicine clinic more than 15 miles from their home; or
- living in the Isles of Scilly or the Scottish Highlands.

*(SI 1988 No 551.)*

# 8 Other Forms of Support

## Community care 8.1

When it comes to the attention of a local authority that a person for whom they could provide community care services may be in need of such services, the authority is under a duty to carry out an assessment. (*National Health Service and Community Care Act 1990, s 47*). Community care services are available to those who are old, ill or disabled, and may therefore be of benefit to those who suffer illness or injury. Legislation on community care also includes provision for carers.

Community care services consist of the following:

- The provision of accommodation under *National Assistance Act 1948, s 21* for those who, by reason of age, illness, disability or other circumstances, are in need of care and attention which is not otherwise available to them.
- The provision of domiciliary services to those who are disabled as defined in *National Assistance Act 1948, s 29*. The services to be provided include those comprised in *Chronically Sick and Disabled Persons Act 1970, s 2*.
- Services for older people under *Health Services and Public Health Act 1968, s 45*.
- Provision of services under the *National Health Service Act 1977* for those who are ill.
- Provision of after care services for those who have been detained under the *Mental Health Act 1983*. The services are provided under *section 117* of that Act.

This discussion concentrates on the provision of services at home under *National Assistance Act, s 29* and *National Health Service Act 1977*. Other provision is outside the scope of this work.

## *Section 29 of the National Assistance Act 1948* 8.2

*Section 29(1)* as amended now reads as follows:

> 'a local authority may, with the approval of the Secretary of State, and to such extent as he may direct in relation to persons ordinarily resident in the area of the local authority shall, make arrangements for promoting

> the welfare of persons to whom this section applies, that is to say persons aged 18 or over who are blind, deaf or dumb or who suffer from mental disorder of any description, and other persons aged 18 or over who are substantially and permanently handicapped by illness, injury or congenital deformity or such other disabilities as may be prescribed by the Minister.'

The services are required to be supplied only to persons aged 18 or over who are ordinarily resident in the local authority's area.

The terminology employed in the definition of disability is of its time. However, certain comments can be made on extensions to, and interpretations of, that terminology. *Section 29* itself makes no reference to people who are partially sighted or partially deaf, but guidance (*LAC 13/74 Para 11 (I)*) confirms that those who are partially sighted, and those who are hard of hearing, may be included in the term 'other persons who are substantially and permanently handicapped'.

Under *section 29*, local authorities have duties and powers to provide certain services. The services which they have a duty to provide are as follows:

- Social work service, advice and support.
- Social rehabilitation or adjustment to disability.
- Compiling and maintaining registers.
- Occupational, social, cultural and recreational facilities.
- Workshop and workshop hostel services.

The services which Social Services departments have power to provide are as follows:

- Holiday homes.
- Free or subsidised travel.
- Assistance in finding accommodation.
- Subsidy award and costs.
- Award and services.
- Information on disability services.

The *Chronically Sick and Disabled Persons Act 1970* was a private members bill sponsored by Alf Morris MP, and was intended to convert the generalities of *section 29* into a set of specific entitlements for people who are disabled. The list of such services is contained in *section 2(1)* of the *Chronically Sick and Disabled Persons Act*, and provides that, where the person concerned is ordinarily resident in the local authority's area, then the authority is under a duty to make arrangements for the following:

- The provision of practical assistance for that person in the home.
- The provision of radio, television and library facilities.
- The provision of lectures, games, outings or other recreational facilities outside the home (including providing assistance to enable a person to take advantage of them).
- The provision of facilities for travelling to and from home in order to participate in any services provided under *section 29* or in similar services.
- The provision of assistance in arranging for carrying out adaptation to the home.
- Facilitating the taking of holidays.
- The provision of meals, either at home or elsewhere.
- The provision of a telephone and necessary special equipment.

## *NHS Act 1977* 8.3

Where the disablement is not permanent, services under *section 29* and *section 2* are not available. Domiciliary and community-based services to such people are therefore provided under *Schedule 8* to the above Act. They are still provided by Social Services departments.

The specific service provided under *section 21* and *Schedule 8* is the provision of home helps and laundry facilities. *Paragraph 3(1) of Schedule 8* provides that it is the duty of every Social Services authority to provide home help 'on such a scale as is adequate for the needs of their area' to meet the needs of those who are ill, old, or 'handicapped as a result of having suffered from illness or by congenital deformity'. Authorities also have power to arrange for the provision of laundry facilities for those households to which they are providing home help.

There are no age restrictions. The handicap need not be either substantial or permanent (cf. *section 29*) as long as it is caused by illness or congenital deformity. If the disability is caused by injury, therefore, it is excluded. Asylum seekers are excluded from provision if their need for services is on account of their being destitute, but not if it is for other reasons (*Westminster City Council v National Asylum Support Service, [2002] UKHL 38, House of Lords*).

## *Provision for carers* 8.4

There are now two principal Acts which deal with carers for those who are in need of community care services. These are the *Carers (Recognition and Services) Act 1995*, and the *Carers and Disabled Children Act 2000*.

Under the former Act, during any assessment for community care services of any disabled adult or child, a carer (that is someone who provides, or intends to provide, a substantial amount of care on a regular basis) can request an assessment. The local authority must assess the ability of the carer or potential carer to provide, or to continue to provide, care.

The Act can only operate in the context of an assessment of the disabled person or child. It is aimed at the needs of the disabled person rather than the carer, and is concerned primarily to ensure that the caring needs of the disabled person are met. There is little scope under the *1995 Act* for the provision of services direct to carers.

The Act applies to young carers, ie those under 18. Such young carers may well be entitled to an assessment of their own needs as 'children in need' under the *Children Act 1989*.

The *Carers and Disabled Children Act 2000* came into force on 1 April 2001. It applies to informal carers aged 16 or over who provide or intend to provide a substantial amount of care on a regular basis for another person aged 18 or over. The carer has a right to an assessment even where the person being cared for has refused an assessment, or has refused delivery of community care services.

The Act gives local authorities power to provide services to carers, following a carer's assessment. Services to carers are not defined in the Act and authorities have a broad scope to provide any services which help the carer provide care for the person cared for. Because the services are 'power-based', the key is the exercise of the local authority's discretion. Services may take the form of physical help or assistance. The local authority may charge the carer for services provided.

The Department of Health has issued a briefing, dealing with respite care and short-term breaks. These are described as remaining a community care service for the cared-for person and <u>not</u> a carers service.

Under the Act, direct payments under the *Community Care (Direct Payments) Act 1996* are made available to carers covered by the Act. This enables the provision of finance to the carer to enable them to buy in their own service. This mirrors the underused power in the Act to provide finance direct to a disabled person.

### ***Payment for services provided*** 8.5

Under *Health and Social Services and Social Security Adjudication Act 1983, s 17*, the local authority has the power to charge for the provision of the domiciliary services covered in this section.

### *Obtaining community care services* 8.6

Application should be made to the local social services authority for an assessment. Where someone living in their area has a possible need for community care services which comes to their attention, the authority must carry out an assessment (*National Health Service and Community Care Act 1990, s 47*) and must also decide whether the needs of the person concerned call for the provision of any services by them.

## Disabled facilities grants 8.7

Where adaptations to the home are required, there are parallel duties under the *Housing Grants Construction and Regeneration Act 1996* and the *Chronically Sick and Disabled Persons Act 1970*.

The 1996 Act provides for a system of grants for adaptations which are required to meet the needs of a disabled person. The local housing authority is the body responsible for the administration of the system. Grants are available where occupants are 'substantially and permanently handicapped' within the meaning of *section 29* of the *National Assistance Act 1949*.

Grants may be either mandatory or discretionary. Mandatory grants are available for:

- Facilitating access to the dwelling.
- Making the dwelling safe.
- Facilitating access to the principal family room and to a bedroom.
- Facilitating access to a toilet, a bathroom or shower room, and a room with a wash basin.
- Facilitating the preparation and cooking of food.
- Improving the heating system to meet the disabled person's needs.
- Facilitating the use of sources of power, light or heat by relocating the controls or providing additional controls.
- Facilitating access and movement around the dwelling to enable the disabled person to care for someone else.

Mandatory grants also require the authority to determine whether the proposed works are reasonable and practicable, and are necessary and appropriate to meet the needs of the disabled person. The local authority has a duty to meet the cost of disabled facilities grants irrespective of resources: *R v Birmingham City Council ex parte Taj Mohammed (1998) 1 CCLR 441*.

Local authorities also have discretion to make grants to make the dwelling suitable for the accommodation, welfare or employment of the disabled person in any other respect.

Eligibility for a disabled facilities grant is determined by a means test. Only the financial resources of the disabled person and his or her partner are taken into account. In the case of a child, the resources of the parent(s) (or other person with whom the child lives) are taken into account.

Under the *Chronically Sick and Disabled Persons Act 1970, s 2(1)(e)*, the authority is required to provide assistance in arranging works of adaptation or additional facilities 'designed to secure greater safety, comfort and convenience'. *Section 2(1)(e)* creates a specific duty to help a disabled person arrange for adaptations. Local authority guidance (*LAC(90)7*) refers to Social Services as the lead body in arranging adaptations.

The duty under the *Chronically Sick and Disabled Persons Act* exists independently of the *1996 Act*. A circular from the Department of the Environment *(Circular 17/96)* provides that where an application for a disabled facilities grant has been made, Social Services authorities can be called on to assist in cases where the needs exceed the provision comprised in the *1996 Act*, or where the applicant finds it difficult to meet a contribution.

## Criminal injuries compensation 8.8

The purposes of the Criminal Injuries Compensation Scheme is to make provision for injury to the victims of crime. The present scheme came into operation on 1 April 1996, and is governed by the *Criminal Injuries Compensation Act 1995*.

In cases where there is a separate personal injury claim, any damages or settlement received must be paid to the Criminal Injuries Compensation Authority to reimburse any payments or any made under the scheme. The rules regarding compensation for personal injuries being disregarded as capital for income based benefits apply to criminal injuries compensation as well (see **Chapter 7**).

The scheme is administered by the Criminal Injuries Compensation Authority, which is made up of claims officers and adjudicators. Initial decisions are made by Claims Officers with an Appeal to the Criminal Injury Compensation Appeal Panel made up of Adjudicators.

References are to the paragraphs of the compensation scheme.

## Eligibility 8.9

*Paragraph 8* defines a criminal injury as an injury sustained in Great Britain which is directly attributable to:

- a crime of violence;
- an offence of trespass on a railway; or
- the apprehension of, or the attempt to apprehend, an offender, the prevention of an offence, or the aiding of a Police Officer in any of these activities.

A crime of violence is one in which the definition of the crime itself involves either direct infliction of force on the victim, or a hostile act towards the victim (*R v CICB, ex p Webb [1986] QB 184*).

Personal injury includes death, physical injury, mental injury and disease. Where the only injury sustained is a mental injury, compensation is only payable when any of the following circumstances apply:

- the applicant was put in reasonable fear of immediate physical harm;
- the applicant had a close relationship of love and affection with another who sustained a criminal injury, the applicant was present at the incident or the immediate aftermath and the close relationship still exists, or would do but for the death of the victim;
- the crime is a sexual offence; or
- the applicant was employed in the business of the railway and witnessed an injury caused by trespass on a railway line (*Paragraph 9*).

There are restrictions on those persons who are eligible to make an application. Where the applicant failed to take reasonable steps to inform the police of the crime, or failed to co-operate with the police or with the CICA, or where the conduct of the applicant or his character as shown by criminal convictions makes any form of award inappropriate, the authority will take these issues into account in determining the suitability of any award. These restrictions are contained in *Paragraph 13*. By *Paragraph 14*, where the applicant is a non-victim applicant in a fatal case, these same conditions also apply.

In addition, by *Paragraph 16*, where the victim and the assailant were living in the same household as members of the same family, any award is withheld unless the assailant has been prosecuted (or there is evidence of a good reason for no prosecution being taken), and the parties no longer live together and it is not foreseen that they will do so in the future.

The application must be made in writing on a form issued by the Authority. The time for doing so is two years from the date of the incident. The claims officer may waive the time limit if it is in the interests of justice so to do (*Paragraph 17*). The claims officer will investigate the claim, including verifying details with the Police as to the circumstances of the crime. The claims officer may also require the claimant to submit to a medical examination (*Paragraph 20*).

Although the two year time limit is not binding in every case, difficulties in investigation may mean that the CICA is reluctant to accept an application outside that time limit. The CICA comments in particular that they will view sympathetically applications by those who were under 18 at the time of the incident, and those whose ability to help themselves is impaired. Careful consideration will also be given to an application which is made in respect of injuries which did not become apparent until some time after the incident complained of.

When the victim is a child, an adult with parental responsibility may apply on behalf of the child. The child's original birth certificate must be enclosed with the application. Where the applicant is an adult who is legally incapable of managing their own affairs, the CICA may appoint an applicant to deal with the claim on that persons behalf. This will only be done once the CICA is satisfied by medical evidence that the applicant is incapable by reason of mental disorder as defined in the *Mental Health Act 1983* of managing and administering his or her property and affairs.

The term 'Crimes of Violence' includes shock sustained by employees of a railway company who see another person killed or injured as a result of trespassing on a railway, or who find bodies on or beside the railway track; those who are injured accidentally in the prevention of crimes; and those who are injured in respect of attempting to catch an offender or a suspected offender. People who are injured as a direct result of a crime of arson, or who are accidentally injured whilst fighting a fire which was the result of arson, may be compensated, in the latter case if they were taking an exceptional risk.

Someone who is injured by an animal will be able to claim, but only if the animal is deliberately set on the applicant or if the person with control of the animal is reckless as to maintaining control of an animal which is known to be vicious towards other humans (see also **Chapter 9**).

An injury inflicted by a vehicle is not a criminal injury unless the vehicle is used as a weapon (*Paragraph 11*). Other claims for injuries by motor vehicles should be addressed to the Motor Insurers Bureau (see below).

The injury must be sufficiently serious to qualify for the minimum amount, which is £1,000 (*Paragraph 24*), but must not exceed in total £500,000 in respect of the same injuries (*Paragraph 23*).

## *Level of award* 8.10

The level of award is determined by a tariff which sets different levels of injuries and allocates appropriate amounts to them. The present tariff is as follows:

| Level of Compensation | Compensation |
|---|---|
| Level 1 | £1,000 |
| Level 2 | £1,250 |
| Level 3 | £1,500 |
| Level 4 | £1,750 |
| Level 5 | £2,000 |
| Level 6 | £2,500 |
| Level 7 | £3,000 |
| Level 8 | £3,500 |
| Level 9 | £4,000 |
| Level 10 | £5,000 |
| Level 11 | £6,000 |
| Level 12 | £7,500 |
| Level 13 | £10,000 |
| Level 14 | £12,500 |
| Level 15 | £15,000 |
| Level 16 | £17,500 |
| Level 17 | £20,000 |
| Level 18 | £25,000 |
| Level 19 | £30,000 |
| Level 20 | £40,000 |
| Level 21 | £50,000 |
| Level 22 | £75,000 |
| Level 23 | £100,000 |
| Level 24 | £175,000 |
| Level 25 | £250,000 |

Different injuries are allocated to different levels. Only two injuries are placed at Level 25, namely the loss of all four limbs and extremely serious and permanent brain damage. Examples of injuries at other levels are as follows.

| Injury | Level of award | Amount |
|---|---|---|
| Loss of foetus | 10 | £5,500 |
| Paraplegia | 24 | £175,000 |
| Disabling mental illness, confirmed by psychiatric diagnosis, lasting up to 28 weeks | 6 | £2,500 |
| Persistent pattern of repetitive violence to a child resulting in moderate multiple injuries (eg bruising and minor fractures) and/or minor disfigurement | 10 | £5,500 |
| Severe burns to the head | 15 | £16,500 |
| Scarring to face, minor disfigurement | 3 | £1,500 |
| Loss of sight in one eye | 17 | £22,000 |
| Loss of index finger | 12 | £8,200 |
| Fractured radius, one arm, substantial recovery | 7 | £3,300 |
| Fractured clavicle, substantial recovery | 5 | £2,000 |
| Investigative surgery to knee, no fracture | 5 | £2,000 |

When the applicant's injuries do not reach the level of £1,000, the applicant may nevertheless be compensated if they have suffered three separate injuries which can be added together. The effects of one such injury must last for at least six weeks, and must require at least two visits to a doctor. A combination of three such injuries is placed at level one.

Where an applicant has sustained multiple injuries, each of which is contained in the classification, then the award is calculated as follows:

- the tariff amount for the highest rate of injury; *plus*
- 10% of the next highest rated injury; *plus*
- 5% of the third highest rated injury.

The Secretary of State is empowered to determine an award in circumstances where the injury is not classified, provided the claims officer considers it to be sufficiently serious to attract at least a Level 1 award *(Paragraph 28)*.

Where the victim is a woman who has been raped, and where she is made pregnant as a result, she is also entitled to receive a Level 10 award for each child born alive that she intends to keep *(Paragraph 27)*.

## Loss of Earnings 8.11

The scheme makes provision for compensation in respect of lost earnings as a result of the injury. This is covered in *Paragraphs 30 to 34*. No compensation for loss of earnings is recoverable for the first 28 weeks. This is intended to avoid double recovery in respect of statutory sick pay. However, no provision is made for people who are not entitled to statutory sick pay, such as self employed people. After 28 weeks, the applicant is entitled to actual and future loss of net earnings.

## Care 8.12

Additional compensation may be awarded to an applicant who is incapacitated for over 28 weeks and who requires special care (*Paragraph 35 (d)*), including special equipment, the adaptation of accommodation and the cost of care, either in residential accommodation or at home. Costs attributable to NHS treatment may also be recovered (*Paragraph 35 (b)*), and also, when it is reasonable, the cost of private health treatment (*Paragraph 35 (c)*).

## Fatal cases 8.13

In cases of fatal injury, applications may be received from dependants or relatives of the victim. A dependant or relative is someone who was at the time of the death of the deceased that person's spouse, unmarried but long-term (normally two years) partner of either sex, parent, child of any age, or former husband or wife who was financially supported by the deceased. Awards may be made in the form of a Fatal Injury Award, a Dependency Award or an Award for Loss of Parental Services, or any combination. Awards can be made to a dependant even though the victim has him or herself received compensation before their death.

The estate of a victim is entitled to claim for the cost of a funeral. With regard to funeral expenses, see in addition **Chapter 11** for an account of the right to claim funeral expenses as part of a personal injury claim, and also the right to a Social Fund funeral expenses payment.

The calculation is similar to that under the *Fatal Accidents Act 1976*. Financial dependency is calculated on the basis of loss of earnings (*Paragraph 40*). A child receives a further award at Level 5 for each year during which they are deprived of their parent, until the point when they reach adulthood, based on the multiplier. There is also a set payment in respect of bereavement. Where there is a single bereaved claimant, the Award is Level 13. If there is more than one, each receives a payment at Level 10.

When the victim has died for reasons not connected with the criminal injury, a dependant may apply for supplementary compensation to cover loss of earnings, expenses and liabilities incurred by the victim before death as a result of a crime. A tariff injury award cannot be paid in these circumstances.

### Deductions 8.14

Other benefits received from the injury are deducted, with the exception of privately financed insurance payments and charitable payments.

### Review and appeal 8.15

Where the applicant is dissatisfied with the award, he or she may apply for a review within 90 days of the decision. The application must be in writing on a form supplied by the CICA and must include reasons for the application. The decision is reviewed by a more senior claims officer. The decision of the review is sent to the applicant, together with an application form for appeal.

If the applicant is still unsatisfied, then he or she may appeal on the form provided. Appeals are governed by *Paragraphs 61* to *71* of the scheme. The appeal form must be returned within 30 days of the review decision.

If the appeal concerns time limits, or the reopening of a case, it is dealt with by the Chairman of the Authority. Appeals concerning the award going to an oral hearing or to an adjudicator. An adjudicator may personally consider an appeal unless it has been deemed not serious enough for a Level 1 Award or there is a dispute on a material fact or conclusion. In either of these cases, the adjudicator must refer to the appeal to an oral hearing.

### Oral hearing 8.16

At an oral hearing, the application is reconsidered in its entirety. The burden of proof is on the applicant. The applicant should receive 21 days' notice of the appeal hearing, and is entitled to be present and represented. The appeal hearing is usually fairly informal. The decision of the panel is final and the only recourse for a disappointed applicant is judicial review.

The panel has wide powers to withhold expenses and/or to reduce a previous award if the appeal is considered to be frivolous.

There is power to make an interim payment where the eventual outcome is not clear. In cases of a high value award, payments can be made through the purchase of an annuity or annuities. Any expenses incurred in obtaining such an annuity are met from the award.

The CICA has discretion to reopen a case after a final decision has been made. This will be done where the medical condition has deteriorated to the extent that injustice would occur if the original award were allowed to stand (*Paragraph 56*). If the application to reopen a case is made more than two years after the date of the final decision, the case would be reopened only if the CICA is satisfied that it would not involve extensive enquiries.

The scheme provides for discretion for the CICA to withhold an award in cases where the applicant has a significant criminal record (*Paragraph 13(e)*) or where the applicant's own conduct has led to their being injured (*Paragraphs 13(d)* and *14*). An award may also be withheld where someone fails to co-operate in bringing an offender to justice. It is expected that an applicant will have notified the police of the incident, and will have done so personally as soon as possible. Conduct before, during or after the event is a relevant factor in this situation, and this can include voluntary participation in a fight, situations where the applicant struck the first blow without reasonable cause, situations where the applicant had been the assailant on a previous occasion or was injured whilst attempting to obtain revenge against the assailant, situations where the applicant used offensive language or behaved in an aggressive of threatening manner, or situations where excessive consumption of alcohol or use of drugs contributed to the attack which caused the injuries.

In the case of someone with previous criminal convictions, penalty points are allocated according to the sentence imposed and the total number of penalty points will result in a percentage reduction on the award. The number of penalty points varies according to the time which has elapsed since the conviction. Where a figure of ten penalty points is imposed, no compensation is awarded. This happens in every case where imprisonment is ordered, and where the incident complained of takes place within the period of that sentence, whether actually served in prison or not. The system of points is not binding, but is intended to give a guide to the significance of the claimant's criminal record.

### *Violence within the family* 8.17

As noted above, where the applicant is an adult, compensation will not be awarded where the applicant and the assailant lived in the same household at the time of the incident unless the assailant has been prosecuted (or there are good reasons why they were not prosecuted) and where the applicant and the assailant have permanently ceased to live together. For this purpose, a man and a woman who live together as husband and wife are regarded as members of the same family (*Paragraphs 16* and *17*).

Where a child is injured, it is not necessary for the parties to have ceased permanently to live together for an award to be made, but the Board must be satisfied that the offender does not benefit from the award. Furthermore, the Board must be satisfied that it is in the child's interest to make an award. The example given by the Board is of a young child who makes a full recovery from an assault, when the reopening of an award at the child's eighteenth birthday may cause considerable distress.

## Motor Insurers Bureau 8.18

The Motor Insurers Bureau is a private company which has entered into agreements with the Government to provide compensation for people who are victims of negligent drivers who are uninsured, or of drivers who cannot be traced. The MIB offers a guarantee fund which meets claims made on behalf of such individuals within the United Kingdom, the Channel Islands and Gibraltar, and includes claims made against liable individuals who are insured in another European country.

There are two separate agreements. The uninsured driver's agreement requires the MIB to meet court judgements against identified motorists who were not insured in accordance with the *Road Traffic Act 1988*. The untraced driver's agreement (the most recent version of which came into force on 14 February 2003) meets applications from victims of 'hit and run' drivers. Applications under the untraced driver's agreements must be made within three years of the accident.

Claims may not be made by owners of uninsured vehicles, nor by passengers in such vehicles.

Where the injuries suffered are bodily injuries, there is no limit to the amount of compensation. Where the claim is for property damage, the MIB does not pay the first £300 of any such claim. There is an upper limit on claims for property damage of £250,000.

The MIB is an insurer of last resort and will not compensate a victim where there is other compensation available to that person. There can now be claims for compensation for damage to property since the latest revision to the untraced driver's agreement, and the Bureau will also entertain claims for a hire car. The £300 excess applies. Payments for property, however, will not be made unless there is an 'identified vehicle' – that is, where there is evidence that a collision actually took place.

The police must be notified within five days in the case of property claims, and within 14 days in the case of injury claims. Claims for personal injury must be made within three years, but claims for property damage must be made within nine months. There is an absolute time limit of two years for a property claim and fifteen years for a personal injury claim.

If the vehicle is stolen, there is an obligation under the *Road Traffic Act 1988, s 151(2)* for the insurers of the legal owner of a stolen vehicle to meet a judgement made against the driver of that vehicle. Where the driver cannot be traced, an application can be made under the untraced driver's agreement.

## Vaccine damage payments

### *Who qualifies?* 8.19

Vaccine damage payments are a non-contributory, non income based scheme which makes payments to those who have become at least 60% disabled as the result of a vaccination. Disablement is assessed in the same way as for industrial injuries payments (see **Chapter 3**).

The scheme covers disability which results from vaccinations against the following diseases:

- diphtheria;
- tetanus;
- pertussis (whooping cough);
- poliomyelitis;
- rubella (German measles);
- measles;
- Haemophilus Influenzae type b;
- mumps;
- tuberculosis;
- meningitis C; or
- smallpox (vaccination up to August 1971).

(*Vaccine Damage Payments Act 1979 (VDPA 1979), s 1(2).*)

Claims can also be made where the disability has resulted from:

- the claimant's mother being vaccinated against one of the above diseases while pregnant; or
- the claimant's being in close physical contact with a person who has been given the oral vaccine against poliomyelitis.

(*Vaccine Damage Payments Act 1979, s 1(3)*; *Vaccine Damage Payments Regulations 1979 (SI 1979 No 432), Reg 5A.*)

### *Age limits* 8.20

The disabled person must be aged over two years when the claim is made. (*VDPA 1979, s 2(c)*).

The vaccination must have been given before they became 18, unless it was against rubella, poliomyelitis or meningitis C, or was given during an outbreak of the disease concerned (*VDPA 1979, s 2(b)*).

### *Where the vaccination was given* 8.21

The vaccination must have been given in the United Kingdom or the Isle of Man (*VDPA s 1(a)(i)*), or under the auspices of the armed forces medical services to a serving member of the forces or a member of their family (*VDPA 1979, s 2(5);Vaccine Damage Payments Regulations 1979 (SI 1979 No 432), Reg 5*).

### *How to claim* 8.22

A claim form is obtainable from:

Vaccine Damage Payments Unit

Palatine House

Lancaster Road

Preston PR1 1HB

Tel: 01772 899944

The form should be completed and returned to that address within six years of the date of vaccination or by age 21, whichever is later.

A payment is made in the form of a lump sum payable to the claimant (*VDPA 1979, s 6(1)*). If the claimant has died, payment is made to their personal representative (*VDPA 1979, s 6(2)*). If the claimant is under 18 or is incapable of managing their own affairs, payment is made to a trustee appointed by the Secretary of State (*VDPA 1979, s 6(3)*).

### *Amount of award* 8.23

For claims made on or after 22 July 2000, the amount payable is £100,000. (*VDPA 1979, s 1(1A)*).

### *Amendments to regulations* 8.24

The time limits for claiming, and the disability threshold, have been changed (*Regulatory Reform Order (Vaccine Damage Payments Act 1979) Order 2002 (SI 2002 No 1592)*) with effect from 16 June 2002. Anyone whose claim was rejected on either of these grounds may reclaim under the new criteria. For those who received lower payments because their claims predated the amendments, top-up payments are being made.

### *Effect on other benefits* 8.25

An award counts as capital for the purpose of income based benefits and tax credits. An award which is placed in trust for the disabled person, however, is disregarded.

An award can affect entitlement to income based benefits. The rules are the same as for personal injury payments (see **Chapter 7**).

Where the claimant is dissatisfied with the outcome of a claim, they can ask for the decision to be reviewed. If they are still dissatisfied they have the right to appeal to a tribunal constituted under the *Social Security Act 1998 (SSA 1998)* (see **Chapter 2**).

## Other forms of provision

### *The Independent Living Funds* 8.26

The Independent Living Funds provide financial assistance to severely disabled people. The Trusts are funded by government, but are independent and are managed by boards of trustees. The trustees work in partnership with social services departments to develop joint care packages, which combine services and/or direct payments under the community care legislation (see above) with cash payments from the Funds. Provision from the Funds is discretionary.

The conditions of eligibility are as follows. The claimant:

- must be severely disabled so as to need help with personal care or household duties;
- must live alone, or with others who are unable fully to meet their care needs;
- must be aged between 16 and 65;
- must be receiving the higher care rate of disability living allowance (see **Chapter 5**);
- must be receiving income support or jobseekers allowance, or an income at around that level;
- must have less than £18,500 in savings (jointly with their partner, if they have one);

- must be receiving (or be about to receive) services funded by a social services authority. The services must cost at least £200 a week, and no more than £665 a week including a payment from the fund;
- must have care needs which are likely to remain stable for six months and which can be met by the package.

The maximum payment from the fund is £395 a week.

Applications are made through the social services department which will provide or pay for the services.

### *The Macfarlane and Eileen Trusts* 8.27

The Macfarlane Trust, the Macfarlane (Special Payments) Trust, and the Macfarlane (Special Payments) (No 2) Trust make payments for people with haemophilia. The Fund was set up on 24 April 1992 to provide for people who do not have haemophilia, but who contracted HIV through blood transfusions or tissue transplants. The Eileen Trust is for people who contracted HIV through NHS blood transfusions or tissue transplants. The Macfarlane Trust is at PO Box 627, London SW1H 0QG (tel 020 7233 0342).

### *The Family Fund* 8.28

The Family Fund makes grants to or for severely disabled children. It can help with holidays, furniture and equipment, and transport. It can be contacted at PO Box 50, York YO1 1UY (Tel 01904 621115).

## Private provision 8.29

There are numerous other possible sources of financial and practical support. A large number of medical conditions have their own charitable institution, which may not itself provide financial assistance, but provides expertise in dealing with the condition (which can be very valuable to someone encountering a condition for the first time), support, and advice on dealing with specialist benefit and legal issues, as well as knowledge of sources of financial support. Appropriate organisations can be found by searching on the internet under the name of the condition.

A person who is in employment when they sustain the injury should check their contract of employment for provisions on occupational sick pay. All employers are required to pay statutory sick pay (see **Chapter 6**), but many pay all or a proportion of salary or wages during sickness.

The law on employment limits the opportunities which an employer has to dismiss someone who is away from work because of sickness or injury. An employee who is threatened with dismissal should seek advice from an employment specialist. There may also be aspects of disability discrimination in an employer's response to sickness or disability.

An occupational or private pension is normally payable only from retirement, but may include provisions for payment during long-term sickness, and also for early retirement occasioned by ill-health.

Many private insurance policies include a provision for a lump sum payment in the event of an accident, and all household insurance policies should be checked to see whether such a provision is in place.

As well as the funds listed in the previous section, charities can make payments to those who are in need and whose requirements are not covered by the support systems listed in this book – for example, by making a payment for a specialist piece of equipment. Advice as to possible sources of payments can be obtained from advice centres, from charities specialising in the kind of condition mentioned, and from the internet. The *Guide to Grants for Individuals in Need* and the *Charities Digest* are available in local libraries. The *Disability Rights Handbook* (see **Appendix 5**) also contains much useful information as to possible sources of help.

An injured person who is a member of a trade union should check with their union handbook and local union office for provisions for those who are injured or sick. A trade union can usually also provide help with finding a specialist lawyer who can pursue any claim, and are normally a source of specialist information on matters relating to industrial injuries benefits.

# 9 Liability and Negligence

## Introduction 9.1

Many forms of compensation for personal injury are obtainable without reference to the fault of any party. Social security benefits generally do not require fault as a condition of payment. However, in order to make a successful claim for damages for personal injury, it will usually be necessary to prove fault on the part of some other party. There are specific forms of fault which are applicable to particular types of injuries (for example, breach of statutory duty which is a common cause of action in work injuries, and specific statutory responsibilities such as the liability for defective products) but the most common cause of action is usually one based on negligence.

The principles of negligence are set out below.

These principles will apply to loss, damage or personal injuries in any circumstances at all. In practice negligence is a common form of action in respect of injuries at work and on the road, and in respect of medical matters.

There are also a number of areas of law where liability is established, not by the common law principles of negligence, but by statute. These various areas of statutory liability for personal injury form the concluding part of this chapter.

## Liability due to negligence

### *Principles of negligence* 9.2

A claim in negligence is based on the principle that the law is entitled to expect a certain standard of care to be taken by people in their dealings with one another. Where conduct falls short of that standard, and damage results, liability is imposed. There are three criteria for a negligence claim to succeed. These are as follows:

- that the person responsible (the defendant) owes a duty of care to the person injured (the claimant);
- that the defendant has breached that duty;

- that damage has resulted from that breach.

A duty of care will not exist in all circumstances. It is therefore firstly necessary to establish that such a duty of care exists. The establishment of a duty of care depends upon three factors; foreseeability, proximity and the 'just and reasonable' test.

The general principle with regard to foreseeability is based on a duty to take reasonable care. A person owes a duty of care to all other persons who might be injured by his or her failure to take reasonable care in any situation (either by an act or by an omission) provided that it was foreseeable that the injured party would suffer damage from a failure to take such care.

Thus, in *Roe v Minister of Health [1954] 2 QB 66*, anaesthetic was stored in glass ampoules in jars of phenol. Unknown to anyone, the glass ampoules developed hairline cracks, and as a result the anaesthetic was contaminated with phenol. Damage resulted to those people who were injected with the contaminated anaesthetic. It was held by the Court of Appeal that there was no liability on the part of the defendants because it was not foreseeable that such injuries would occur. Once the problem in question became a matter of general medical knowledge, however, the duty of care would thereafter arise in respect of all medical practitioners in any circumstances.

The term 'proximity' refers to a legal, rather than a geographical, state of affairs. Lord Keith described this in *Yuen Kun Yeu v Attorney General of Hong Kong ([1987] 2 All ER 705*, Judicial Committee of the Privy Council) as 'such close and direct relations that the act complained of directly affects a person whom the person alleged to be bound to take care would know would be directly affected by his careless act'.

In addition to the requirements of foreseeability and proximity, the judges have now developed a requirement that it be just and reasonable to impose a duty upon the defendant – see *Caparo Industries Plc v Dickman [1990] 2 AC 605*.

In most situations it will be clear from previous cases whether a duty is owed. However, in novel cases, the three requirements of foreseeability, proximity and the just and reasonable requirement will be needed to establish that a duty of care exists.

## Secondary victims 9.3

The duty of care clearly extends to those people who are immediately injured or damaged by the failure to take reasonable care. Does the duty also extend to third parties? In the case of *McLoughlin v O'Brian [1983] 1 AC 410*, Mr McLoughlin and his children were involved in a car accident for which Mr O'Brian was responsible. Mr O'Brian clearly was liable to Mr McLoughlin and the injured children. Mrs McLoughlin, who was alerted by a neighbour to the accident, visited the hospital an hour later, and discovered that her daughter was dead, heard her son screaming in pain, and saw her husband sobbing with grief. As a result she suffered psychological trauma. It was held by the House of Lords that she was entitled to recover damages for her own injury, and that Mr O'Brian's liability extended not only to those people directly injured by his negligence, but also to close relatives who were affected by the consequences.

This whole issue was explored further by the House of Lords in the case of *Alcock v Chief Constable of South Yorkshire [1992] 1 AC 310* (the Hillsborough case). This case rose out of the deaths and injuries to Liverpool supporters attending an F A Cup semi-final at Hillsborough Football Ground, Sheffield, which injuries were caused by the admitted negligence of South Yorkshire Police. The Lords held that, for there to be recovery for psychiatric illness (or 'nervous shock' as the courts normally describe it) by a person witnessing or hearing about a shocking event, a number of conditions had to be fulfilled. Firstly, the claimant had to have 'such a close and intimate relationship (with the victim) as gave rise to that very special bond of affection which would make shock-induced psychiatric illness reasonably foreseeable'. It would be assumed that such a bond existed between parent and child, and between spouses. In other circumstances, the injured party would have to prove that such a relationship existed.

Secondly, the claimant would have to witness the entire incident or its immediate aftermath with their own unaided senses. To witness an incident (as a number of the claimants did) on live television, the Lords considered, is not the same thing as being present in the stadium and witnessing the whole event first hand. While the Lords considered that the pictures would give rise to feelings of deep anxiety or distress, they were no more shocking than receiving information from a third party. Thirdly, the 'secondary victims' would have to come within the 'immediate aftermath' of the event to recover damages. Those who identified the bodies in the mortuary some nine hours later could not establish that they were within the immediate aftermath of the shocking event. In the event, none of the fifteen plaintiffs in the case succeeded.

**Chapter 12** includes a discussion of some of the recent cases on secondary victims and psychological trauma.

The requirement that the parties should be closely related to each other has one exception. Where a person suffers psychological trauma as a result of coming on a case of death or injury and stopping to help, that person will also be entitled to recover. These are known as the 'rescuer' cases. See for example the case of *Chadwick v British Transport Commission ([1967] 2 All ER 945*, Court of Appeal) where the claimant's claim was based on psychological injures which he suffered as a result of helping out at a train accident.

If the existence of the duty of care is about foreseeability, then the question whether that duty has been breached is one of reasonableness or its absence. The defendant may foresee that he or she owes a duty of care to an individual, but is not bound to guard against damage to that individual in all circumstances. He or she is only required to act reasonably. So, for example, in the case of *Bolton v Stone [1951] AC 850*, the claimant was injured by a cricket ball which was hit out of a cricket ground. The ball was hit over a wall seventeen feet high, an event which had happened only six times in the preceding 30 years. She argued that the cricket club should put a roof on the ground to prevent this kind of incident, but the court held that this would be an unreasonable response given the nature and extent of the risk. On the other hand, in *Paris v Stepney Borough Council [1951] AC 367*, Mr Paris was a local authority employee who worked under buses. He had only one eye. His employers failed to provide him with goggles, as a result of which he lost his other eye when sustaining an injury while working for his employers. It was held that the employers were liable. The risk was significant and the cost of guarding against it was minimal. It would therefore have been reasonable for the employers to take the minimal steps required of them to prevent the risk to Mr Paris' sight.

It will be appreciated that these cases are towards the opposite ends of a continuum. Liability will depend on where on the continuum the actions of the defendant fall.

It may be added that, in the case of professional work, the standard is that of the trained operator, and not the lesser standard to be expected of a trainee. If a trainee does not achieve the standard of a trained person, then he or she will be negligent. See for example *Wilsher v Essex Area Health Authority [1986] 3 All ER 801*, where a junior and inexperienced doctor made a mistake in treating a baby. The majority of the Court of Appeal held that his conduct had to be judged against the objective standard of care to be expected from someone providing a specialist service, rather than the objective standard of the inexperienced junior doctor. The professional person is expected to rise above the standard of care expected of the non-professional, but not necessarily too far; the standard of care expected of a doctor who stops by a road accident is less than that expected of the eminent consultant in Harley Street.

## Medical negligence 9.4

For a number of years the standard of care expected of medical practitioners has been that of the sensible practitioner. This has led to protests that there will be no 'levelling up' as long as this is the duty, but it is only recently that the courts have begun to reconsider the standard of care required in a medical case.

What is the standard of care required? For many years this has been determined by reference to the case of *Bolam v Friern Hospital Management Committee [1957] 1 WLR 582*. Mr Bolam suffered from mental illness, and it was proposed to put him through a course of electroconvulsive therapy (ECT). At the time, there were two contrary bodies of thought as to the proper procedure to be followed in such a case. One school of thought considered that the patient should be under some sort of control, whether manual or by administration of drugs, while the other school thought that such restraint would be dangerous. No relaxant drugs were used on Mr Bolam who in consequence dislocated both hip joints and sustained fractures of the pelvis during the course of treatment. Mr Justice McNair held that in a case of professional liability such as this, a doctor would not be guilty of negligence if he or she acted in accordance 'with the practice accepted as proper by a responsible body of medical men skilled in that particular art'.

The effect of this is that a doctor complies with the duty of care, and is not negligent, if he or she acts in accordance with a competent body of medical opinion. The court will not concern itself with arguments as to which of the two conflicting professional views should be preferred. A Judge who sought to prefer one body of medical opinion over another had his decision overruled by the House of Lords, who held that this was an unsatisfactory way to solve the question (*Maynard v West Midlands Regional Health Authority [1984] 1 WLR 634*). However, in recent years the court has shown some willingness to depart from this approach; see for example the case of *Bolitho v The City and Hackney Health Authority [1997] 3 WLR 1151*.

An error of clinical judgement may amount to negligence, but will not necessarily do so. The strongly protectionist views of Lord Denning, expressed in the case of *Whitehouse v Jordan [1980] 1 All ER 650, CA; [1981] 1 WLR 246, HL*, were to the effect that, in Lord Denning's words in the Court of Appeal 'in a professional man an error of judgement is not negligent'. This view was rejected, both by Lord Justice Donaldson in the Court of Appeal, and by Lord Fraser of Tullybelton in the House of Lords. Lord Fraser said that 'the true position is that an error of judgement may, or may not, be negligent; it depends upon the nature of the error. If it is one that would not have been made by a reasonably competent professional man professing to have the standard and type of skill that the defendant held himself out as having, and acting with ordinary care, then it is negligent. If, on the other hand, it is an error that such a man, acting with ordinary care, might have made, then it is not negligent'.

## Stress 9.5

In order to pursue a successful claim on the basis of stress as a workplace injury, a claimant will have to show negligence on the part of the employer. As mentioned in **Chapter 1**, the case which prompted a number of claims based on stress was that of *Walker v Northumberland County Council [1995] 1 All ER 737*. In that case, it will be recalled, Mr Walker, having suffered a breakdown, advised his employers of the stress he was under, and as a result the employers agreed to provide assistance for him. This they failed to do, and were found liable in consequence. Cases of stress are particularly difficult, not least because a person may undergo stress as a result of many different factors or a combination of factors, not all of which are related to his or her work.

The Court of Appeal has recently taken the opportunity to give guidance on the law on liability for stress at work, in the case of *Hatton v Sutherland [2002] EWCA Civ 76*; reported as *Sutherland (Chairman of the Governors of St Thomas Becket RC High School) v Hatton and other cases [2002] IRLR 263*. It is clear that, in order to establish a claim, the claimant will have to show firstly that he or she has suffered a psychiatric injury, and not merely (non-clinical) depression; and secondly, that this must have been reasonably foreseeable to the employer. The court rejected the view that any particular occupation is by its nature so stressful that an employer will be liable if he or she does not have in place systems which will enable a person with difficulties to seek help. The same rules, it was said, apply to all occupations. (The particular occupation under consideration was teaching.)

The Court stated that an employer is entitled to assume that an employee is able to cope with all the normal stresses of their occupation unless that employer knows of some factor concerning either the job or the individual concerned that should alert him or her to the possibility of psychiatric injury. The court listed factors related both to the job and to the circumstances of the particular employee. The factors relating to the demands of the job include:

- The nature and extent of the work done by the employee.
- Whether the employee's workload is much greater than normal for that kind of job.
- Whether the work is particularly intellectually or emotionally demanding.
- Whether the demands made of the employee are comparable with those made of employees in similar jobs.
- Whether there are signs that others doing the same job are suffering from stress.

- Whether there is an abnormal level of sickness or absenteeism in the department.

The factors relating to the circumstances of the individual employee are:

- Whether the employee is showing signs of impending harm to health.
- Whether the employee has a particular problem or is especially vulnerable.
- Whether the employee has already suffered from illness attributable to stress at work.
- Whether the employee has been taking uncharacteristic frequent or prolonged absences, and whether there is reason to believe these may be related to stress at work.

The employer will nevertheless not be liable unless it was reasonably foreseeable that the employee in question would suffer such an injury as the result of stress. The employer is not bound to make intrusive enquiries and is entitled to accept what he or she is told at face value. Where the employee returns after taking time off, the employer is entitled to assume, unless told otherwise, that the employee is again fit to return to work.

It is clear from the decisions of the Court of Appeal that an employee who believes that he or she is suffering from workplace stress which may lead to psychiatric injury is under a duty to do something about it, and to communicate the facts to the employer. A failure to do so may result in the employer escaping liability.

Other decisions which have been reported after Hatton are considered in **Chapter 12**.

## *Causation and remoteness of damage* 9.6

The final requirement for a successful negligence claim is resulting damage. The damage must result from the breach of duty by the defendant, and not from some other cause. A new intervening act may serve to remove liability from the original wrongdoer.

In order for the claim to succeed, the breach must be a cause of the damage, although it need not necessarily be the sole or even the principal cause. The test usually applied is the 'but for' test. For a recent interpretation by the House of Lords of the 'but for' test (admittedly in a rare set of circumstances), see the discussion of *Fairchild v Glenhaven Funeral Services [2002] 3 WLR 89* in **Chapter 12**.

The defendant is not liable for all the consequences of his or her breach of duty. In *The Wagon Mound [1961] AC 388* the courts laid down that the test was one of reasonable foresight. The precise nature of the damage need not be foreseeable, providing that the damage is of a type that could be foreseen.

Provided that the actual damage is foreseen, the extent of the damage is irrelevant, and the defendant will be liable to compensate the claimant for all such damage. This is known as 'the eggshell skull rule', and lays down the principle that the defendant 'takes his victim as he finds him'. If the claimant is unduly sensitive, then the defendant will be liable for all damage caused, provided it falls within the test of reasonable foresight outlined above.

## *Volenti non fit injuria* 9.7

There is no liability for negligence where the claimant has brought about his or her own downfall. For example, a claimant who takes part in a hazardous sport is deemed to accept the consequences of the normal hazards of the sport.

Mere knowledge of the risk does not amount to consent. In order for the defendant to be able to rely on the defence of *volenti*, the claimant must be shown to have had full knowledge of the nature and extent of the risk, but freely and voluntarily to have agreed to incur it.

Where an employee makes a claim against their employer for negligence, a plea of *volenti* on the part of the employer is almost certain to fail, in view of the unequal nature of the relationship (*Smith v Baker and Sons HL [1891] AC 325*). A negligent car driver who seeks to plead *volenti* on the part of a passenger who was aware of the driver's inexperience or impaired ability to drive because of alcohol or drugs will not succeed in that defence because of the provisions of *section 149* of the *Road Traffic Act 1988*. This prohibits any restriction on the driver's liability to his passenger such as is required to be covered by insurance. This may be compared with the case of *Morris v Murray [1991] 2 QB 6*, Court of Appeal, where the defendant, who to the claimant's knowledge was extremely drunk, took an aeroplane for a flight in poor weather conditions and crashed soon after take off. The other circumstance in which *volenti* will not apply is the situation of a rescuer (see for example *Chadwick v British Transport Commission*, above).

As noted above one of the principal areas in which *volenti* is relevant is in the area of sports injuries.

## Negligence and sports injuries 9.8

As between two players in, say, a football match, the proper standard of care is one of reasonable care in all the circumstances, taking into account the fact that both parties are involved in a competitive sport. Where a player is injured in a tackle which falls within the rules of the game, there can be no action, as a player is clearly deemed to accept the risk of injury caused legitimately. However, where the tackle is outside the laws of the game – where it is 'reckless and dangerous', as in *Condon v Basi (CA) [1985] 1 WLR 866* – it may be held to be negligent. Clearly an assault by one player on another is unlawful.

Recently other cases have pursued action against third parties who have been held to blame for injury. Thus the referee in a colts rugby match who allowed the collapse of the scrum was liable in negligence to a player who was injured as a result (*Smoldon v Whitworth (The Times, 18 December 1996)*), Court of Appeal, a decision which was applied in *Vowles v David Evans and The Welsh Rugby Union [2003] EWCA Civ 318* (see **Chapter 12**). Perhaps more importantly, the boxer Michael Watson, who was deemed to consent to injury by his opponent in the boxing ring, was held not to consent to his injuries being caused or exacerbated by the inadequate safety arrangements provided by the sport's governing body after he was hit by his opponent (*Watson v British Boxing Board of Control [2001]*).

A spectator at a sporting event does not consent to negligence by either the participants or the organisers, though a valid notice excluding liability may defeat a claim. In *White v Blackmore [1972] 2 QB 651*, Court of Appeal, a spectator at a motor race was killed. He did not know of the negligence which produced the fatal accident, and therefore the *volenti* rules could not apply. However, an exclusion notice placed at the entrance to the stadium removed his rights despite his lack of knowledge. He was free to decide whether to enter the stadium or not. On the other hand, someone entering the stadium in the course of their employment would have no such freedom, and so the notice would probably not apply to restrict their rights.

A spectator accepts the risks incidental to the game, such as injury by a cricket ball hit into the crowd (though it is unlikely that such a hit would be deemed to be negligent). However, *White v Blackmore* illustrates the fact that a spectator cannot necessarily be said to consent to the risks of negligence.

## *Contributory negligence* 9.9

Where injury is caused without any fault whatever on the part of the claimant, then he or she will be awarded damages to represent their loss. The amount of such damages is considered elsewhere in this book. If the claimant is not to blame at all, then he or she will be able to claim 100% of their assessed losses. However, if the claimant is in part responsible for their own loss or damage, then their award will be reduced by a percentage to represent the percentage contribution which they have made to their injuries. This is known as contributory negligence. It is possible for an award to be reduced by 100% where contributory negligence is sufficiently serious.

Contributory negligence is dealt with in *section 1(1)* of the *Law Reform (Contributory Negligence) Act 1945* which provides that:

> 'where any person suffers damage as the result partly of his own fault and partly of the fault of any other person or persons . . . the damages recoverable in respect thereof shall be reduced to such an extent as the Court thinks just and equitable having regard to the claimant's share in the responsibility for the damage.'

Proof of contributory negligence depends upon a finding that the claimant failed to take reasonable care of his or her own safety.

In a similar way to *volenti*, contributory negligence is theoretically available as an argument for an employer in a works accident case, but again, the unequal relationship between employer and employee is relevant. It is the responsibility of the employer to provide proper safety equipment, to provide necessary instructions to employees, and to guard against employees who take unnecessary risks.

It is not necessary for the plaintiff to be directly at fault for the contributory negligence principle to have applied. For example, it has been established since the case of *Froom v Butcher [1976] QB 286* that it is contributory negligence to fail to wear a seatbelt in a car. A driver who, not wearing a seatbelt, nevertheless drives with proper care and attention, will nonetheless face a reduction on account of contributory negligence if his injuries are made worse by the fact that he was not wearing a seatbelt, even though the collision itself was entirely the fault of another person.

The rules on contributory negligence are not applied uniformly to all claimants, and there may be concessions in the case of, for example, children and older people. Furthermore, it is unlikely that damages awarded to a rescuer will be reduced by reasons of contributory negligence.

## *Vicarious liability* 9.10

Vicarious liability is the principle whereby one person is responsible for the actions of another. Its most common application in negligence is the liability of an employer for the acts of his or her employees. For example, where injury is caused to a worker by the negligence of a fellow worker, the employer will be liable to compensate the employee.

This may be seen as part of a public policy decision to spread risks, which is also reflected in the compulsory insurance obligations associated both with employment and with driving.

The liability on the employer is strict, and no negligence on the part of the employer need be proved. Once negligence has been established on the part of the employee, the employer will have no defence to say that he or she endeavoured to avoid the incident. It will not even necessarily avail the employer to say that the employee was acting beyond instructions. Provided the actions of the employee were carried out in the course of his or her employment, the employer is liable for the employee's actions.

It may be noted that there may be a separate claim in negligence against the employer directly, for example in a situation where the employer was himself or herself negligent by failing to provide proper training for employees, which resulted in the injury caused by one employee to another. It is likely that the courts will regard even an express prohibition by the employer as being directed to the methods by which a job is done. Thus a driver who gives a lift in contravention of the employer's instructions not to do so may nevertheless render the employer vicariously liable provided that the employee was at the time engaged in carrying out work for the purposes of his or her employment (*Rose v Plenty [1976] 1 All ER 97, Court of Appeal*).

## Occupiers liability 9.11

Reference is made above to liability which is caused due to the fault of an occupier of premises in respect of an injury sustained by a person using those premises. Liability in such cases is imposed on the defendant by the *Occupiers Liability Acts 1957* and *1984*, which impose a specific duty of care on the occupier's premises, and which overcomes the issue of whether or not a duty of care exists in such a case.

An occupier is a person who has sufficient degree of control over premises to put him or her under a duty to those who lawfully come on to the premises. It is not necessary that the defendant has any legal interest in the land or premises.

The statutory duty under the *Occupiers Liability Act 1957* is owed to lawful visitors, which includes not simply those who are actually invited on to the property, but those whose presence is accepted by implication (such as a person delivering post). Repeated trespass does not imply that the person becomes a lawful visitor.

The duty owed to a lawful visitor is the common duty of care, which is defined by *section 2(2)* as 'a duty to take such care as in all the circumstances of the case is reasonable to see that the visitor will be reasonably safe in using the premises for the purposes for which he is invited or permitted to be there'. The duty may extend to taking steps to see that others present on the premises do not harm lawful visitors by foreseeably likely misconduct (*Cunningham v Reading Football Club (1991)*).

The occupier must be prepared for children to be less careful than adults (*section 2(3)(a)*). In the case of a very young child, however, the occupier is entitled to expect that a prudent parent will ensure that such a child is supervised where there is potential danger (*Phipps v Rochester Corporation [1955] 1 QB 450*).

Where the visitor has special skills, the occupier is entitled to rely on such a visitor taking measures to guard against any particular risks (*section 2(3)(b)*).

The occupier may discharge his or her duty to the visitor by placing a warning (*section 2(4)(a)*), provided that the warning is sufficient to enable the visitor to be reasonably safe; and will have a defence where the damage is due to faulty construction, repair or maintenance work carried out by an independent contractor employed by the occupier (*section 2(4)(b)*).

The *Occupiers Liability Act 1984* applies to persons other than visitors. The occupier owes a duty to such persons if:

- He or she is aware of the danger or has reasonable grounds to believe that it exists.
- He or she knows or has reasonable grounds to believe that the non-visitor is in the vicinity of the danger, or may come in to the vicinity of the danger.
- The risk is one against which the occupier might, in all the circumstances of the case, be reasonably expected to offer the non-visitor some protection.

(*Section 1(3)*.)

This will operate in certain circumstances to impose on an occupier a duty to a trespasser. Whether the occupier has discharged that duty will depend on factors such as the method of entry used by the non-visitor, the age of the entrant, and the extent of the risk, including the burden that would be imposed on the occupier in taking steps to eliminate the risk. See for example the cases on swimming in public or semi-public lakes discussed in **Chapter 12**.

## Statutory liability

### *Liability for defective products – general common law principles* 9.12

Where a person is injured by a defective product, the normal principles of common law apply. This will normally offer two possible causes of action to the injured party; an action for breach of contract, or an action in negligence.

The principles for negligence are outlined above. Liability in respect of breach of contract is frequently founded on the *Sale of Goods Act 1979*. Where goods are supplied in the course of a business in exchange for money, then the *Sale of Goods Act 1979, s 14* implies into the contract a number of conditions regarding the quality of the goods. The two principal conditions implied are firstly that the goods shall be of satisfactory quality, and secondly that they shall be fit for the purpose for which they are required. The requirement of satisfactory quality applies unless the vendor has indicated a particular defect, or the purchaser has examined the goods and has discovered, or should have discovered, that defect. The condition of fitness for purpose operates on the principle that the purchaser is entitled to rely on the vendors skill and judgement in producing goods which are suitable for the purpose for which the purchaser requires them.

If the goods then turn out to be unsatisfactory in either respect, liability on the vendor is strict. The *Unfair Contract Terms Act 1977, section 6(1)* prevents a vendor from excluding liability under the Act.

These provisions will only apply where there is a contract between the provider of the goods and the injured party. If this is not the case, then it is more likely that the law of negligence will be brought into play.

### ***Statutory protection*** 9.13

The principal statutory protection for a consumer is the *Consumer Protection Act 1987*, which was introduced following the *European Product Liability Directive*. It applies to products made after 1 March 1988. It does not apply to agricultural produce, nor to game that has not undergone an industrial process.

A producer of goods which cause damage (namely death, personal injury or loss or damage to property) is liable under the *Act*. Where injury is caused, wholly or partly, by a defective product, the producers of the product are strictly liable without proof of negligence. In addition to the producers, liability also falls on any persons who, by putting their names on the product, have held themselves out as being the producers of the product, and also on any persons who have imported the product into an EC member state in order to supply it to another person in the course of business. Where more than one such person is involved, liability is joint and shareable between them. A 'product' is any goods or electricity (*section 1(2)*). Component parts and raw materials are also covered by the definition.

Frequently it will be the case that the injured party has no information enabling them to identify any of the above parties. In such a case, liability also falls on the supplier of the product. The injured party must have requested the support of the supplier to identify one or more of the persons who are liable.

The request must have been made within a reasonable period after the incident occurred and at a time when it was not reasonably practicable for the injured party to identify such persons. The supplier must then have failed to identify the appropriate person within a reasonable time of the request. In such a case the supplier is liable in the same way as if he or she were the producer of the product.

A product is defective if its safety 'is not such as persons generally are entitled to expect' (*section 3(1)*). The risks covered include damage to property as well as damage to individuals.

This leaves the question of what 'persons generally are entitled to expect'. This will depend on issues such as the manner in which the product has been marketed, and the purposes for which it has been marketed, issues such as any instructions for use of the product, or warnings supplied with it; what might reasonably be expected to be done with the product; and the time at which the product was supplied to the customer (*section 3(2)*).

*Section 4* of the Act provides certain statutory defences. The onus of proof is on the producer (etc) to show:

- that the defect is attributable to compliance with either domestic or Community law;
- that the defendant did not at any time supply the product to another;
- that the defendant did not supply the goods in the course of a business, and either he or she does not fall within the definition of a producer contained in *section 2(2)*, or does so only by providing goods other than for profit;
- that the defects did not exist in the product at the relevant time;
- that the state of scientific and technical knowledge at the relevant time was not such that a producer of products of the same description as the product in question might be expected to have discovered the defects if it had existed in the products while they were under his or her control (the so-called 'state of the art' defence); or
- that the producer has provided raw materials or components but the defect is due to the design of the overall product, or to instructions given by the producer of the overall product to the producer.

## *Employers' liability for defective equipment* 9.14

In *Davie v New Merton Board Mills [1959] AC 604*, a worker was using a tool supplied by the employer when a chip sheered off and flew into his eye. He was blinded in that eye as a result, and sued the employer. However, the House of Lords found in favour of the employer, as the tool in question had been purchased from a reputable supplier.

This situation was clearly unsatisfactory, and Parliament legislated to overturn it in the *Employers Liability (Defective Equipment) Act 1969*. Under that Act, where an employee sustains personal injury in the course of their employment owing to defective equipment which has been supplied by the employer for the purposes of his or her business, the employer will be liable. The defect must be attributable to the actions of a third party, whether identified or not (if the defect is due to the actions of the employer, then ordinary principles of negligence apply). If these conditions are fulfilled, the employer is liable regardless of fault.

Equipment includes plant and machinery, vehicles, aircraft, and clothing. It has also been held to include a ship (*Coltman v Bibby Tankers Ltd, The Derbyshire [1988] AC 276*). The equipment must be defective, and not merely inappropriate or inadequate.

## Animals 9.15

The *Animals Act 1971* provides that the keeper of an animal may be liable in damages for any damage that the animal does. The Act divides animals into dangerous and non-dangerous species.

The keeper of an animal which belongs to a dangerous species is liable for all the damage which it does. An animal belongs to a dangerous species if it is one which is not commonly domesticated in the British Isles, and if the fully-grown animals of that species are either likely to cause severe damage (if they are of a ferocious species) or alternatively if any damage which they do cause is likely to be severe. A zoo keeper, for example, is thus under a duty to restrain all his or her dangerous animals on pain of being liable for any damage they cause if they escape. Liability under *section 2(1)* is strict.

Under *section 2(2)*, the keeper of an animal which does not belong to a dangerous species is nevertheless strictly liable for any damage which it causes if certain conditions are fulfilled. The keeper is liable for damage caused by such an animal if:

- the damage was of a kind which the animal, unless restrained, was likely to cause, or which, if caused by the animal, was likely to be severe; and
- the likelihood of the damage, or of its being severe, was due to characteristics of the animal which are not normally found in animals of that species, or are not normally so found except at particular times or in particular circumstances; and

- those characteristics were known to the keeper, or to an employee of his or hers, or to a person under 16 in his or her household.

This places liability on the keeper of an animal which does not belong to a dangerous species where the keeper knew, or is deemed to have known, of any particular tendency of his or her animals to cause damage. Thus a person who is bitten by a dog will have an action against its keeper if the keeper was aware, or should have been aware, of its tendency to behave in a dangerous manner – hence the (rather unsatisfactory) rule of thumb that 'every dog is allowed one bite'.

The case of *Curtis v Betts [1990] 1 All ER 769*, Court of Appeal, illustrates the operation of the section. The plaintiff was attacked and savaged by the defendant's bull mastiff which was being placed in a car. The animal was normally docile. The damage was of a kind which was likely to be severe, in that a bite from a bull mastiff was likely to be severe. The likelihood of the damage was due to characteristics which are found only in particular circumstances, in that bull mastiffs are known to be territorially defensive, and the dog in question was defending its territory. The defendant had not been negligent, but since on the evidence he knew of the dog's characteristics, he was liable.

Possible defences to the keeper include contributory negligence (*section 10*), and situations where the damage is entirely the claimant's own fault (*section 5(1)*) or the claimant voluntarily accepts the risk (*section 5(2)*).

A claim to the Criminal Injuries Compensation Authority (see **Chapter 8**) may also be considered.

### *Defective premises* **9.16**

In most cases where someone is injured by the defective state of premises, they will have a cause of action in negligence or under the *Occupiers Liability Acts*. The *Defective Premises Act 1972* adds another possible cause of action. The *Act* imposes a duty on architects, engineers and others who carry out work for or in connection with the provision of a dwelling to see that their work ' is done in a workmanlike or . . . professional manner, with proper materials . . . so that as regards the work the dwelling will be fit for habitation when completed'. There is no requirement of negligence on the part of the builder or architect, on whom the duty is to 'see that' the work is done properly. In most cases the loss will be an economic one, but the *Act* is not limited to economic loss and also covers personal injury.

## Limitation **9.17**

In any claim for damages, the claim must be brought within a reasonable time of the accrual of the cause of action. The time appropriate in any one case is governed by the *Limitation Act 1980* which provides that, in a claim for damages for negligence, nuisance or breach of statutory duty which includes a claim for personal injuries, the time limit for the issue of proceedings is three years from the date on which the cause of action accrued, or if it is later, from the date when the injured person acquired the relevant knowledge.

The date at which the action accrues is the date of the act or omission that causes the damage. It there is a series of actions, then it may be necessary to determine which of them was the proximate cause of the injury.

If the issue in question is the date of the claimant's knowledge, then the relevant date is the date on which he or she knew the following:

- That the injury was significant.
- That the injury was attributable to the act or omission which is alleged to constitute negligence, either in whole or in part.
- The identity of the defendant.
- If the act or omission causing the damage is not that of the defendant, the identity of such person and the facts giving rise to liability on the part of the defendant.

(*Section 14(1)*.)

Knowledge can be either actual or constructive.

The date of actual knowledge is the date at which the claimant was in possession of information which he or she might even necessarily have had interpreted by some medical or other expert advice. Constructive knowledge, covered by *section 14(3)* of the Act, is knowledge which he or she is reasonably expected to have acquired.

If the defendant, or any agent of the defendant, takes steps deliberately to conceal any relevant facts, then the primary limitation period does not begin to run until after the claimant has discovered the concealment.

Where the claimant is under a disability, the limitation period does not begin to run until the disability comes to an end. In the case of a minor, this would be from the point at which he or she attains the age of 18. In the case of someone under a mental disability, so that he or she is deemed incapable of managing or administering his or her own property and affairs under the *Mental Health Act 1983*, the limitation period will not run while the disability remains in place. A claimant who is a formal or informal patient in a psychiatric institution is conclusively presumed to be of unsound mind.

If the disability occurs after the course of action has accrued, then it does not interfere with the three year period. So, for example, where a claimant becomes of unsound mind after the date of the incident giving rise to the claim, but before proceedings are issued, the three year period nevertheless continues to run. However, the Court should take the supervening disability into account in determining whether to extend the period.

Under *section 33* of the *Limitation Act 1980* the Court has an equitable discretion to disapply the limitation period. In so doing, the Court is required to have regard to all the circumstances of the individual case, in particular the following:

- The length of the delay and the reason for it on the claimant's part. This is a purely subjective test and there is no requirement that the reasons are reasonable.
- The effect of the delay on the cogency of the evidence.
- The conduct of the defendant.
- The duration of any disability to the claimant.
- The extent to which the claimant has acted promptly or reasonably once he or she has acquired the relevant knowledge.
- The steps taken to obtain medical, legal or other expert advice and the nature of such advice.

# 10 Compensation and Damages

## Introduction 10.1

The normal outcome of a personal injury claim is an award of damages to the injured party. The aim is firstly to compensate the victim fully for all their financial losses, and to attempt to predict their future loss so that compensation can be awarded which will enable them as far as possible to live in the way in which they had become accustomed. Secondly, the aim is to provide fair compensation for non-pecuniary loss such as pain and suffering.

## Awards for damages 10.2

Damages are assessed on a once and for all basis and until comparatively recently were payable in a single lump sum. Since the *Damages Act 1996* it has become possible to pay damages by way of periodic payments known as a structured settlement, which is considered further below. However, the damages award is still a once for all assessment. The only escape from this principle is by way of an interim payment, which can be awarded if the court is satisfied that the defendant is liable to pay the plaintiff a substantial sum, and has the means to meet it.

It is also possible for a provisional damages award to be made, under *section 6* of the *Administration of Justice Act 1982*. This can happen where there is a possibility that a claimant will develop a serious disease, or will suffer serious mental or physical deterioration, as a result of the injury. The court may then assess damages on the basis that the contingency will not occur, but may declare that if it does occur a further payment will be made. This is in effect a split lump sum award, rather than an ongoing assessment, and is of use in only a limited number of cases.

Damages are a matter for assessment by the court, and are grouped under a number of headings. Damages which are ascertainable by reference to a specific pecuniary loss (for example, loss of earnings) are known as special damages, and damages awarded as compensation for non-pecuniary items such as pain and suffering are known as general damages.

## ***Pain, suffering and loss of amenity*** **10.3**

This element of damages is intended, not to punish the defendant, but to provide some compensation for the victim, based upon the pain which he or she has suffered, the disruption of their life which follows from the injury (the suffering element), and the loss arising form the fact of physical injury and the impairment of bodily functions (the loss of amenity element).

The amount awarded for pain is determined on a subjective basis, and will be higher the greater the amount of pain which is suffered. If the pain is controlled by drugs, or if the victim is unconscious, the amount awarded will be proportionately less. Suffering can be relevant even if the victim suffers no pain. It represents the claimant's appreciation of the disruption to his or her life caused by the injury, and includes items such as the loss of the ability to have children, the disfigurement which follows from the injury, and the loss of expectation of life. This is again measured on a subjective basis, and will be less for someone who has suffered severe brain damage and who has no appreciation of their situation than for someone with less severe injuries who is nevertheless fully aware of their implications.

Loss of amenity, on the other hand, is measured objectively, and will apply even to the victim who is unaware of their fate. Items which may be covered by the heading include:

- loss of job enjoyment (*Morris v Johnson Matthey & Co Ltd (1968) 112 Sol Jo 32*);
- the loss of a good education (*Jones v Lawrence [1969] 3 All ER 267*);
- loss of status through the claimant's inability to complete an apprenticeship (*Dunk v George Waller & Son [1970] 2 QB 163*); and
- loss of the chance to enhance a person's reputation (*Marbey v Daly's Theatre [1928] 1 KB 269*).

The figure for damages for pain, suffering and loss of amenity is normally derived from a tariff. This in turn is derived from previous cases, and makes reference to the guidelines laid down by the Judicial Studies Board. The aim of the assessment is to arrive at a global figure which represents the pain and suffering to the claimant, and will vary according to the seriousness of the injury and its likely outcome.

In a case involving multiple injuries, the overall award is usually lower than the sum of the awards for each different injury.

Interest is payable on general damages at a flat rate of 3% per annum from the date of service of a claim until trial.

## *Past loss* 10.4

The general principle of past loss is that a claimant should, as nearly as possible, be put in the same position as he or she would have been in if he or she had not sustained the injury. This heading will cover matters such as loss of earnings.

Since the intention is to put the claimant back into the same position as he or she would have been in, past earnings are assessed net of Income Tax and National Insurance. See below for the rules on the recovery of benefits.

Where the claimant is made redundant, and the redundancy is to some extent attributable to the injury, then a redundancy payment is deductible from lost earnings, but this is not the case if the redundancy is not attributable to the injury (*Colledge v Bass, Mitchells & Butlers Ltd [1988] 1 All ER 536*; *Mills v Hassoll [1983] ICR 330*).

Sick pay and payments received under a permanent health insurance scheme are normally set off against an award for past loss. Where the claimant has taken out private insurance, then they are allowed to keep the proceeds without accounting for it to the other party. Other payments which the claimant is allowed to keep include charitable and benevolent payments, pension entitlements, and assistance from friends and relatives.

## *Future loss* 10.5

Damages will also include an element in respect of future loss. This will be a lump sum which is calculated to represent the value of the losses which the claimant is likely to sustain in the future. The net annual earnings loss is taken and is multiplied by a figure which represents the number of years over which the loss will run. This figure will not in practice be the entire period over which the loss will run (which in some cases will be the rest of the claimant's life) for two reasons. Firstly, it is assumed that the capital award of damages will be invested to produce income. The claimant's needs should be met from a combination of income and capital, and the aim should be that the fund is exhausted at the end of the period. Second, it cannot be assumed that the claimant would avoid other interference with his or her earnings, such as unemployment and illness.

As well as expected loss of earnings, future loss will include estimates of increased costs, and the necessity for capital expenditure such as adaptations to a house or a car (although in so far as the adaptations enhance the value of the item, this will not be the case).

The calculation takes no account of the need to protect the award against its decline in real terms due to inflation. The House of Lords has rejected attempts to increase the multiplier to do so, arguing for example that the interest produced by investing the lump sum will tend to exceed the effects of inflation (*Cookson v Knowles [1979] AC 556*).

### Loss of earning capacity 10.6

Finally, a damages award is likely to include damages for loss of earning capacity, where the claimant's ability to earn in the future has been significantly impaired.

### Expenses 10.7

The main expense which may be incurred is the cost of medical treatment and nursing care. An expenses claim for the future is calculated in the same way as loss of earnings, that is, an annual estimate multiplied by a multiplier. Where care is provided entirely by the National Health Service, it will be provided free of charge, but account should be taken of the fact that personal care (as opposed to health care) may be charged for by a local authority which provides such services by way of community care services, under *Health and Social Services and Social Security Adjudication Act 1983, s 17*. The Court of Appeal has considered the relationship between nursing care and personal care in *R v North and East Devon Health Authority ex parte Coughlan (1999) 2 CCLR 285*.

Where the claimant chooses to opt for private care, the cost will form part of the award. No account is taken of whether it was reasonable to opt for private care rather than relying on National Health Service care.

This also raises a particular issue where the care is not provided by a professional, but by a relative of the injured person. The case of *Hunt v Severs [1994] 2 All ER 385* illustrates the problem. Mr Severs negligently crashed his motor bike, on which Ms Hunt was a pillion passenger. She sued him for damages, payable by his insurers. She had been rendered paraplegic and needed constant nursing care. He in fact provided that care, and they later married. A figure of £60,000 was awarded by the trial judge in respect of care expenses, but the insurers appealed on the basis that the award of £60,000 was, in effect, being made to the wrongdoer, and that this was contrary to public policy. The claimant argued that the award was for her care, and it was not a matter for the court as to how the need was met.

The House of Lords held that the central purpose of the award was to compensate the voluntary carer to whom she entrusted her care. It would be wrong to order Mr Severs to pay £60,000 in damages to Ms Hunt which she would then return to him (although in point of fact it was the insurers who would pay, and not Mr Severs). As a result Ms Hunt and her husband were

£60,000 worse off because she had relied on his care instead of seeking private nursing care, which would have the added outcome of freeing him to seek paid employment.

## Amounts of awards for general damages 10.8

As indicated above, items of general damages will normally reflect guidelines laid down by the courts and by the Judicial Studies Board. The current issue of the guidelines groups injuries under the headings:

- injuries involving paralysis;
- head injuries;
- psychiatric damage;
- injuries affecting the senses;
- injuries to internal organs;
- orthopaedic injuries;
- facial injuries;
- scarring to other parts of the body;
- damage to hair; and
- dermatitis.

Different types of injuries are quite commonly placed within a range of possible awards, and the position of the actual reward within that bracket will depend on its seriousness and other factors. For example in the case of quadriplegia (which is placed within a bracket of £165,000 to £205,000), the level of the award is affected by considerations such as the extent of any residual movement, the presence and extent of pain, depression, age and life expectancy. The top of the bracket is considered to be appropriate only where there is significant effect on senses or ability to communicate.

## Recovery of benefits 10.9

Where the claimant receives a benefit representing a particular loss and where that is also included in an award of damages, the amount agreed or awarded must be paid over to the Compensation Recovery Unit of the Department for Work and Pensions. This applies to all payments in respect of personal injury, whether they are received as the result of a court order or in voluntary settlement of a claim.

The law on the recovery scheme is principally contained in the *Social Security (Recovery of Benefits) Act 1997*.

No sum is deductible from an award for pain and suffering. Where the amount of compensation in respect of a particular head is less than the amount to be recovered, the compensator is nevertheless required to pay the difference.

EXAMPLE

| **Compensation award** | **Listed benefits** |
| --- | --- |
| Loss of earnings £10,000 | Incapacity benefit £12,000 |
| Pain and suffering £12,000 | DLA care component £5,000 |

The compensation for loss of earnings is reduced to nil because incapacity benefit can reduce compensation under that head (see table below). The compensator must pay £12,000 to the CRU, but cannot recover the remaining £2,000 from the award for pain and suffering. The £5000 for DLA care is not recoverable either because only the pain and suffering award remains.

The injured person gets the full pain and suffering award of £12,000, but nothing for loss of earnings.

The compensator must pay £17,000 to the CRU.

Note that retirement pension is not a recoverable benefit, but that payments of listed benefits made after retirement age nevertheless continue to be subject to recovery. War pensions are not recoverable benefits either, but an award will normally be adjusted under the Secretary of State's discretion (see **Chapter 4**).

The onus is on the person or body paying compensation to apply to the Compensation Recovery Unit for a Certificate of Recoverable Benefits. The compensator is then liable to repay the amount stated to the Compensation Recovery Unit. There is no obligation on the claimant to pay this amount if the compensator does not.

The type of compensation, and the benefits for which payments of each are recoverable, are as follows:

| Compensation | Recoverable Benefits |
|---|---|
| Loss Of Earnings | Disability Working Allowance<br>Disablement Benefit<br>Incapacity Benefit<br>Income Support<br>Invalidity Pension<br>Job Seekers Allowance<br>Reduced Earnings Allowance<br>Severe Disablement Allowance<br>Sickness Benefit<br>Statutory Sick Pay paid before 6 April 1994<br>Unemployment Benefit<br>Unemployability Supplement<br>Invalidity Allowance |
| Cost of Care | Attendance Allowance<br>Disability Living Allowance<br>Care Component<br>Disablement Benefit for Constant Attendance<br>Disablement Benefit for Exceptionally Severe Disablement |
| Loss of Mobility | Mobility Allowance<br>DLA Mobility Component |

Benefit is recoverable when it is paid in consequence of the injury or disease from which the claimant suffered during the relevant period. The complicating factor in determining whether benefit is paid in consequence of the injury is where the claimant has another disability or health problem which has affected his or her entitlement to benefits. This is dealt with as follows.

Where the claimant is entitled to benefit both because of the relevant incident and because of another problem, then the benefit is recoverable provided that the relevant incident is at least partially responsible for the illness or disability.

The benefit is not recoverable where the relevant incident would not have given the entitlement to the benefit, but where the other unconnected event would do so.

Where the claimant's condition is a pre-existing disability which was exacerbated by the relevant incident, then once the claimant reaches the point at which he or she would have suffered that level of pain in any event, benefit is no longer recoverable.

Where benefit is wrongly paid, the amount of that benefit is not recoverable from the compensator.

The 'relevant period' is a period of five years from the date of the accident or injury, if the claimant is claiming damages for an accident or injury, or five years from the date when the claimant first claimed their recoverable benefit because of a disease. The relevant period ends when a final payment of compensation is made, or when compensation already paid is accepted in full and final settlement.

Certain compensation payments are exempt from recovery. These include the following:

- Compensation ordered by a criminal court against a convicted person.
- Payments made out of certain trusts.
- Payments made by insurance companies before either the occurrence of the injury or disease, or the first claim for a listed benefit.
- A redundancy payment which is taken into account in assessing damages.
- Payments for legal costs.
- Payments from the Macfarlane Trusts or the Eileen Trust (see **Chapter 8**).
- Payments made under the *Fatal Accidents Act* (but not the *Law Reform (Miscellaneous Provisions) Act 1934* – see **Chapter 11**).
- Payments made under the *Vaccine Damage Payments Act 1979*.
- Payments made under the Criminal Injuries Compensation Scheme.
- Compensation paid by British Coal under the NCB Pneumoconiosis Scheme.
- Payment made for hearing loss of less than 50 dB in one or both ears.
- Contractual sick pay.
- Payments made under the National Health Service Industrial Injuries Scheme.

Both the claimant and the compensator may appeal against a Certificate of Recoverable Benefits. Appeals are on the grounds that:

- the amount, rate, or period of benefit given in the Certificate are wrong; or
- the benefits were not paid because of an accident, injury or disease; or
- benefits listed which have been brought into account have not been paid to the claimant and are not likely to be;

- the compensation payment was not made as a result of the accident, injury or disease.

An appeal cannot be made until the compensation claim has been finally settled and payment of any recoverable benefits has been made by the compensator. The time limit for the appeal is one month from the date when the compensator makes full payment of recoverable benefits to the CRU.

## Structured settlements 10.10

Instead of a lump sum of money being handed over to the claimant, compensation may be paid by way of a structured settlement. This is set up pursuant to the *Damages Act 1996* and consists of the payment of a sum by way of damages in periodic instalments. This is normally done by way of an annuity linked to the life of the claimant. Provided that it is the defendant, rather than the claimant, that purchases the annuity, payments will be treated by the Inland Revenue as repayment of capital, and will thus be free of Income Tax.

A structured settlement may only be made if the parties agree to periodical payments. A formal agreement will be entered into, which will be subject to the approval of the Inland Revenue.

The main advantage of a settlement is security for the claimant. Payments are guaranteed for life and may be increased for inflation. Because the payments are made at intervals, there is less risk of the claimant being exploited by family or friends, which may be particularly relevant in cases of brain injury. The periodical payments are tax free. Payments under a structured settlement may not always be effective to avoid benefit penalties, but in many cases, this can be arranged (see **Chapter 7**).

The disadvantage from the point of the claimant is the inflexibility of such an arrangement. Once the capital sum is used to buy an annuity, it cannot be recovered. There is no provision for the claimant to be able to acquire a lump sum for a single purchase.

Payments made under a structured settlement are disregarded as income for the purposes of income-based benefits provided they are not for everyday living expenses; where they are, the first £20 per week of any such payment is disregarded. See **Chapter 7**. This provision followed the decision in the Court of Appeal in the case of *Beattie v Secretary of State for Social Security, April 9, 2001*, to the effect that payments from structured settlements counted as income for income support purposes.

# 11 Fatalities

## Introduction 11.1

The principles of negligence which apply to personal injury apply in precisely the same way to occurrences which result in death. However, calculation of damages are different, and there are also differences in the available benefits.

## Inquests 11.2

In the case of a sudden, violent or unexplained death, there is a general duty to report the facts to the Coroner. Certain deaths are required by statute to be reported, while the practice of coroners in particular areas may determine that other types of death should be reported. Examples of deaths that should be reported are those where death cannot readily be certified as resulting from natural causes, where the death may be linked to an accident, where death occurred during a surgical operation, or where death may be due to lack of proper medical care. Where someone is admitted to hospital, other than for purely terminal care, and death occurs within 24 hours, this death too should be reported.

The Coroner will carry out initial investigations. If death is due to natural causes no further action is taken. Where it is not obviously the case that death is due to natural causes, a post mortem is ordered.

The Coroner must hold an inquest where there is reasonable cause to suspect that the deceased died a violent or unnatural death, or died a sudden death of which the cause is unknown, or died in prison. In addition the Coroner may hold an inquest in any case where death cannot be certified as due to natural causes. If criminal charges may follow, the Coroner must refer the matter to the Crown Prosecution Service before proceeding.

Most inquests take place before a Coroner sitting alone, but a jury must be summoned where death occurred in prison or police custody, or in circumstances where the death was one which required to be reported to a government inspector. A jury may be summoned if issues of public interest are likely to be raised.

The inquest is directed to finding out who the deceased was, and how, when and where he or she died. The Coroners Rules prevent the Coroner or the jury making a finding on issues of blame or guilt, and the verdict may not be framed so as to indicate criminal or civil liability on the part of a named person.

Where there may be a compensation claim, it is important for solicitors acting in the claim to know about the inquest, as it offers an opportunity to find out information and to question witnesses which might not otherwise be available.

Verdicts available to the Coroner include:

- Accidental death.
- Death by misadventure.
- Suicide.
- Death by natural causes.
- Unlawful killing.
- Death due to lack of care.
- Open verdict.

Where a death is reported to the coroner, no organs may be removed from the body without the Coroner's permission.

## Actions by survivors 11.3

An incident resulting in death, and possibly in a claim on behalf of the deceased, may also give rise to claims on behalf of others involved, which should not be ignored. For example, the principles expressed in *McLoughlin v O'Brian* (above) may be of assistance in pursing a claim on behalf of a close relative who suffers psychological trauma as a result, either of the fatal occurrence itself, or of its immediate aftermath. In this connection see also the recent case of *Walters v North Glamorgan NHS Trust [2002] EWCA Civ 1792,* discussed in **Chapter 12**. There may also be claims for direct physical injuries, for example, in respect of people who were passengers in the car involved in the fatal collision.

### *Damages* 11.4

There are two headings of claim for damages in respect of a fatality. Under the *Law Reform (Miscellaneous Provisions) Act 1934* the cause of action which the deceased had against the negligent party survives for the benefit of the deceased estate. In addition, dependants of the deceased are entitled to claim for loss of support under the *Fatal Accidents Act 1996*.

## *Law Reform (Miscellaneous Provisions) Act 1934* 11.5

The estate of a deceased person inherits the right to sue on that person's behalf in respect of the cause of death. The action will often be commenced after death by the personal representatives of the deceased person. If, however, a person who has already begun an action dies after the action has commenced, the action can be amended into the name of the personal representatives.

There are four headings of damages under the *Law Reform (Miscellaneous Provisions) Act 1934*. These are as follows.

1. **Special Damages**. This heading covers loss of earnings of the deceased and damage and loss to property occurring between the date of the occurrence resulting in death and the date at which the deceased dies.
2. **Pain and suffering**. The claim may incorporate a claim on behalf of the deceased for pain, injury and suffering incurred between the date of the occurrence and the date of death. If death is instantaneous, or virtually so, there will be little or no claim under this heading. In cases involving disease, there may be long periods of suffering to consider.
3. **Damages for loss of expectation of life**. Where the deceased has become aware that his or life is likely to be shortened, and of the effect that this will have on his or her family, further damages are able to be awarded for that awareness.
4. **Funeral expenses**. The estate may also claim for the funeral expenses of the deceased.

## *Fatal Accidents Act 1976* 11.6

As indicated above, this is a claim brought by a dependent or dependants of the deceased in respect of the loss of support. For this purpose a dependant includes a spouse or former spouse, a child, a parent, a grandchild, a grandparent and a co-habitee of the opposite sex who lived with the deceased for more than two years. Note that the Court of Appeal decision in the case of *Antonio Mendoza v Ahmad Raja Ghaidan (5 November 2002)* may mean that same sex relationships in due course acquire a similar right. In addition, persons who are not blood relatives, but who have been treated as either parents or children, will be able to sustain a claim.

The claim is for damages under three headings. These are as follows:

1. **Value of the dependency**. Dependency is assessed by a mathematical formula and covers loss from the date of death to the date of trial and also for the future after the trial is concluded.
2. **Funeral expenses** are the second head of damages. As indicated above, funeral expenses also form a head of damages in respect of a *Law*

*Reform (Miscellaneous Provisions) Act* claim and insofar as there is any duplication between the two heads, there will be an appropriate reduction.

3. **Damages for bereavement**. This is a set amount in respect of a bereavement sustained by a surviving spouse, the parents of a legitimate child, or the mother of a illegitimate child. The sum allowed is £3,500 in respect of a cause of action which accrues before 1 April 1991; £7,500 from that date until 1 April 2002, and £10,000 thereafter. If more than one person is bereaved, the sum allowed is shared.

The normal principles of liability outlined above will apply to any claim under either of the above two heads.

## Bereavement benefits 11.7

Bereavement benefits are social security benefits which are based on the contributions of the deceased person. The contribution record of the survivor and that person's earnings or financial status are irrelevant to the claim. The same rules apply to both men and women, and the previous arrangement whereby bereavement benefits were available only to widows has been discontinued. However, certain women who were widowed before April 2001 may be in receipt of a widows pension in place of the benefits described below.

Bereavement benefits are not payable to the survivor(s) of a polygamous marriage. However, the survivor of a marriage which is only potentially polygamous may claim.

There are three bereavements benefits. These are payable to bereaved persons under retirement age only. The benefits are as follows.

### *Bereavement payment* 11.8

This is a lump sum of £2000 payable on the death of the deceased person (*SSCBA 1992, ss 36, 60(2), 60(3)*). It is irrelevant whether the surviving spouse has paid contributions of his or her own, whether or not he or she has children, and whether or not he or she has other sources of income. The fact that the spouses were separated at the date of death does not affect entitlement. However, if the surviving spouse is co-habiting with another person of the opposite sex as his or her wife or husband at the date of death, then the bereavement payment is not payable. The survivor is not entitled to a payment if he or she is over pension age at the date of death, unless the deceased person was not then getting a Category A retirement pension (*SSCBA 1992, s 36(1)(a)*).

The contribution condition is that, in any one year before he or she attained pension age or died, the deceased spouse must have paid Class 1 National Insurance Contributions on earnings amounting to at least 25 times the lower earnings limit for that year; or 25 Class 2 or Class 3 contributions (*SSCBA 1992, Sch 3 Part I para 4*). Note that credited contributions are insufficient. Alternatively, a payment may be made irrespective of contributions if the death was as a result of an industrial injury or disease.

A person whose spouse died outside Great Britain is not entitled to a payment unless they were in Great Britain at the date of their spouse's death, or returned within four weeks of the spouse's death, or the spouse's national insurance contribution record is sufficient to qualify for widowed parents allowance or bereavement allowance (*Social Security Benefit (Persons Abroad) Regulations 1975 (SI 1975 No 563), Reg 4(2B)*).

## ***Widowed parents allowance*** **11.9**

This is a weekly sum payable to the surviving spouse for as long as he or she has dependent children (*SSCBA 1992, s 39A, 60(2), 60(3)*). The surviving spouse must be under pensionable age.

The claimant must be entitled to child benefit for a child who is:

- a son or daughter of the deceased spouse; or
- a child in respect of whom the deceased was entitled to child benefit; or
- a child in respect of whom the surviving spouse was entitled to child benefit, provided the spouses were living together at the date of death.

(*SSCBA 1992, s 39A(2)(a)*.)

Alternatively, a widow who is pregnant by her late husband may claim (*SSCBA 1992, s 39A(2)(b)*).

A child remains a dependant for as long as the bereaved parent receives child benefit for at least one child. Widowed parents allowance is not affected by capital, or by any earnings or other income of the surviving spouse. The surviving spouse will also be entitled to claim child tax credit in respect of the child.

The contribution conditions are as follows:

- in any one year, the deceased spouse must have paid Class 1 contributions on earnings amounting to 52 times the lower earnings limit for that year, or paid 52 Class 2 or Class 3 contributions; and

- for each year of their working life the deceased spouse must have paid or been credited with Class 1 contributions on 52 times the lower earnings limit for that year, or 52 Class 2 or Class 3 contributions. The contributor is allowed one year for every ten years of their working life during which they did not fulfil this condition. The condition is also deemed satisfied if the deceased spouse had fulfilled the condition for at least half of the years in his or her working life (or 20 years if that is less than half) and had been prevented from undertaking regular employment in the remaining years by responsibilities at home (*SSCBA 1992, Sch 3 para 5*).

Alternatively, death from an industrial injury or disease provides qualification regardless of the deceased spouse's contributions.

## Bereavement allowance 11.10

Bereavement allowance is paid for a period of 12 months after the death of a spouse to their surviving spouse, providing he or she is aged at least 45 and under pension age at the date when his or her spouse died. Where the surviving spouse is aged at least 55, the amount payable is £77.45 per week. Where he or she is below that age at the date of death of their spouse, then the amount payable is reduced. This is done on a sliding scale at a rate of a 7% reduction for each year by which the surviving spouse is below the age of 55. Where the surviving spouse is below the age of 45, no bereavement allowance is payable.

The bereavement allowance is also payable to a surviving spouse who has previously been entitled to widowed parents allowance, provided that he or she is aged at least 45 when the widowed parents allowance runs out. It may therefore be seen that a young widow or widower with children may receive several years' payment of widowed parents allowance followed by 12 months worth of whole or partial bereavement allowance.

The contribution conditions are the same as those for widowed mothers allowance, as is qualification on the basis of industrial injury or disease.

The bereavement benefits are not taxable. They are counted as income for the purpose of income based benefits, but the first £10 of a widowed parents allowance is disregarded in calculating income support.

Both widowed parents allowance and the bereavement allowance terminate on the remarriage of the surviving spouse and are suspended during a period of co-habitation.

### *Income support* 11.11

A surviving spouse who has dependent children will be in a prescribed category for the purpose of obtaining income support. For details of the calculation of income support, see **Chapter 7**. Older widows and widowers will be entitled to claim a bereavement premium when calculating the amount of income support to which they are entitled.

## Guardians allowance 11.12

Guardians allowance is a benefit payable in respect of a child both of whose parents are either dead or otherwise unavailable. It is payable to the person looking after the child.

### *Who can claim* 11.13

The person claiming must be entitled to child benefit for the child, or be treated as entitled to it (*SSCBA 1992, s 77(1)(a)*).

The claimant may not be a parent of the child (but may be a step-parent: *section 6* of the *National Insurance Act 1957*). Adoptive parents who have jointly adopted a child are treated as parents for guardians allowance purposes (*SS(GA) Regs reg 2(2)(a)*). An adoptive parent who was entitled to the guardians allowance immediately before the date of the adoption order may retain it (*SSCBA 1992, s 77(11)*). Where a child has been adopted by one person, the allowance is payable if that person dies (*Social Security (Guardians Allowance) Regulations 1975 (SI 1975 No 515), Reg 2(2)(b)*). On the death of an adoptive parent, a surviving natural parent may claim the allowance (*Secretary of State for Social Services v F [1983] 3 All ER 173, Court of Appeal*).

The child must be a qualifying child.

The child must be living with the claimant or the claimant must be contributing to the child's maintenance by at least £11.55 a week, in addition to any maintenance which qualifies them for child benefit (*SSCBA 1992, s 77(5)(a)*).

The claimant must satisfy residence conditions. Since entitlement to guardians allowance depends on entitlement to child benefit, the residence conditions for child benefit must be satisfied. In addition, at least one of the child's parents must have been born in the UK, or must have spent a total of 52 weeks in any two-year period in the UK at some time after reaching the age of 16 (*SI 1975 No 515, Reg 6(1)*).

### *Qualifying children* 11.14

A child is a qualifying child if:

- both their parents have died (*SSCBA 1992, s 77(2)(a)*); or
- one of their parents has died, and at the date of death the claimant did not know the whereabouts of the other. The claimant is expected to demonstrate that they have taken reasonable steps to trace that parent (*SSCBA 1992, s 77(2)(b)*); or
- one of the child's parents has died and the other is sentenced to a term of imprisonment (including detention in hospital) for two years or more (*SSCBA 1992, s 77(2)(c)*).

Once the whereabouts of the second parent have been ascertained, the claim cannot proceed, even if that parent later disappears again (*R(G) 2/83*). The onus is on the claimant to show that he or she has made 'all reasonable efforts' (*SSCBA 1992, s 77(2)(b)*) to find the missing parent. A Northern Ireland Commissioner has held that 'whereabouts' means 'a place identifiable with some particularity', so that mere knowledge that the second parent is alive will not by itself suffice to defeat the claim (*R 3/74 (P)*). It is irrelevant to the requirement to make reasonable efforts that it is not in the interests of the child that the surviving parent be found.

In determining the length of sentence where the surviving parent is in prison, no account is taken of any part of the sentence served before the death of the other parent (*SI 1975 No 515, Reg 5(2)(a)*). Where the condition is satisfied, any payments made by the imprisoned parent for the maintenance of the child are deducted from any guardians allowance payable (*SI 1975 No 515, Reg 5(6)*).

If the child's parents were not married at the date of birth of the child, and paternity has been established either by admission or by court order, both count as the child's parents for guardians allowance purposes. Otherwise guardians allowance is payable after the death of the mother (*SI 1975 No 515, Reg 3(1)*).

Where the parents are divorced, guardians allowance is payable on the death of the parent with care of the child, provided that the other did not have custody of the child (the term custody is still used in the legislation) and was not maintaining the child under a child support maintenance assessment or under a court order (*SI 1975 No 515, Reg 4*). However, guardians allowance is not payable to the surviving parent.

Where benefit is paid while one parent is serving a prison sentence, it ceases to be payable when that parent is released, unless release is merely temporary.

## Age 11.15

There are no upper or lower age limits for claiming guardians allowance.

### *Claims* 11.16

Claims must be made on Form BG1, obtainable from the Child Benefit office, Inland Revenue Enquiry Centres, and from Jobcentre Plus offices. The benefit is the responsibility of the Inland Revenue. The decision maker can treat a claim for child benefit as a claim for guardians allowance. A claim can be backdated for up to three months.

## Social Fund funeral expenses payments 11.17

The regulatory part of the Social Fund provides for grants to be made in three situations, including payments for funeral expenses.

A grant can be made to cover certain specified expenses where the claimant is receiving a qualifying benefit at the date of claim, and accepts responsibility for the cost of a funeral.

Qualifying benefits are:

- Income support.
- Income based jobseekers allowance.
- Housing benefit.
- Council tax benefit (this includes a second adult rebate where the claimant is the second adult).
- Pension credit.
- Child tax credit which includes elements other than the family element.
- Working tax credit which includes elements for disability or severe disability.

(*Social Fund Maternity and Funeral Expenses (General) Regs 1987 reg 7(1)(a).*)

The deceased must have been ordinarily resident in the UK and the funeral must usually take place there (it can take place in another European Economic Area country where the responsible person is an EC worker) (*Social Fund Maternity and Funeral Expenses (General) Regulations 1987 (SI 1987 No 481), Reg 7(1)*).

The claim must be made within three months of the date of the funeral (*Social Security (Claims and Payments) Regulations 1987 (SI 1987 No 1968), Sch 4 para 9*).

The claimant must be accepted as the responsible person. A claimant is eligible if he or she is:

- The partner of the deceased.

- Someone who was responsible for a child who has died, provided there is no absent parent who is not themselves eligible.
- A close relative or close friend of the deceased, where it is reasonable for that person to accept responsibility for the funeral.

(*Social Fund Maternity and Funeral Expenses (General) Regulations 1987 (SI 1987 No 481), Reg 7(1)(e)*.)

Close relatives or friends are excluded if there is anyone else who might have taken responsibility for the funeral. A claimant is excluded if the deceased:

- left a partner; or
- left a parent or child, unless that person:
  - is under 18;
  - is receiving a qualifying benefit;
  - is estranged from the deceased when they died;
  - is a student, or anyone under pension age studying on a full-time course;
  - is a member of a religious order which fully maintains them;
  - is in prison, and was getting a qualifying benefit immediately before being detained;
  - is in hospital, and was getting a qualifying benefit immediately before going into hospital; or
  - is an asylum seeker being supported by the National Asylum Support Service.
- has a close relative who was in closer contact with the deceased; or
- has a close relative who was in equally close contact (unless that person was getting a qualifying benefit).

References above to people receiving a qualifying benefit include being the partner of someone who receives such a benefit.

(*SI 1987 No 481, Reg* 7.)

The claimant must accept responsibility for funeral costs (*SI 1987 No 481, Reg 7(1)(e)*.)

The payment includes the necessary costs of:

- Purchasing a new burial plot and burial fees (but not for the burial of ashes following cremation).

- Cremation, including medical references and certificates.
- Costs of documentation to release the deceased's assets.
- Reasonable costs of transport for journeys in excess of 50 miles.
- One round trip for the responsible person to arrange or attend the funeral.
- Up to £700 for other expenses.

(*SI 1987 No 481, Reg 7A(1)*.)

Any assets of the deceased available to the responsible person without taking out a grant of probate or letters of administration are deducted from the amount of any award, as are sums from insurance policies or occupational pension schemes, contributions made by a charity or a family member, a funeral grant paid to a war disablement pensioner, or an amount paid under a funeral plan. Capital of the responsible person is ignored. (*SI 1987 No 481, Reg 8(1)*.)

Claims are made on Form SF200.

# 12 Recent Personal Injury Cases

## Principles of negligence

### *Repair of highways* 12.1

*Gulliksen v Pembrokeshire CC [2002] 4 All ER 450.* The local authority had built a path on a council estate which was dedicated as a public right of way. The building of the path was part of the laying out of the estate, and the council argued that it was part of its provision of housing rather than its provision of highways. It was held that the dedication of the path as a public right of way made the council liable for disrepair under the *Highways Act 1980, s 41*, because under *section 36(2)(a)* a highway constructed 'by a highway authority' became a highway maintainable at public expense.

### *Secondary victims* 12.2

It will be recalled that the House of Lords in *Alcock v Chief Constable of South Yorkshire [1992] 1 AC 310* held that there were three requirements for liability to a secondary victim in respect of psychiatric injury. Firstly, the claimant had to have close ties of love and affection with the person killed, injured or imperilled. Secondly, the claimant had to be close to the incident, both in time and in space. Thirdly, he or she had to perceive the incident through his or her unaided senses. (To this Lord Lloyd, in *Page v Smith [1996] AC 155*, added that the claimant should be of reasonable fortitude.)

In *Walters v North Glamorgan NHS Trust [2002] EWCA Civ 1792*, Ms Walters was in hospital with her son Elliott, aged nine months. She awoke at 3 a.m. to find that he had had a fit, and he was placed in the intensive care unit within a very short time. At 4.45 a.m., she was told that it was 'very unlikely' that he had suffered any serious brain damage as a result of his fit. At 11 a.m. she was told that the CAT scan had shown no sign of brain damage, but that he would be transferred to Kings College Hospital in London. Mrs Walters and her partner travelled with him. At 9 p.m., following a further CAT scan, she was told that he had suffered severe brain damage and was on a life support machine. She was told he was unlikely to survive with any sort of quality of life, and the life support machine was switched off the following day.

The result for Ms Walters was a severe pathological grief reaction. The particular issue for the Court of Appeal was whether the events over a period of 36 hours could properly be described as 'one horrifying event'. It was held that they could. Lord Justice Ward held that there had been 'an inexorable progression from the moment when the fit occurred as the result of the failure of the hospital to properly diagnose and then treat the baby, the fit causing the brain damage which shortly thereafter made termination of the child's life inevitable, and the dreadful climax when the child died in her arms'. The control mechanisms in *Alcock* should not be applied too rigidly or mechanistically.

The waters are somewhat muddied by the decision of the Court of Appeal in *Atkinson v Seghal (21 March 2003)*. In that case Ms Atkinson had been asked by her daughter, aged 16, to give her a lift to ballet class. She had refused, telling her that she could walk. On her way there, a car mounted the pavement and knocked the daughter over. This was at 7.05 p.m. She was pronounced dead at 7.40 p.m. and taken to the mortuary at the local hospital.

Her father and mother arrived independently at the scene and were told by a police officer that she was dead. They were driven to the mortuary, arriving at 9.15 p.m., where they saw the body. Ms Atkinson cradled the body in her arms. Subsequently she visited her grave regularly and made her home a shrine to her daughter.

In *McLoughlin v O'Brian [1983] 1 AC 410*, Mrs McLoughlin had arrived at the hospital within one hour of the accident. What actually counts as 'the immediate aftermath' of the accident? The House of Lords, in *McLoughlin*, stressed that this was on the limit of what was allowable (although there is some confusion in the judgements, which could lead to a conclusion that up to two hours would be regarded as in the immediate aftermath). Although reference was made by the Court of Appeal in *Atkinson* to the approach taken in *Walters*, the two cases are very different. Unlike *Walters*, there is no series of shocking events, no inexorable progression. The time limit imposed in *McLoughlin* is purely arbitrary, but if one hour was 'on the margin', as in *McLoughlin*, can the period be extended to two hours and ten minutes, as in *Atkinson* – and if so, how much further can it be extended?

The result is that it is by no means clear in what circumstances a secondary claimant can recover damages for psychiatric injury which occurs following events over a period of time.

## Stress 12.3

Since the decision of the Court of Appeal in *Hatton v Sutherland [2002] EWCA Civ 76* (**Chapter 9**), a number of decisions have attempted to apply the guidance laid down in that case. In *Young v Post Office [2002] IRLR 660*, Court of Appeal, Mr Young was in a stressful job with the post office. From 1994 he was beginning to show signs of stress and was prescribed anti-depressants by his doctor. In January 1997 he informed his employers that he needed help. Matters did not improve and he took four months off work from May 1997 due to depression. His employers held a meeting to consider how to respond. It was agreed that he should come back to work on a flexible basis, but within two weeks of his return the acting manager had gone on holiday, leaving Mr Young to run the workshop. When the acting manager returned, he had a lot of other work to catch up on and Mr Young remained in charge. After seven weeks he went off sick again and did not return. He took early retirement in May 1998.

The trial judge found that the Post Office knew that he needed to be looked after on his return, and rejected the argument by the Post Office that Mr Young should have spoken up if he had been having problems on his return to work. The Court of Appeal upheld the finding. It was reasonably foreseeable that an employee who had just taken four months off work with stress would be at risk of further stress-related injury. It was not up to the employee to take the initiative in informing the employer that he was not coping.

In *Croft v Broadstairs & St Peter's Town Council [2003] EWCA Civ 676*, Ms Croft, an employee of the council, was undergoing psychiatric counselling. She had not informed the council of her problems, but senior officials of the council knew of them from their personal relationships with her. She got into disciplinary difficulties at work, and was given a verbal warning. She became upset and depressed at this. There were discussions about whether to remove the warning, but it was eventually ratified, and she suffered a nervous breakdown. She said that both the previous mayor and the current mayor knew of her personal difficulties. The High Court ruled in her favour, but the Court of Appeal allowed the council's appeal. The employers were entitled to proceed on the basis that she was a person of ordinary robustness, and the fact that one of the officials knew in a personal capacity of her situation was not enough to import knowledge to the council.

## Causation and remoteness of damage

### *New intervening act* 12.4

Damage must be due to the breach of the duty of care. A new intervening act breaks the 'chain of causation' and relieves the defendant of liability, in whole or in part.

Where negligent medical treatment makes the injury worse, the negligent act does not break the chain of causation and relieve the original wrongdoer of liability unless the treatment is so grossly negligent as to be a totally inappropriate response to the injury. The original wrongdoer is therefore still liable, but may be able to recover a contribution from the provider of the negligent medical treatment. *Webb v Barclays Bank and Portsmouth Hospitals NHS Trust [2001] EWCA Civ 1141.*

In *Wilson v Coulson [2002] PIQR 300* the claimant was brain damaged as a result of negligence. He worsened its effects by taking heroin, in order to relieve his headaches, but to which he became addicted. The original injury was not so severe that he was no longer able to decide whether to take drugs or not. His decision to take drugs was voluntary, informed, deliberate and unreasonable. The defendant should not have to pay for his unreasonable conduct, which broke the chain of causation. Furthermore, to allow the claim would have been contrary to public policy.

In *Horton v Caplin Contracts Ltd [2003] PIQR 180* the claimant was injured following a fall of scaffolding, which had been maliciously arranged by a colleague with whom he had argued. Because this was not reasonably foreseeable, there was no breach of statutory duty relating to the construction of the scaffold by the employer in accordance with regulations. Even if there had been such a breach, the act of the colleague was a new intervening act which broke the chain of causation.

## *Mesothelioma* 12.5

The House of Lords found in favour of three claimants (two being personal representatives of deceased workers) who had failed to show in the lower courts how their mesothelioma had been caused. It is considered that mesothelioma is caused by the inhalation of asbestos fibre, and that a single fibre will suffice. Since all the claimants had worked with asbestos for more than one employer, they were unable to show in which employment the inhalation had taken place, and thus were unable to satisfy the 'but for' test, which requires the claimant to show that his or her injuries would not have been caused but for the negligence of the employer.

The problem was put by Lord Bingham as follows. 'If C is employed successively by A and B and is exposed to asbestos dust and fibres during each employment and develops a mesothelioma, the very strong probability is that this will have been caused by the inhalation of asbestos dust containing fibres. But C could have inhaled a single fibre giving rise to his condition during employment by A, in which case his exposure by B will have no effect on his condition, or he could have inhaled a single fibre giving rise to his condition during his employment by B, in which case his exposure by A will have had no effect on his condition; or he could have inhaled fibres during his employment by A and B which together gave rise to his condition; but medical science cannot support the suggestion that any of these probabilities is to be regarded as more probable than any other.'

The House of Lords held that the 'but for' test worked injustice in the particular cases. They chose to follow the decision in *McGhee v NCB [1973] 1 WLR 1*, which says that there should be flexibility in the rules of causation in special circumstances. The decision is strictly limited to mesothelioma cases because of the unusual nature of medical causation applicable to the disease (the theory that a single fibre can cause the illness). In most cases of industrial disease, such as deafness, the effect of exposure is cumulative, and liability can be apportioned to different employers. In this case it would have been unjust to deny compensation to the claimants because there were multiple employers, whereas a claimant who had worked for a single employer would have been able to recover. *Fairchild v Glenhaven Funeral Services [2002] 3 WLR 89.*

## Negligence and sports injuries 12.6

In *Chittock v Woodbridge School [2003] PIQR 6*, the claimant was a schoolboy who was injured due to his own misjudgement while skiing unsupervised, but on the piste, during a school skiing trip. The Court of Appeal held that the duty of care owed by the staff was that of a reasonably careful parent. There was on the facts no breach of the school's duty, and the Court set aside the trial judge's award of damages subject to a deduction for 50% contributory negligence.

In *Vowles v David Evans and the Welsh Rugby Union [2003] EWCA Civ 318*, the claimant was a rugby player who was seriously injured when a scrum collapsed. He took action against the referee. The Court of Appeal held that a referee did indeed owe a duty of care to the players, although the threshold was high. On the facts of the particular case, the referee was liable.

A stewards' enquiry following a horse race had made a finding of careless riding against two jockeys, and a third who was injured brought a claim. His claim failed. The Court of Appeal held that the stress of a race means that the liability threshold is in practice high. An error of judgement or momentary lapse in the standards of skill required will not be sufficient to give rise to liability. *Caldwell v Maguire [2002] PIQR 45.*

## Contributory negligence 12.7

*Williams v Devon CC [2003] EWCA Civ 365* concerned a tripping accident indoors. The claimant, a school kitchen manager, walked through a stable type door into the hall after gym equipment had been tidied away. A bench had been left across the doorway 'in an extremely silly place'. The trial judge made a deduction of one third for her contributory negligence. The Court of Appeal set this finding aside and held that there was no contributory negligence. In the reality of the work environment, and given the absence of any reason to suspect that the hall had not been properly cleared away, there was no reason for her to watch out for any obstruction; this would be 'a counsel of perfection'.

## *Occupiers liability* **12.8**

Earlier decisions denied claims made by trespassers under the *Occupiers Liability Act 1984* while swimming. In *Tomlinson v Congleton Borough Council (The Times, 22 March 2002)* the claimant was seriously injured when he dived into shallow water and hit his head. The lake was a disused quarry in a public park, with beach areas alongside to add to the attraction. There were prominent warning signs, wardens were employed to warn the public, and works were being undertaken to prevent access to the beaches. The Council was found liable by a majority of the Court of Appeal, reversing the trial judge, with a contribution of two thirds for contributory negligence. In *Donoghue v Folkstone Properties [2003] EWCA Civ 231*, however, the Court of Appeal adopted a more conventional approach, and held that no duty of care was owed to a claimant who dived into shallow water late at night on Boxing Day. Notices had been erected since the occupiers were aware that people sometimes swam there in the summer.

In *Gwilliam v West Herts Hospitals, The Times, 7 August 2002*, a hospital arranged for an independent contractor to provide staff for a dangerous fairground game. The hospital checked whether there was a policy of public liability insurance in place, but failed to determine that the policy had expired several days before the event. The Court of Appeal held that, under the *Occupiers Liability Act 1957, s 2(4)*, the hospital was under a duty to ensure that the independent contractor had proper public liability insurance, although on the facts reasonable care had been taken and the claim failed.

## *Procedure*

### *Asbestos disease and Crown immunity* **12.9**

Under the *Crown Proceedings Act 1947, s 10*, a member of the forces could not make a civil claim in respect of an injury which had been certified as attributable to service, so as to give rise to a war pension. This provision was repealed by the *Crown Proceedings (Armed Forces) Act 1987*, but the repeal was not retrospective. Mr Matthews served in the Royal Navy between 1955 and 1968, and was exposed to asbestos, but the existence of an asbestos-related disease did not become apparent until many years later. The House of Lords held that the provisions did not breach the *European Convention on Human Rights, Article 6*.

# Appendix 1

## Schedule 2 – Prescribed Degrees of Disablement

| Description of injury | Degree of disablement per cent |
|---|---|
| 1 Loss of both hands or amputation at higher sites | 100 |
| 2 Loss of a hand and a foot | 100 |
| 3 Double amputation through leg or thigh, or amputation through leg or thigh on one side and loss of other foot | 100 |
| 4 Loss of sight to such an extent as to render the claimant unable to perform any work for which eyesight is essential | 100 |
| 5 Very severe facial disfiguration | 100 |
| 6 Absolute deafness | 100 |
| 7 Forequarter or hindquarter amputation | 100 |
| *Amputation cases—upper limbs (either arm)* | |
| 8 Amputation through shoulder joint | 90 |
| 9 Amputation below shoulder with stump less than 20.5 centimetres from tip of acromion | 80 |
| 10 Amputation from 20.5 centimetres from tip of acromion to less than 11.5 centimetres below tip of olecranon | 70 |
| 11 Loss of a hand or of the thumb and four fingers of one hand or amputation from 11.5 centimetres below tip of olecranon | 60 |
| 12 Loss of thumb | 30 |
| 13 Loss of thumb and its metacarpal bone | 40 |
| 14 Loss of four fingers of one hand | 50 |
| 15 Loss of three fingers of one hand | 30 |
| 16 Loss of two fingers of one hand | 20 |
| 17 Loss of terminal phalanx of thumb | 20 |
| *Amputation cases—lower limbs* | |
| 18 Amputation of both feet resulting in end-bearing stumps | 90 |

| | |
|---|---|
| 19 Amputation through both feet proximal to the metatarsophalangeal joint | 80 |
| 20 Loss of all toes of both feet through the metatarsophalangeal joint | 40 |
| 21 Loss of all toes of both feet proximal to the proximal inter-phalangeal joint | 30 |
| 22 Loss of all toes of both feet distal to the proximal inter-phalangeal joint | 20 |
| 23 Amputation at hip | 90 |
| 24 Amputation below hip with stump not exceeding 13 centimetres in length measured from tip of great trochanter | 80 |
| 25 Amputation below hip and above knee with stump exceeding 13 centimetres in length measured from tip of great trochanter, or at knee not resulting in end-bearing stump | 70 |
| 26 Amputation at knee resulting in end-bearing stump or below knee with stump not exceeding 9 centimetres | 60 |
| 27 Amputation below knee with stump exceeding 9 centimetres but not exceeding 13 centimetres | 50 |
| 28 Amputation below knee with stump exceeding 13 centimetres | 40 |
| 29 Amputation of one foot resulting in end-bearing stump | 30 |
| 30 Amputation through one foot proximal to the metatarsophalangeal joint | 30 |
| 31 Loss of all toes of one foot through the metatarsophalangeal joint | 20 |
| *Other injuries* | |
| 32 Loss of one eye, without complications, the other being normal | 40 |
| 33 Loss of vision of one eye, without complications or disfigurement of eyeball, the other being normal | 30 |
| *Loss of:* | |
| *A Fingers of right or left hand* | |
| Index finger— | |
| 34 Whole | 14 |
| 35 Two phalanges | 11 |
| 36 One phalanx | 9 |
| 37 Guillotine amputation of tip without loss of bone | 5 |
| Middle finger— | |

| | |
|---|---|
| 38 Whole | 12 |
| 39 Two phalanges | 9 |
| 40 One phalanx | 7 |
| 41 Guillotine amputation of tip without loss of bone | 4 |
| Ring or little finger— | |
| 42 Whole | 7 |
| 43 Two phalanges | 6 |
| 44 One phalanx | 5 |
| 45 Guillotine of tip without loss of bone | 2 |
| B. Toes of right or left foot | |
| Great toe— | |
| 46 Through metatarso-phalangeal joint | 14 |
| 47 Part, with some loss of bone | 3 |
| Any other toe— | |
| 48 Through metatarso-phalangeal joint | 3 |
| 49 Part, with some loss of bone | 1 |
| Two toes of one foot, excluding great toe— | |
| 50 Through metatarso-phalangeal joint | 5 |
| 51 Part, with some loss of bone | 2 |
| Three toes of one foot, excluding great toe— | |
| 52 Through metatarso-phalangeal joint | 6 |
| 53 Part, with some loss of bone | 3 |
| Four toes of one foot, excluding great toe— | |
| 54 Through metatarso-phalangeal joint | 9 |
| 55 Part, with some loss of bone | 3 |

# Appendix 2

## Part I – List of Prescribed Diseases and the Occupations for which they are prescribed

| | Occupation |
|---|---|
| A Conditions due to physical agents | Any occupation involving: |
| [A1 Leukaemia (other than chronic lymphatic leukaemia) or cancer of the bone, female breast, testis or thyroid. | Exposure to electro-magnetic radiations (other than radiant heat) or to ionising particles where the dose is sufficient to double the risk of the occurrence of the condition.] |
| A2 . . . cataract. | [Frequent or prolonged exposure to radiation from red-hot or white-hot material.] |
| A3 Dysbarism, including decompression sickness, barotrauma and osteonecrosis. | Subjection to compressed or rarefied air or other respirable gases or gaseous mixtures. |
| A4 Cramp of the hand or forearm due to repetitive movements. | Prolonged periods of handwriting, typing or other repetitive movements of the fingers, hand or arm. |
| A5 Subcutaneous cellulitis of the hand (beat hand). | Manual labour causing severe or prolonged friction or pressure on the hand. |
| A6 Bursitis or subcutaneous cellulitis arising at or about the knee due to severe or prolonged external friction or pressure at or about the knee (beat knee). | Manual labour causing severe or prolonged external friction or pressure at or about the knee. |
| A7 Bursitis or subcutaneous cellulitis arising at or about the elbow due to severe or prolonged external friction or pressure at or about the elbow (beat elbow). | Manual labour causing severe or prolonged external friction or pressure at or about the elbow. |
| A8 Traumatic inflammation of the tendons of the hand or forearm, or of the associated tendon sheaths. | Manual labour, or frequent or repeated movements of the hand or wrist. |

| | |
|---|---|
| A9 Miner's nystagmus. | Work in or about a mine. |
| [A10 Sensorineural hearing loss amounting to at least 50 dB in each ear, being the average of hearing losses at 1, 2 and 3 kHz frequencies, and being due in the case of at least one ear to occupational noise (occupational deafness).] | [(a) The use of powered (but not hand powered) grinding tools on [metal (other than sheet metal or plate metal)] < . . . > , or work wholly or mainly in the immediate vicinity of those tools whilst they are being so used; or<br><br>(b) the use of pneumatic percussive tools on metal, or work wholly or mainly in the immediate vicinity of those tools whilst they are being so used; or<br><br>(c) the use of pneumatic percussive tools for drilling rock in quarries or underground or in mining coal [or in sinking shafts or for tunnelling in civil engineering works], or work wholly or mainly in the immediate vicinity of those tools whilst they are being so used; or<br><br>[(ca) the use of pneumatic percussive tools on stone in quarry works, or work wholly or mainly in the immediate vicinity of those tools whilst they are being so used; or]<br><br>(d) work wholly or mainly in the immediate vicinity of plant (excluding power press plant) engaged in the forging (including drop stamping) of metal by means of closed or open dies or drop hammers; or<br><br>(e) work in textile manufacturing where the work is undertaken wholly is undertaken wholly or mainly in rooms or sheds in which there are machines engaged in weaving man-made or natural (including mineral) fibres or in the high speed false twisting of fibres; or] |

(f) the use of, or work wholly or mainly in the immediate vicinity of, machines engaged in cutting, shaping or cleaning metal nails; or

(g) the use of, or work wholly or mainly in the immediate vicinity of, plasma spray guns engaged in the deposition of metal; or

(h) the use of, or work wholly or mainly in the immediate vicinity of, any of the following machines engaged in the working of wood or material composed partly of wood, that is to say: multi-cutter moulding machines, planing machines, automatic or semi-automatic lathes, multiple cross-cut machines, automatic shaping machines, double-end tenoning machines, vertical spindle moulding machines (including high speed routing machines), edge banding machines, bandsawing machines with a blade width of not less than 75 millimetres and circular sawing machines in the operation of which the blade is moved towards the material being cut; or

(i) the use of chain saws in forestry[; or]

[(j) air arc gouging or work wholly or mainly in the immediate vicinity of air arc gouging; or

(k) the use of band saws, circular saws or cutting discs for cutting metal in the metal founding or forging industries, or work wholly or mainly in the immediate vicinity of those tools whilst they are being so used; or

(l) the use of circular saws for cutting products in the manufacture of steel, or work wholly or mainly in the immediate vicinity of those tools whilst they are being so used; or

(m) the use of burners or torches for cutting or dressing steel based products, or work wholly or mainly in the immediate vicinity of those tools whilst they are being so used; or

(n) work wholly or mainly in the immediate vicinity of skid transfer banks; or

(o) work wholly or mainly in the immediate vicinity of knock out and shake out grids in foundries; or

(p) mechanical bobbin cleaning or work wholly or mainly in the immediate vicinity of mechanical bobbin cleaning; or

(q) the use of, or work wholly or mainly in the immediate vicinity of, vibrating metal moulding boxes in the concrete products industry; or

(r) the use of, or work wholly or mainly in the immediate vicinity of, high pressure jets of water or a mixture of water and abrasive material in the water jetting industry (including work under water); or

(s) work in ships' engine rooms; or

(t) the use of circular saws for cutting concrete masonry blocks during manufacture or work wholly or mainly in the immediate vicinity of those tools whilst they are being so used; or

(u) burning stone in quarries by jet channelling processes, or work wholly or mainly in the immediate vicinity of such processes; or

| | |
|---|---|
| | (v) work on gas turbines in connection with— |
| | (i) performance testing on test bed; |
| | (ii) installation testing of replacement engines in aircraft; |
| | (iii) acceptance testing of Armed Service fixed wing combat planes; or |
| | (w) the use of, or work wholly or mainly in the immediate vicinity of— |
| | (i) machines for automatic moulding, automatic blow moulding or automatic glass pressing and forming machines used in the manufacture of glass containers or hollow ware; |
| | (ii) spinning machines using compressed air to produce glass wool or mineral wool; |
| | (iii) continuous glass toughening furnaces.] |
| A11 Episodic blanching, occurring throughout the year, affecting the middle or proximal phalanges or in the case of a thumb the proximal phalanx, of— | (a) the use of hand-held chain saws in forestry; or |
| (a) in the case of a person with 5 fingers (including thumb) on one hand, any 3 of those fingers, or | (b) the use of hand-held rotary tools in grinding or in the sanding or polishing of metal, or the holding of material being ground, or metal being sanded or polished, by rotary tools; or |
| (b) in the case of a person with only 4 such fingers, any 2 of those fingers, or | (c) the use of hand-held percussive metal-working tools, or the holding of metal being worked upon by percussive tools, in riveting, caulking, chipping, hammering, fettling or swaging; or |

| | |
|---|---|
| (c) in the case of a person with less than 4 such fingers, any one of those fingers or, as the case may be, the one remaining finger (vibration white finger). | (d) the use of hand-held powered percussive drills or hand-held powered percussive hammers in mining, quarrying, demolition, or on roads or footpaths, including road construction; or |
| | (e) the holding of material being worked upon by pounding machines in shoe manufacture. |
| [A12 Carpal tunnel syndrome. | The use of hand-held powered tools whose internal parts vibrate so as to transmit that vibration to the hand, but excluding those which are solely powered by hand.] |
| B. Conditions due to biological agents | Any occupation involving |
| B1 Anthrax. | Contact with animals infected with anthrax or the handling (including the loading or unloading or transport) of animal products or residues. |
| B2 Glanders. | Contact with equine animals or their carcases. |
| B3 Infection by leptospira. | (a) Work in places which are, or are liable to be, infested by rats, field mice or voles, or other small mammals; or |
| | (b) work at dog kennels or the care or handling of dogs; or |
| | (c) contact with bovine animals or their meat products or pigs or their meat products. |
| B4 Ankylostomiasis. | Work in or about a mine. |
| B5 Tuberculosis. | Contact with a source of tuberculous infection. |
| B6 Extrinsic allergic alveolitis (including farmer's lung). | Exposure to moulds or fungal spores or heterologous proteins by reason of employment in:— |
| | (a) agriculture, horticulture, forestry, cultivation of edible fungi or malt-working; or |

| | |
|---|---|
| | (b) loading or unloading or handling in storage mouldy vegetable matter or edible fungi; or |
| | (c) caring for or handling birds; or |
| | (d) handling bagasse. |
| B7 Infection by organisms of the genus brucella. | Contact with— |
| | (a) animals infected by brucella, or their carcases or parts thereof, or their untreated products; or |
| | (b) laboratory specimens or vaccines of, or containing, brucella. |
| B8 Viral hepatitis. | Any occupation involving: Contact with— |
| | (a) human blood or human blood products; or |
| | (b) a source of viral hepatitis. |
| B9 Infection by Streptococcus suis. | Contact with pigs infected by Streptococus suis, or with the carcases, products or residues of pigs so infected. |
| [B10 | |
| (a) Avian chlamydiosis | Contact with birds infected with chlamydia psittaci, or with the remains or untreated products of such birds. |
| B10 | |
| (b) Ovine chlamydiosis | Contact with sheep infected with chlamydia psittaci, or with the remains or untreated products of such sheep. |
| B11 Q fever | Contact with animals, their remains or their untreated products.] |
| [B12 Orf. | Contact with sheep, goats or with the carcasses of sheep or goats. |
| B13 Hydatidosis. | Contact with dogs.]. |

C Conditions due to chemical agents

C1

| | |
|---|---|
| [(a) Anaemia with a haemoglobin concentration of 9g/dL or less, and a blood film showing punctate basophilia;<br>(b) peripheral neuropathy;<br>(c) central nervous system toxicity]. | The use or handling of, or exposure to the fumes, dust or vapour of, lead or a compound of lead, or a substance containing lead. |
| C2 [Central nervous system toxicity characterised by parkinsonism]. | The use or handling of, or exposure to the fumes, dust or vapour of, manganese or a compound of manganese, or a substance containing manganese. |
| C3 Poisoning by phosphorus or an inorganic compound of phosphorus or poisoning due to the anti-cholinesterase or pseudo anti-cholinesterase action of organic phosphorus compounds. | The use or handling of, or exposure to the fumes, dust or vapour of, phosphorus or a compound of phosphorus, or a substance containing phosphorus. |
| [C4 Primary carcinoma of the bronchus or lung. | Exposure to the fumes, dust or vapour of arsenic, a compound of arsenic or a substance containing arsenic.] |
| [C5A Central nervous system toxicity characterised by tremor and neuropsychiatric disease. | Exposure to mercury or inorganic compounds of mercury for a period of, or periods which amount in aggregate to, 10 years or more. |
| C5B Central nervous system toxicity characterised by combined cerebellar and cortical degeneration. | Exposure to methylmercury.] |
| [C6 Peripheral neuropathy. | The use or handling of, or exposure to, carbon disulphide (also called carbon disulfide).] |
| [C7 Acute non-lymphatic leukaemia. | Exposure to benzene.] |
| C8 . . . | . . . |
| C9 . . . | . . . |
| C10 . . . | . . . |
| C11 . . . | . . . |

| | |
|---|---|
| [C12 | |
| (a) Peripheral neuropathy;<br>(b) central nervous system toxicity. | Exposure to methyl bromide (also called bromomethane).] |
| [C13 Cirrhosis of the liver. | Exposure to chlorinated naphthalenes.] |
| C14 . . . | . . . |
| C15 . . . | . . . |
| [C16 | |
| (a) Neurotoxicity;<br>(b) cardiotoxicity. | Exposure to the dust of gonioma kamassi.] |
| [C17 Chronic beryllium disease. | Inhalation of beryllium or a beryllium compound.] |
| [C18 Emphysema. | Inhalation of cadmium fumes for a period of, or periods which amount in aggregate to, 20 years or more.] |
| [C19 | |
| (a) Peripheral neuropathy;<br>(b) central nervous system toxicity. | Exposure to acrylamide.] |
| C20 Dystrophy of the cornea (including ulceration of the corneal surface) of the eye. | [Exposure to quinone or hydroquinone.] |
| [C21 Primary carcinoma of the skin. | Exposure to arsenic or arsenic compounds, tar, pitch, bitumen, mineral oil (including paraffin) or soot.] |
| [C22 | |
| (a) Primary carcinoma of the mucous membrane of the nose or paranasal sinuses;<br>(b) primary carcinoma of the bronchus or lung. | Work before 1950 in the refining of nickel involving exposure to oxides, sulphides or water-soluble compounds of nickel.] |
| [C23 Primary neoplasm of the epithelial lining of the urinary tract. | (a) the manufacture of 1-naphthylamine, 2-naphthylamine, benzidine, auramine, magenta or 4-aminobiphenyl (also called biphenyl-4-ylamine); |

| | |
|---|---|
| | (b) work in the process of manufacturing methylene-bis-orthochloroaniline (also called MbOCA) for a period of, or periods which amount in aggregate to, 12 months or more;<br><br>(c) exposure to 2-naphthylamine, benzidine, 4-aminobiphenyl (also called biphenyl-4-ylamine) or salts of those compounds otherwise than in the manufacture of those compounds;<br><br>(d) exposure to orthotoluidine, 4-chloro 2-methylaniline or salts of those compounds; or<br><br>(e) exposure for a period of, or periods which amount in aggregate to, 5 years or more, to coal tar pitch volatiles produced in aluminium smelting involving the Soderberg process (that is to say, the method of producing aluminium by electrolysis in which the anode consists of a paste of petroleum coke and mineral oil which is baked *in situ*).] |
| [C24 | |
| (a) Angiosarcoma of the liver;<br>(b) acro-osteolysis characterised by<br>(i) lytic destruction of the terminal phalanges,<br>(ii) in Raynaud's phenomenon, the exaggerated vasomotor response to cold causing intense blanching of the digits, and<br>(iii) sclerodermatous thickening of the skin;<br>(c) liver fibrosis. | Exposure to vinyl chloride monomer in the manufacture of polyvinyl chloride.] |

| | |
|---|---|
| [C25 Vitiligo. | The use or handling of, or exposure to, paratertiary-butylphenol (also called 4-*tert* butylphenol), paratertiary-butylcatechol (also called 4-*tert*-butylcatechol), para-amylphenol (also called *p*-pentyl phenol isomers), hydroquinone, monobenzyl ether of hydroquinone (also called 4-benzyloxyphenol) or mono-butyl ether of hydroquinone (also called 4-butoxyphenol).] |
| [[C26 | |
| (a) Liver toxicity;<br>(b) kidney toxicity. | The use or handling of, or exposure to, carbon tetrachloride (also called tetrachloromethane).] |
| [C27 Liver toxicity. | The use or handling of, or exposure to, trichloromethane (also called chloroform).] |
| C28 . . . | . . . |
| [C29 Peripheral neuropathy. | The use or handling of, or exposure to, n-hexane or n-butyl methyl ketone.]] |
| [C30 | |
| (a) Dermatitis;<br>(b) ulceration of the mucous membrane or the epidermis. | The use or handling of, or exposure to, chromic acid, chromates or dichromates.] |
| D. Miscellaneous Conditions | |
| D1 Pneumoconiosis. | Any occupation—<br>(a) set out in Part II of this Schedule;<br>(b) specified in regulation 2(b)(ii). |
| D2 Byssinosis. | Any occupation involving:<br>Work in any room where any process up to and including the weaving process is performed in a factory in which the spinning or manipulation of raw or waste cotton or of flax, or the weaving of cotton or flax, is carried on. |

| | |
|---|---|
| D3 Diffuse mesothelioma (primary neoplasm of the mesothelium of the pleura or of the pericardium or of the peritoneum). | [Exposure to asbestos, asbestos dust or any admixture of asbestos at a level above that commonly found in the environment at large.] |
| [D4 Allergic rhinitis which is due to exposure to any of the following agents—<br>(a) isocyanates;<br>(b) platinum salts;<br>(c) fumes or dusts arising from the manufacture, transport or use of hardening agents (including epoxy resin curing agents) based on phthalic anhydride, tetrachlorophthalic anhydride, trimellitic anhydride or triethylenetetramine;<br>(d) fumes arising from the use of rosin as a soldering flux;<br>(e) proteolytic enzymes;<br>(f) animals including insects and other arthropods used for the purposes of research or education or in laboratories;<br>(g) dusts arising from the sowing, cultivation, harvesting, drying, handling, milling, transport or storage of barley, oats, rye, wheat or maize, or the handling, milling, transport or storage of meal or flour made therefrom;<br>(h) antibiotics;<br>(i) cimetidine;<br>(j) wood dust;<br>(k) ispaghula;<br>(l) castor bean dust;<br>(m) ipecacuanha;<br>(n) azodicarbonamide; | Exposure to any of the agents set out in column 1 of this paragraph.] |

| | |
|---|---|
| (o) animals including insects and other arthropods or their larval forms, used for the purposes of pest control or fruit cultivation, or the larval forms of animals used for the purposes of research or education or in laboratories;<br>(p) glutaraldehyde;<br>(q) persulphate salts or henna;<br>(r) crustaceans or fish or products arising from these in the food processing industry;<br>(s) reactive dyes;<br>(t) soya bean;<br>(u) tea dust;<br>(v) green coffee bean dust;<br>(w) fumes from stainless steel welding.] | |
| D5 Non-infective dermatitis of external origin ( . . . excluding dermatitis due to ionising particles or electro-magnetic radiations other than radiant heat). | Exposure to dust, liquid or vapour or any other external agent [except chromic acid, chromates or bi-chromates,] capable of irritating the skin (including friction or heat but excluding ionising particles or electro-magnetic radiations other than radiant heat). |
| D6 Carcinoma of the nasal cavity or associated air sinuses (nasal carcinoma). | (a) Attendance for work in or about a building where wooden goods are manufactured or repaired; or<br>(b) attendance for work in a building used for the manufacture of footwear or components of footwear made wholly or partly of leather or fibre board; or<br>(c) attendance for work at a place used wholly or mainly for the repair of footwear made wholly or partly of leather or fibre board. |
| | Any occupation involving: |
| D7 Asthma which is due to exposure to any of the following agents:— | Exposure to any of the agents set out in column 1 of this paragraph. |

(a) isocyanates;

(b) platinum salts;

(c) fumes or dusts arising from the manufacture, transport or use of hardening agents (including epoxy resin curing agents) based on phthalic anhydride, tetrachlorophthalic anhydride, trimellitic anhydride or triethylenetetramine;

(d) fumes arising from the use of rosin as a soldering flux;

(e) proteolytic enzymes;

[(f) animals including insects and other arthropods used for the purposes of research or education or in laboratories]

(g) dusts arising from the sowing, cultivation, harvesting, drying, handling, milling, transport or storage of barley, oats, rye, wheat or maize, or the handling, milling, transport or storage of meal or flour made therefrom (occupational asthma

[(h) antibiotics;

(i) cimetidine;

(j) wood dust;

(k) ispaghula;

(l) castor bean dust;

(m) ipecacuanha;

(n) azodicarbonamide]

[(o) animals including insects and other arthropods or their larval forms, used for the purposes of pest control or fruit cultivation, or the larval forms of animals used for the purposes of research, education or in laboratories;

(p) glutaraldehyde;

(q) persulphate salts or henna;

| | |
|---|---|
| (r) crustaceans or fish or products arising from these in the food processing industry; | |
| (s) reactive dyes; | |
| (t) soya bean; | |
| (u) tea dust; | |
| (v) green coffee bean dust; | |
| (w) fumes from stainless steel welding; | |
| (x) any other sensitising agent.] | |
| D8 Primary carcinoma of the lung where there is accompanying evidence of one or both of the following— | (a) The working or handling of asbestos or any admixture of asbestos; or |
| (a) asbestosis; | (b) the manufacture or repair of asbestos textiles or other articles containing or composed of asbestos; or |
| [(b) unilateral or bilateral diffuse pleural thickening extending to a thickness of 5mm or more at any point within the area affected as measured by a plain chest radiograph (not being a computerised tomography scan or other form of imaging) which— | (c) the cleaning of any machinery or plant used in any of the foregoing operations and of any chambers, fixtures and appliances for the collection of asbestos dust; or |
| (i) in the case of unilateral diffuse pleural thickening, covers 50% or more of the area of the chest wall of the lung affected; or | |
| (ii) in the case of bilateral diffuse pleural thickening, covers 25% or more of the combined area of the chest wall of both lungs.] | |
| | (d) substantial exposure to the dust arising from any of the foregoing operations. |

| | |
|---|---|
| [D9 Unilateral or bilateral diffuse pleural thickening extending to a thickness of 5mm or more at any point within the area affected as measured by a plain chest radiograph (not being a computerised tomography scan or other form of imaging) which— | (a) The working or handling of asbestos or any admixture of asbestos; or |
| (i) in the case of unilateral diffuse pleural thickening, covers 50% or more of the area of the chest wall of the lung affected; or | (b) the manufacture or repair of asbestos textiles or other articles containing or composed of asbestos; or |
| (ii) in the case of bilateral diffuse pleural thickening, covers 25% or more of the combined area of the chest wall of both lungs.] | (c) the cleaning of any machinery or plant used in any of the foregoing operations and of any chambers, fixtures and appliances for the collection of asbestos dust; or Any occupation involving: |
| | (d) substantial exposure to the dust arising from any of the foregoing operations. |
| [D10 [Primary carcinoma of the lung] | (a) Work underground in a tin mine; or |
| | (b) exposure to bis(chloromethyl)ether produced during the manufacture of chloromethyl methyl ether; or |
| | (c) exposure to zinc chromate calcium chromate or strontium chromate in their pure forms.] |
| [D11 Primary carcinoma of the lung where there is accompanying evidence of silicosis. | Exposure to silica dust in the course of— |
| | (a) the manufacture of glass or pottery; |
| | (b) tunnelling in or quarrying sandstone or granite; |
| | (c) mining metal ores; |
| | (d) slate quarrying or the manufacture of artefacts from slate; |
| | (e) mining clay; |

(f) using siliceous materials as abrasives;

(g) cutting stone;

(h) stonemasonry; or

(i) work in a foundry.]

[D12 Except in the circumstances specified in regulation 2(d)—

Exposure to coal dust by reason of working underground in a coal mine for a period or periods amounting in aggregate to at least 20 years (whether before or after 5th July 1948) and any such period or periods shall include a period or periods of incapacity while engaged in such an occupation.]

(a) chronic bronchitis; or

(b) emphysema; or

(c) both,

where there is accompanying evidence of a forced expiratory volume in one second (measured from the position of maximum inspiration with the claimant making maximum effort) which is—

[(i) at least one litre below the appropriate mean value predicted, obtained from the following prediction formulae which give the mean values predicted in litres—

For a man, where the measurement is made without back-extrapolation, (3.62 × Height in metres) – (0.031 × Age in years) – 1.41; or, where the measurement is made with back-extrapolation, (3.71 × Height in metres) – (0.032 × Age in years) – 1.44;

For a woman, where the measurement is made without back-extrapolation, (3.29 × Height in metres) – (0.029 × Age in years) – 1.42; or, where the measurement is made with back-extrapolation, (3.37 × Height in metres) – (0.030 × Age in years) – 1.46; or]

(ii) less than one litre.

## Notes

### Amendment

Entry A1: substituted by SI 2000/1588, reg 6(1), (2). Date in force: 10 July 2000: see SI 2000/1588, reg 1(1).

Entry A2: word omitted revoked by SI 2000/1588, reg 6(1), (3)(a). Date in force: 10 July 2000: see SI 2000/1588, reg 1(1).

Entry A2: words from "Frequent or prolonged" to "or white-hot material." in square brackets substituted by SI 2000/1588, reg 6(1), (3)(b). Date in force: 10 July 2000: see SI 2000/1588, reg 1(1).

Entry A10: words in square brackets in column 1 substituted by SI 1989/1207, reg 4(5); paras (a)–(e) substituted by SI 1987/2112, art 2; words in square brackets in para (a) substituted by SI 1994/2343, reg 4, words omitted revoked by SI 1996/425, reg 5(4); in para (c) words in square brackets inserted, and paras (ca), (j)–(w) inserted, by SI 1994/2343, reg 4.

Entry A12: inserted by SI 1993/862, reg 6(2); substituted by SI 1996/425, reg 5(5).

Entries B10, B11: inserted by SI 1989/1207, reg 6, Schedule.

Entries B12, B13: inserted by SI 1991/1938, reg 2(1).

Entry C1: in column 1 sub-paras (a)–(c) substituted by SI 2003/270, reg 5(1), (3). Date in force: 17 March 2003 (except in relation to claims made, or treated as made, before that date): see SI 2003/270, regs 1(1), 6.

Entry C2: in column 1 words "Central nervous system toxicity characterised by parkinsonism" in square brackets substituted by SI 2003/270, reg 5(1), (4). Date in force: 17 March 2003 (except in relation to claims made, or treated as made, before that date): see SI 2003/270, regs 1(1), 6.

Entry C4: substituted by SI 2003/270, reg 5(1), (5). Date in force: 17 March 2003 (except in relation to claims made, or treated as made, before that date): see SI 2003/270, regs 1(1), 6.

Entries C5A, C5B: substituted, for entry C5 as originally enacted, by SI 2003/270, reg 5(1), (6). Date in force: 17 March 2003 (except in relation to claims made, or treated as made, before that date): see SI 2003/270, regs 1(1), 6.

Entry C6: substituted by SI 2003/270, reg 5(1), (7). Date in force: 17 March 2003 (except in relation to claims made, or treated as made, before that date): see SI 2003/270, regs 1(1), 6.

Entry C7: substituted by SI 2003/270, reg 5(1), (8). Date in force: 17 March 2003 (except in relation to claims made, or treated as made, before that date): see SI 2003/270, regs 1(1), 6.

Entries C8–C11: (omitted) revoked by SI 2003/270, reg 5(1), (2). Date in force: 17 March 2003 (except in relation to claims made, or treated as made, before that date): see SI 2003/270, regs 1(1), 6.

Entry C12: substituted by SI 2003/270, reg 5(1), (9). Date in force: 17 March 2003 (except in relation to claims made, or treated as made, before that date): see SI 2003/270, regs 1(1), 6.

Entry C13: substituted by SI 2003/270, reg 5(1), (10). Date in force: 17 March 2003 (except in relation to claims made, or treated as made, before that date): see SI 2003/270, regs 1(1), 6.

Entries C14, C15: (omitted) revoked by SI 2003/270, reg 5(1), (2). Date in force: 17 March 2003 (except in relation to claims made, or treated as made, before that date): see SI 2003/270, regs 1(1), 6.

Entry C16: substituted by SI 2003/270, reg 5(1), (11). Date in force: 17 March 2003 (except in relation to claims made, or treated as made, before that date): see SI 2003/270, regs 1(1), 6.

Entry C17: substituted by SI 2003/270, reg 5(1), (12). Date in force: 17 March 2003 (except in relation to claims made, or treated as made, before that date): see SI 2003/270, regs 1(1), 6.

Entry C18: substituted by SI 2003/270, reg 5(1), (13). Date in force: 17 March 2003 (except in relation to claims made, or treated as made, before that date): see SI 2003/270, regs 1(1), 6.

Entry C19: substituted by SI 2003/270, reg 5(1), (14). Date in force: 17 March 2003 (except in relation to claims made, or treated as made, before that date): see SI 2003/270, regs 1(1), 6.

Entry C20: in column 2 words "Exposure to quinone or hydroquinone." in square brackets substituted by SI 2003/270, reg 5(1), (15). Date in force: 17 March 2003 (except in relation to claims made, or treated as made, before that date): see SI 2003/270, regs 1(1), 6.

Entry C21: substituted by SI 2003/270, reg 5(1), (16). Date in force: 17 March 2003 (except in relation to claims made, or treated as made, before that date): see SI 2003/270, regs 1(1), 6.

Entry C22: substituted by SI 2003/270, reg 5(1), (17). Date in force: 17 March 2003 (except in relation to claims made, or treated as made, before that date): see SI 2003/270, regs 1(1), 6.

Entry C23: substituted by SI 2003/270, reg 5(1), (18). Date in force: 17 March 2003 (except in relation to claims made, or treated as made, before that date): see SI 2003/270, regs 1(1), 6.

Entry C24: substituted by SI 2003/270, reg 5(1), (19). Date in force: 17 March 2003 (except in relation to claims made, or treated as made, before that date): see SI 2003/270, regs 1(1), 6.

Entry C25: substituted by SI 2003/270, reg 5(1), (20). Date in force: 17 March 2003 (except in relation to claims made, or treated as made, before that date): see SI 2003/270, regs 1(1), 6.

Entries C26, C27, C28, C29: inserted by SI 1987/2112, reg 2, Schedule.

Entry C26: substituted by SI 2003/270, reg 5(1), (21). Date in force: 17 March 2003 (except in relation to claims made, or treated as made, before that date): see SI 2003/270, regs 1(1), 6.

Entry C27: substituted by SI 2003/270, reg 5(1), (22). Date in force: 17 March 2003 (except in relation to claims made, or treated as made, before that date): see SI 2003/270, regs 1(1), 6.

Entry C28: (omitted) revoked by SI 2003/270, reg 5(1), (2). Date in force: 17 March 2003 (except in relation to claims made, or treated as made, before that date): see SI 2003/270, regs 1(1), 6.

Entry C29: substituted by SI 2003/270, reg 5(1), (23). Date in force: 17 March 2003 (except in relation to claims made, or treated as made, before that date): see SI 2003/270, regs 1(1), 6.

Entry C30: inserted by SI 1996/425, reg 5(6).

Entry C30: substituted by SI 2003/270, reg 5(1), (24). Date in force: 17 March 2003 (except in relation to claims made, or treated as made, before that date): see SI 2003/270, regs 1(1), 6.

Entry D3: in column 2 words in square brackets substituted by SI 1997/810, reg 6(2).

Entry D4: substituted by SI 1996/425, reg 5(7).

Entry D5: words omitted revoked, and words in square brackets inserted, by SI 1996/425, reg 5(8).

Entry D7: sub-para (f) substituted, and sub-paras (h)–(n) inserted, by SI 1986/1374, reg 2(2): sub-paras (o)–(x) inserted by SI 1991/1938, reg 2(2).

Entry D8: in column 1 sub-para (b) substituted by SI 1997/810, reg 6(3).

Entry D9: in column 1 words in square brackets substituted by SI 1997/810, reg 6(4).

Entry D10: inserted by SI 1987/335, reg 2(1), Schedule; words in square brackets substituted by SI 1993/862, reg 6(4).

Entry D11: inserted by SI 1993/862, reg 6(5).

Entry D12: inserted by SI 1993/1985, reg 6.

Entry D12: substituted by SI 1997/810, reg 6(5).

Entry D12: para (i) substituted by SI 2000/1588, reg 6(1), (4). Date in force: 10 July 2000: see SI 2000/1588, reg 1(1).

# Appendix 3

## Disabilities which may make a person incapable of work

| (1) | (2) | (3) |
|---|---|---|
| Activity | Descriptor | Points |
| 1 Walking on level ground with a walking stick or other aid if such aid is normally used. | 1(a) Cannot walk at all. | 15 |
| | (b) Cannot walk more than a few steps without stopping or severe discomfort. | 15 |
| | (c) Cannot walk more than 50 metres without stopping or severe discomfort. | 15 |
| | (d) Cannot walk more than 200 metres without stopping or severe discomfort. | 7 |
| | (e) Cannot walk more than 400 metres without stopping or severe discomfort. | 3 |
| | (f) Cannot walk more than 800 metres without stopping or severe discomfort. | 0 |
| | (g) No walking problem. | 0 |
| 2 Walking up and down stairs. | 2(a) Cannot walk up and down one stair. | 15 |
| | (b) Cannot walk up and down a flight of 12 stairs. | 15 |
| | (c) Cannot walk up and down a flight of 12 stairs without holding on and taking a rest. | 7 |
| | (d) Cannot walk up and down a flight of 12 stairs without holding on. | 3 |

| | | |
|---|---|---|
| | (e) Can only walk up and down a flight of 12 stairs if he goes sideways or one step at a time. | 3 |
| | (f) No problem in walking up and down stairs. | 0 |
| 3 Sitting in an upright chair with a back, but no arms. | 3(a) Cannot sit comfortably. | 15 |
| | (b) Cannot sit comfortably for more than 10 minutes without having to move from the chair [because the degree of discomfort makes it impossible to continue sitting]. | 15 |
| | (c) Cannot sit comfortably for more than 30 minutes without having to move from the chair [because the degree of discomfort makes it impossible to continue sitting]. | 7 |
| | (d) Cannot sit comfortably for more than 1 hour without having to move from the chair [because the degree of discomfort makes it impossible to continue sitting]. | 3 |
| | (e) Cannot sit comfortably for more than 2 hours without having to move from the chair [because the degree of discomfort makes it impossible to continue sitting]. | 0 |
| | (f) No problem with sitting. | 0 |
| 4 Standing without the support of another person or the use of an aid except a walking stick. | 4(a) Cannot stand unassisted. | 15 |
| | (b) Cannot stand for more than a minute before needing to sit down. | 15 |
| | (c) Cannot stand for more than 10 minutes before needing to sit down. | 15 |

| | | |
|---|---|---|
| | (d) Cannot stand for more than 30 minutes before needing to sit down. | 7 |
| | (e) Cannot stand for more than 10 minutes before needing to move around. | 7 |
| | (f) Cannot stand for more than 30 minutes before needing to move around. | 3 |
| | (g) No problem standing. | 0 |
| 5 Rising form sitting in an upright chair with a back but no arms without the help of another person. | 5(a) Cannot rise from sitting to standing. | 15 |
| | (b) Cannot rise from sitting to standing without holding on to something. | 7 |
| | (c) Sometimes cannot rise from sitting to standing without holding on to something. | 3 |
| | (d) No problem with rising from sitting to standing. | 0 |
| 6 Bending and kneeling. | 6(a) Cannot bend to touch his knees and straighten up again. | 15 |
| | (b) Cannot [either, bend or kneel, or bend and kneel] as if to pick up a piece of paper from the floor and straighten up again. | 15 |
| | (c) Sometimes cannot [either, bend or kneel, or bend and kneel] as if to pick up a piece of paper from the floor and straighten up again. | 3 |
| | (d) No problem with bending or kneeling. | 0 |
| 7 Manual dexterity. | 7(a) Cannot turn the pages of a book with either hand. | 15 |
| | (b) [Cannot turn a sink tap or the control knobs on a cooker with either hand]. | 15 |

| | | |
|---|---|---|
| | (c) Cannot pick up a coin which is 2.5 centimetres or less in diameter with either hand. | 15 |
| | (d) Cannot use a pen or pencil. | 15 |
| | (e) Cannot tie a bow in laces or string. | 10 |
| | (f) [Cannot turn a sink tap or the control knobs on a cooker with one hand, but can with the other]. | 6 |
| | (g) Cannot pick up a coin which is 2.5 centimetres or less in diameter with one hand[, but can with the other]. | 6 |
| | (h) No problem with manual dexterity. | 0 |
| 8 Lifting and carrying [by the use of upper body and arms (excluding all other activities specified in Part I of this Schedule)]. | 8(a) Cannot pick up a paper-back book with either hand. | 15 |
| | (b) Cannot pick up and carry a 0.5 litre carton of milk with either hand. | 15 |
| | (c) Cannot pick up and pour from a full saucepan or kettle of 1.7 litre capacity with either hand. | 15 |
| | (d) Cannot pick up and carry a 2.5 kilogramme bag of potatoes with either hand. | 8 |
| | (e) Cannot pick up and carry a 0.5 litre carton of milk with one hand[, but can with the other]. | 6 |
| | (f) Cannot pick up and carry a 2.5 kilogramme bag of potatoes with one hand[, but can with the other]. | 0 |

| | | |
|---|---|---|
| | (g) No problem with lifting and carrying. | 0 |
| 9 Reaching. | 9(a) Cannot raise either arm [as if] to put something in the top pocket of a coat or jacket. | 15 |
| | (b) Cannot raise either arm to his head [as if] to put on a hat. | 15 |
| | (c) Cannot put either arm behind back [as if] to put on a coat or jacket. | 15 |
| | (d) Cannot raise either arm above his head [as if] to reach for something. | 15 |
| | (e) Cannot raise one arm to his head [as if] to put on a hat[, but can with the other]. | 6 |
| | (f) Cannot raise one arm above his head [as if] to reach for something[, but can with the other]. | 0 |
| | (g) No problem with reaching. | 0 |
| 10 Speech. | 10(a) Cannot speak. | 15 |
| | (b) Speech cannot be understood by family or friends. | 15 |
| | (c) Speech cannot be understood by strangers. | 15 |
| | (d) Strangers have great difficulty understanding speech. | 10 |
| | (e) Strangers have some difficulty understanding speech. | 8 |
| | (f) No problems with speech. | 0 |
| 11 Hearing with a hearing aid or other aid if normally worn. | 11(a) Cannot hear sounds at all. | 15 |
| | (b) Cannot hear well enough to follow a television programme with the volume turned up. | 15 |

| | | |
|---|---|---|
| | (c) Cannot hear well enough to understand someone talking in a loud voice in a quiet room. | 15 |
| | (d) Cannot hear well enough to understand someone talking in a normal voice in quiet room. | 10 |
| | (e) Cannot hear well enough to understand someone talking in a normal voice on a busy street. | 8 |
| | (f) No problem with hearing. | 0 |
| 12 Vision in normal daylight or bright electric light with glasses or other aid to vision if such aid is normally worn. | 12(a) Cannot tell light from dark. | 15 |
| | (b) Cannot see the shape of furniture in the room. | 15 |
| | (c) Cannot see well enough to read 16 point print at a distance greater than 20 centimetres. | 15 |
| | (d) Cannot see well enough to recognise a friend across the room [at a distance of at least 5 metres]. | 12 |
| | (e) Cannot see well enough to recognise a friend across the road [at a distance of at least 15 metres]. | 8 |
| | (f) No problem with vision. | 0 |
| 13 Continence [(other than enuresis (bed wetting)).] | 13(a) No voluntary control over bowels. | 15 |
| | (b) No voluntary control over bladder. | 15 |
| | (c) Loses control of bowels at least once a week. | 15 |
| | (d) Loses control of bowels at least once a month. | 15 |
| | (e) Loses control of bowels occasionally. | 9 |

| | | |
|---|---|---|
| | (f) Loses control of bladder at least once a month. | 3 |
| | (g) Loses control of bladder occasionally. | 0 |
| | (h) No problem with continence. | 0 |
| 14 Remaining conscious [without having epileptic or similar seizures during waking moments]. | 14(a) Has an involuntary episode of lost or altered consciousness at least once a day. | 15 |
| | (b) Has an involuntary episode of lost or altered consciousness at least once a week. | 15 |
| | (c) Has an involuntary episode of lost or altered consciousness at least once a month. | 15 |
| | (d) Has had an involuntary episode of lost or altered consciousness at least twice in the 6 months before the day in respect to which it falls to be determined whether he is incapable of work for the purposes of entitlement to any benefit, allowance or advantage. | 12 |
| | (e) Has had an involuntary episode of lost or altered consciousness once in the 6 months before the day in respect to which it falls to be determined whether he is incapable of work for the purposes of entitlement to any benefit, allowance or advantage. | 8 |

| | | |
|---|---|---|
| | (f) Has had an involuntary episode of lost or altered consciousness once in the 3 years before the day in respect to which it falls to be determined whether he is incapable of work for the purposes of entitlement to any benefit, allowance or advantage. | 0 |
| | (g) Has no problems with consciousness. | 0 |

## Notes

### Amendment

In items 3, 8, 9, 12, 13 words in square brackets inserted, in items 6, 14 words in square brackets substituted, and in item 7 first and second words in square brackets substituted and final words in square brackets inserted, by SI 1996/3207, reg 2(11)(a), (b).

| (1) | (2) | (3) |
|---|---|---|
| Activity | Descriptor | Points |
| 15 Completion of tasks. | 15(a) Cannot answer the telephone and reliably take a message. | 2 |
| | (b) Often sits for hours doing nothing. | 2 |
| | (c) Cannot concentrate to read a magazine article or follow a radio [or television] programme. | 1 |
| | (d) Cannot use a telephone book or other directory to find a number. | 1 |
| | (e) Mental condition prevents him from undertaking leisure activities previously enjoyed. | 1 |

| | | |
|---|---|---|
| | (f) Overlooks or forgets the risks posed by domestic appliances or other common hazards due to poor concentration. | 1 |
| | (g) Agitation, confusion or forgetfulness has resulted in [potentially dangerous] accidents in the 3 months before the day in respect to which it falls to be determined whether he is incapable of work for the purposes of entitlement to any benefit, allowance or advantage. | 1 |
| | (h) Concentration can only be sustained by prompting. | 1 |
| 16 Daily living. | 16(a) Needs encouragement to get up and dress. | 2 |
| | (b) Needs alcohol before midday. | 2 |
| | (c) Is frequently distressed at some time of the day due to fluctuation of mood. | 1 |
| | (d) Does not care about his appearance and living conditions. | 1 |
| | (e) Sleep problems interfere with his daytime activities. | 1 |
| 17 Coping with pressure. | 17(a) Mental stress was a factor in making him stop work. | 2 |
| | (b) Frequently feels scared or panicky for no obvious reason. | 2 |

| | | |
|---|---|---|
| | (c) Avoids carrying out routine activities because he is convinced they will prove too tiring or stressful. | 1 |
| | (d) Is unable to cope with changes in daily routine. | 1 |
| | (e) Frequently finds there are so many things to do that he gives up because of fatigue, apathy or disinterest. | 1 |
| | (f) Is scared or anxious that work would bring back or worsen his illness. | 1 |
| 18 Interaction with other people. | 18(a) Cannot look after himself without help from others. | 2 |
| | (b) Gets upset by ordinary events and it results in disruptive behavioural problems. | 2 |
| | (c) Mental problems impair ability to communicate with other people. | 2 |
| | (d) Gets irritated by things that would not have bothered him before he became ill. | 1 |
| | (e) Prefers to be left alone for 6 hours or more each day. | 1 |
| | (f) Is too frightened to go out alone. | 1 |

## Notes

### Amendment

In item 15 first words in square brackets inserted, and second words in square brackets substituted, by SI 1996/3207, reg 2(11)(c).

# Appendix 4 – Principal Acts and Regulations

## Social Security

### *Acts*

IAA – Immigration and Asylum Act 1999. Removed entitlement to most benefits from asylum seekers and other persons subject to immigration control.

SPCA – State Pension Credit Act 2002. Governs the State Pension Credit, which comes into operation on 6 October 2003.

SSA – Social Security Act 1998. Introduced the revised system of decision making and appeals in the social security system.

SSAA – Social Security Administration Act 1992. Consolidating Act governing procedure and decision making in the social security system. Should now be read in conjunction with the Social Security Act 1998.

SSCBA – Social Security Contributions and Benefits Act 1992. Consolidating Act containing principal qualifying conditions for all benefits including contributions.

TCA – Tax Credits Act 2002. Covers the child tax credit and the working tax credit.

VDPA – Vaccine Damage Payments Act 1979. Sets out the scheme for vaccine damage payments.

### *Regulations*

CTB Regs – Council Tax Benefit (General) Regs 1992 No 1814. Govern the detailed operation of the council tax benefit scheme.

CTC Regs – Child Tax Credits Regs 2002 No 2007. Detailed regulation of the child tax credit scheme.

HB Regs – Housing Benefit (General) Regs 1987 No 1971. Govern the detailed operation of the housing benefit scheme.

IS Regs – Income Support (General) Regs 1987 No 1967. Govern the detailed operation of the income support scheme.

SPC Regs – State Pension Credit Regs 2002 No 1792. Detailed regulation regarding the state pension credit which comes into force on 6 October 2003.

SPO – the Naval, Military and Air Forces etc. (Disablement and Death) Service Pensions Order 1983 No 883. The regulations governing war pensions.

Social Security (Claims and Payments) Regulations 1979 No . No longer the principal claims and payments regulations, but contain the requirement to enter details of accidents in an accident book.

SS (C&P) Regs – Social Security (Claims and Payments) Regs 1987 No 1968. Govern all aspects of claims for benefits, decisions on claims,and payment of benefit.

SS (GA) Regs – Social Security (Guardians Allowance) Regulations 1975 No 515. Regulations concerning the Guardians Allowance.

SS (IB) Regs – Social Security (Incapacity Benefit) Regs 1994 No 2946. Principal regulations covering the detailed operation of the incapacity benefit scheme.

SS (IFW) Regs – the Social Security (Incapacity for Work) (General) Regs 1995 No 311. Covers the personal capability assessment and other aspects of incapacity for work for the purposes of incapacity benefit and income support.

SS (II)(PD) Regs – Social Security (Industrial Injuries) (Prescribed Diseases) Regs 1985 No 967. Contain the full list of prescribed diseases and how they are to be established.

SS (OB) Regs – Social Security (Overlapping Benefits) Regs 1979 No 597. Cover the overlap between different income replacement benefits and how it is dealt with.

SS & CS (DA) Regs – Social Security and Child Support (Decisions and Appeals) Regs 1991 No 991. Governs the procedure of tribunals following the Social Security Act 1998.

SSP Regs – Statutory Sick Pay (General) Regs 1982 No 894. Govern the operation of statutory sick pay.

TC (A) (No 2) Regs – Tax Credits (Appeals) (No 2) Regs 2002 No 3196. Govern the operation of appeals to appeal tribunals for tax credits, under the interim arrangements which are in place until appeals to the Commissioners of Income Tax can be arranged.

TC (C&N) Regs – Tax Credits (Claims and Notification) Regs 2002 No 2014. Covers claims for both working tax credit and child tax credit.

VDP Regs – Vaccine Damage Payments Regulations 1979 No 432. Govern the operation of the vaccine damage scheme under the Vaccine Damage Payments Act 1979.

WTC (EMR) Regs – Working Tax Credits (Entitlement and Maximum Rate) Regs 2002 No 2005. Determine the amount of working tax credit payable.

## Statutes concerning non-social security matters

Animals Act 1971 imposes strict liability for damage caused by animals. Divides animals into dangerous species and others.

Carers (Recognition and Services) Act 1995 and the Carers and Disabled Children Act 2000 provide for the assessment of a carer who cares for a person entitled to services under the National Health Service and Community Care Act 1990 and for the provision to them of services.

Consumer Protection Act 1987 imposes liability on the producer of goods (who may be the manufacturer, importer, or seller) for goods which are not safe.

Criminal Injuries Compensation Act 1995 covers the Criminal Injuries Compensation Scheme and its procedures.

Defective Premises Act 1972 provides that those involved in building a house are liable to later users of the house if it is not fit for habitation.

Employers Liability (Defective Equipment) Act 1969 provides that where a person is injured by equipment supplied by an employer, the employer is liable.

Fatal Accidents Act 1996 provides a remedy for dependants of someone who dies as a result of negligence.

Health and Social Services and Social Security Adjudication Act 1983 permits a local authority to charge for services provided.

Housing Grants Construction and Regeneration Act 1996 provides for grants for the adaptation of accommodation for someone who is sick or disabled.

Law Reform (Contributory Negligence) Act 1945 provides for deductions from damages awards where the claimant has themselves contributed to the injury or damage.

Law Reform (Miscellaneous Provisions) Act 1934 provides that a cause of action by a person who has died survives for the benefit of his or her estate.

Limitation Act 1980 prevents actions for personal injury being commenced more than three years after the incident complained of, or after the date on which the injured party acquired knowledge. The court has a general discreton to exceed the limitation period in suitable cases.

National Assistance Act 1948 covers the provision of services to people who fall within the definition of disabled contained in that section. The section imposes a duty to provide certain services, and operates in conjunction with the Chronically Sick and Disabled Persons Act 1970

National Health Service Act 1977 covers the provision of community care services to those who are ill, but who do not qualify for services under the National Assistance Act 1948.

National Health Service and Community Care Act 1990 s 47 requires a local authority, to whose notice the need for community care services in the case of an individual has come, to assess that person and to decide whether to provide them with any services.

Occupiers Liability Acts 1957 and 1984 impose a duty of care on the occupiers of premises to take care to ensure that their lawful visitors, and others on the premises, are not harmed.

Sale of Goods Act 1979 provides contractual liability for defective goods.

Unfair Contract Terms Act 1977 prevents the exclusion of the liability imposed on a seller by the Sale of Goods Act in a consumer sale.

# Appendix 5 – Useful Publications and Information Sources

This appendix is concerned principally with sources of information regarding the social security benefits outlined in this book. For detailed discussion of issues of legal liability in negligence and other forms of liability, reference should be made to standard legal textbooks on personal injury, or legal advice sought from a specialist in the field.

## Social security benefits – guides and handbooks

- Tonge, Kate (2002); *Tolleys Social Security and State Benefits: A Practical Guide* (Tolley, 2nd edition), ISBN 0 7545 1657 1, £43.00.
- Knipe, Robin, and Tonge, Kate: *Butterworths Welfare Law*, Butterworths, ISBN 0 4069 9660 1, £125.00. Comprehensive looseleaf volume with service.
- Robinson, Alan (2002): *Tolleys Social Security and Family Benefit Law: A Practical Guide* (Tolley), ISBN 0 7545 1894 9, £39.95.
- Child Poverty Action Group (2003): *Welfare Benefits and Tax Credits Handbook 2003/2004* (5th edition), CPAG, 94 White Lion Street, London N1 9PF, ISBN 1 901698 51 3, £30.00.
- Disability Alliance (May 2003), *Disability Rights Handbook,* £14.00.

## Annotated guides to the law

- Multi-author: *Social Security Legislation, Vols 1–4*, Sweet & Maxwell, to be published October 2003; £62 per volume.
- Multi-author: *Social Security Legislation, Vols 1–4 Supplement*, to be published March 2004, £38.00.
- Findlay, L et al, (December 2003): *CPAG'S Housing Benefit and CTB Legislation,* CPAG, £77.00, to include supplement.

## Official publications

- The Law Relating to Social Security, HMSO. The 'Blue Book.'

- The Decision Makers Guide (available on the internet – see below).
- Housing Benefit and Council Tax Benefit Guidance Manual.
- Neligan's Digest of Commissioners Decisions (available on the internet – see below).

## Other useful references

- Clements, Luke, (2000): *Community Care and the Law*, Legal Action Group, ISBN 0 905099 94.

## Computer software

There are a number of computer programmes on the market which claim to enable you to work out benefit, normally by asking questions which you answer from your case papers or by putting them to your client. Some knowledge of the benefit system is still very useful to unravel the complexities.

- Lisson Grove programme enquiries to Tim Blackwell, Lisson Grove Benefits programme, The Basement, 16 Vernon Terrace, Brighton BN1 3JG, tel 012273 711736, website, www.lissongrovebenefits.co.uk
- Ferret CD-ROM, £235. This includes: *The Law of Social Security* (the Blue Book); *The Law of Child Support* (the Orange Book); Acts from 1992 and statutory instruments from 1987; the full text of reported Commissioners' decisions from 1997 and starred Commissioners' decisions from 1990; *Neligan's Digest of Commissioners Decisions: Adjudication Officers Guide* and the *Child Support Adjudication Officers Guide; Disability Rights Handbook;* Derbyshire County Council's *DLA & AA case law pack;* and *Overpayment and Recovery of Benefits* by Paul Stagg.
- CPAG CD-ROM, £266 + VAT for a subscription which includes three updates a year. The CD-Rom includes: the Welfare Benefits Handbook; the Child Support Handbook; Findlay's Housing Benefit (see annotated guides); Legislation, commissioners' decisions, transcripts of High Court judgements, circulars, and articles from the Welfare Rights Bulletin.

## Internet resources

- www.dwp.gov.uk/advisers/index.htm is the Department of Work and Pensions guide for advisers. Many of the official sites can be accessed through this site.

- www.dss.gov.uk/publications/dss/2000/commdecs/contents.pdf gives access to the official site for Commissioners' decisions.
- www.dss.gov.uk/publications/dss/2000/neligans/index.htm for *Neligan's Guide.*
- www.courtservice.gov.uk/tribunals/ossc_frm.htm is the official site for the Social Security and Child Support Commissioners and includes much information about the work of the commissioners as well as decisions.
- www.cpag.org.uk/-CPAG's website.
- www.rightsnet.org.uk/ is the address of the London Advice Services Alliance Rightsnet site, which contains much useful information and regular updates on benefit news.

# Table of Cases

## A

Alcock v Chief Constable of South Yorkshire [1992] 1 AC 310 ....... 9.3, 12.2
Ansell v Minister of Pensions [1947] 2 All ER 501 .............................. 4.2
Antonio Mendoza v Ahmad Raja Ghaidan (5 November 2002) ............ 11.6
Atkinson v Seghal (21 March 2003) ............................................. 12.2

## B

Barnett v Chelsea and Kensington Hospital Management Committee [1969] 1 QB 428 ................................................... 1.4
Ball v Insurance Officer [1995] 1 All ER 833 ................................... 3.10
Beattie v Secretary of State for Social Security, April 9, 2001 ............ 10.10
Bolam v Friern Hospital Management Committee [1957] 1 WLR 582 .......................................................................... 9.4
Bolitho v The City and Hackney Health Authority [1997] 3 WLR 1151 ........................................................................ 9.4
Bolton v Stone [1951] AC 850 ..................................................... 9.3

## C

Caldwell v Maguire [2002] PIQR 45 ............................................. 12.6
Caparo Industries Plc v Dickman [1990] 2 AC 605 ............................ 9.2
Cassidy v Ministry of Health [1951] 2 KB 343 ................................. 1.4
Chadwick v British Transport Commission [1967] 2 All ER 945 ...... 9.3, 9.7
Chief Adjudication Officer v Creighton [2000] NI 222 (Northern Ireland Court of Appeal) ....................................................... 5.25
Chief Adjudication Officer v Faulds [2000] 2 All ER 961 ............... 3.7, 3.8
Chief Adjudication Officer v Palfrey ............................................. 7.7
Chief Adjudication Officer v Rhodes [1999] ICR 178 ........................ 3.10
Chittock v Woodbridge School [2003] PIQR 6 ................................ 12.6
Cockburn v Secretary of State of Social Security [1997] WLR 799 ... 5.7, 9.7
Colledge v Bass, Mitchells & Butlers Ltd [1988] 1 All ER 536 ............ 10.4
Coltman v Bibby Tankers Ltd, The Derbyshire [1988] AC 276 ............. 9.14
Cookson v Knowles [1979] AC 556 ............................................. 10.5
Condon v Basi (CA) [1985] 1 WLR 866 ......................................... 9.8

Croft v Broadstairs & St Peters Town Council [2003] EWCA Civ 676 ........ 12.3
Cunningham v Reading Football Club (1991) ........ 9.11
Curtis v Betts [1990] 1 All ER 769 ........ 9.15

## D

Davie v New Merton Board Mills [1959] AC 604 ........ 9.14
Diment v Chief Adjudication Officer ........ 5.14
Donoghue v Folkstone Properties [2003] EWCA Civ 231 ........ 12.8
Draper v Hodder (CA 1972) ........ 1.11
Duggan v Chief Adjudication Officer ........ 2.16
Dunk v George Waller & Son [1970] 2 QB 163 ........ 10.3

## F

Fairchild v Glenhaven Funeral Services [2002] 3 WLR 89 ........ 9.6, 12.5
Flemming v Secretary of State [2002] EWCA Civ 641 ........ 5.33
Froom v Butcher [976] QB 286 ........ 9.9

## G

Gulliksen v Pembrokeshire CC [2002] 4 All ER 450 ........ 12.1
Gwilliam v West Herts Hospitals The Times, 7 August 2002 ........ 12.8

## H

Hatton v Sutherland [200222] EWCA Civ 76 ........ 1.3, 9.5, 12.3
Hewitt v Chief Adjudication Officer ........ 5.14
Hinchy v Secretary of State for Work and Pensions (EWCA [2003] Civ 138 The Times, 24 February 2003) ........ 2.16
Horton v Caplin Contracts Ltd [2003] PIQR 180 ........ 12.4
Hunt v Severs [1994] 2 All ER 385 ........ 10.7

## J

Jones v Lawrence [1969] 3 All ER 267 ........ 10.3

## M

M (a child) v Chief Adjudication Officer ........ 5.14
Marbey v Daly's Theathre [1928] 1 KB 269 ........ 10.3

Maynard v West Midlands Regional Health Authority [1984] 1 WLR 634 .......... 9.4
McAuley v Department for Social Development, Court of Appeal of Northern Ireland .......... 7.9
McGhee v NCB [1973] 1 WLR 1 .......... 12.5
McLoughlin v O'Brian [1983] 1 AC 410 .......... 9.3, 11.3, 12.2
Mills v Hassoll [1982] ICR 330 .......... 10.4
Moran v Secretary of State for Social Services (1987) Court of Appeal .......... 5.9
Morris v Johnson Matthey & Co Ltd (1968) 112 Sol Jo 32 .......... 10.3
Morris v Murray [1991] 2 QB 6 .......... 9.7
Moyna v Secretary of State [2002] EWCA Civ 408 .......... 5.10
Mullen v Social Security Commissioner (17 January 2002, unreported) .......... 3.8

**N**

Nessa v Chief Adjudication Officer [1999] 4 All ER 677 .......... 7.12

**P**

Page v Smith [1996] AC 155 .......... 12.2
Paris v Stepney Borough Council [1951] AC 367 .......... 9.3
Phipps v Rochester Corporation [1955] 1 QB 450 .......... 9.11

**R**

R v Birmingham City Council ex parte Taj Mohammed (1998) 1 CCLR 441 .......... 8.7
R v CICB ex parte Webb [1986] QB 184 .......... 8.9
R v Industrial Injuries Commissioner [1966] 2 QB 31 .......... 3.10
R v National Insurance Commissioner ex parte Michael [1977] 2 All ER 420 .......... 3.10
R v National Insurance Commissioner ex parte Secretary of State for Social Services [1981] 1 WLR 1017 .......... 5.7, 5.8
R v North and East Devon Health Authority ex parte Coughlan (1999) 2 CCLR 285 .......... 10.7
Roberts v Dorothea Slate Quarries [1948] 2 All ER 201 .......... 3.8
Roe v Minister of Health [1954] 2 QB 66 .......... 9.2
Rose v Plenty [1976] 1 All ER 97 .......... 9.10

## S

Sanders v Minister of Pensions (1948) 4 WPAR 31 .............................. 4.2
Secretary of state for Social Security v Fairey [1997] 1 WLR 799 ........... 5.7
Secretary of State for Social Services v F [1983] 3 All ER 173 ............ 11.13
Secretary of State for Work & Pensions v Hourigan [2002] EWCA Civ 1890 ........................................................................ 7.7
Sherrif v Klyne Tugs (Lowestoft) Limited [1999] IRLR 481 (Court of Appeal) ........................................................................ 1.3
Shipp v Minister of Pensions [1946] KB 386 ...................................... 4.2
Smith v Baker and Sons HL [1891] AC 325 ......................................... 9.7
Smoldon v Whitworth The Times, 18 December 1996) ......................... 9.8
Sutherland (Chairman of the Governors of St Thomas Becket RC High School v Hatton and other cases [2002] IRLR 263 ................. 9.5
Swaddling v Adjudication Officer [1999] All ER (EC) 217 .................. 7.12

## T

The Wagon Mound [1961] AC 388 ...................................................... 9.6
Thomas v Chief Adjudication Officer ................................................ 7.9
Tomlinson v Congleton Borough Council (The Times, 22 March 2002) .......................................................................... 12.8
Trim Joint District School Board of Management v Kelly [1914] AC 667 ........................................................................ 3.7

## V

Vowles v David Evans and the Welsh Rugby Union [2003] EWCA Civ 318 ................................................................ 9.8, 12.6

## W

Walker v Northumberland County Council [1995] 1 All ER 737 ..... 1.3, 9.5
Walters v North Glamorgan NHS Trust [2002] EWCA Civ 1792 . 11.3, 12.2
Watson v British Boxing Board of Control [2001] .............................. 9.8
Webb v Barclays Bank and Portsmouth Hospitals NHS Trust [2001] EWCA Civ 1141 .............................................................. 12.4
Westminster City Council v National Asylum Support Service [2002] UKHL 38, House of Lords ............................................ 8.3
White v Blackmore [1972] 2 QB 651 ............................................... 9.8
Whitehouse v Jordan [1980] 1 All ER 650, CA; [1981] 1 WLR 246, HL ........................................................................................ 9.4
Williams v Devon CC [2003] EWCA Civ 365 .................................. 12.7
Wilsher v Essex Area Health Authority [1986] 3 All ER 801 ................ 9.3

Wilson v Coulson [2002] PIQR 300 .......................................... 12.4

**X**

XY v Minister of Pensions [1947] 2 All ER 501 .................................. 4.2

**Y**

Young v Post Office [2002] IRLR 660 .......................................... 12.3
Yuen Kun Yeu v Attorney General of Hong Kong [1987] 2 All ER
705 ......................................................................... 9.2

# Table of Statutes


A

**Access to Health Records Act 1990** ........ 1.4
s 5(1) ........ 1.4
**Access to Justice Act 1999** ... 7.9
**Administration of Justice Act 1982**
s 6 ........ 10.2
**Animals Act 1971** ....... 1.11, 9.15
s 2(1) ........ 9.15
s 2(2) ........ 9.15
s 5(1) ........ 9.15
s 5(2) ........ 9.15
s 10 ........ 9.15

C

**Carers and Disabled Children Act 2000** ......... 8.4
**Carers (Recognition and Services) Act 1995** ......... 8.4
**Child Support Pensions & Social Security Act 2000**
s 69 ........ 7.45
**Children Act 1989** ........ 8.4
**Children (Leaving Care) Act 2000** ........ 7.35
s 6 ........ 7.16
**Chronically Sick and Disabled Persons Act 1970** ........ 8.2, 8.7
s 2 ........ 8.1
s 2(1) ........ 8.2
s 2(1)(e) ........ 8.7
**Community Care (Direct Payments) Act 1996** . 8.4, 8.7
**Consumer Protection Act 1987** ........ 9.13
s 1(2) ........ 9.13
s 2(2) ........ 9.13
s 3(1) ........ 9.13
s 3(2) ........ 9.13
s 4 ........ 9.13
**Criminal Injuries Compensation Act 1995** ........ 8.8
**Crown Proceedings Act 1947**
s 10 ........ 12.9
**Crown Proceedings (Armed Forces) Act 1987** ........ 12.9

D

**Damages Act 1996** .... 10.2, 10.10
**Defective Premises Act 1972** ........ 1.9, 9.16

E

**Employers Liability (Defective Equipment Act) 1969** ........ 9.14

F

**Factories Act 1961** ....... 1.2, 3.11
**Fatal Accidents Act 1976** ... 8.13, 10.9, 11.4

## H

**Health and Safety at Work Act 1974** ........ 1.2
**Health and Social Services and Social Security Adjudication Act 1983**
s 17 ........ 8.5, 10.7
**Health Services and Public Health Act 1968**
s 45 ........ 8.1
**Highways Act 1980**
s 41 ........ 1.7
s 58(1) ........ 1.7
s 58(2) ........ 1.7
**Housing Grants construction and Regeneration Act 1996** .. 8.7

## I

**Immigration and Asylum Act 1999**
s 115 ........ 5.4, 5.22, 5.29, 7.13, 7.33, 7.47

## L

**Law Reform (Contributory Negligence) Act 1945**
s 1(1) ........ 9.9
**Law Reform (Miscellaneous Provisions) Act 1934** ... 10.9, 11.4, 11.5, 11.6
**Limitation Act 1980** ........ 9.17
s 14(1) ........ 9.17
s 14(3) ........ 9.17
s 33 ........ 9.17

## M

**Mental Health Act 1983** ...... 8.9, 9.17
s 117 ........ 8.1

## N

**National Assistance Act 1948**
s 2 ........ 8.3
s 21 ........ 8.1, 8.3
s 29 ........ 8.1, 8.2, 8.3, 8.7
s 29(1) ........ 8.2
**National Health Service Act 1977** ........ 8.1, 8.3
Sch 8 ........ 8.3
Sch 8, para 3(1) ........ 8.3
Sch 12 ........ 7.62
**National Health Service and Community Care Act 1990**
s 47 ........ 8.1, 8.6
**National Insurance Act 1957**
s 6 ........ 11.13

## O

**Occupiers Liability Act 1957** ........ 1.7, 1.9, 9.11, 9.16
s 2(3)(a) ........ 9.11
s 2(3)(b) ........ 9.11
s 2(4) ........ 12.8
s 2(4)(a) ........ 9.11
s 2(4)(b) ........ 9.11
**Occupiers Liability Act 1984** ....... 1.7, 1.9, 9.11, 9.16, 12.8
s 1(3) ........ 9.11

## R

**Road Traffic 1988** ............... 8.18
s 149 ................................ 9.7
s 151(2) .......................... 8.18


## S

**Sale of Goods Act 1979** ....... 9.12
s 14 ................................ 9.12
**Social Security Act 1998** ..... 2.2, 2.9, 2.15, 3.13, 8.25
s 7(2) .............................. 2.15
s 8(1) .............................. 2.9
s 9(1) .............................. 2.12
s 10(1)(a) ......................... 2.14
s 29 ................................ 3.11
**Social Security Administration Act 1992** ............................. 2.2
s 1 .................................. 2.7
s 1(1A) ............................ 2.7
s 8 .................................. 3.11
s 14(1) ............................ 6.4
s 19 ................................ 3.12
s 71 ................................ 2.16
**Social Security Contributions and Benefits Act 1992** ... 2.2, 7.54
s 2(1)(a) ........................... 3.3
ss 6–10 ........................... 7.54
s 21 ................................ 6.7
s 30 (1)(c) ....................... 6.11
s 30A ............................... 6.6
s 30C ............................... 6.6
s 30C(4)(a) ...................... 6.11
s 30C(5) .......................... 6.11
s 36 ................................ 11.8
s 36(1)(a) ......................... 11.8
s 39A .............................. 11.9
s 39A(2)(a) ...................... 11.9
s 39A(2)(b) ...................... 11.9
s 60(2) .................... 11.8, 11.9
s 60(3) .................... 11.8, 11.9
**Social Security Contributions and Benefits Act 1992** – *contd*
s 64 ................................ 5.23
s 64(4) ............................ 5.23
s 65(1) ............................ 5.23
s 66 ......................... 5.20, 5.23
s 66(2) ............................ 5.13
s 68 ................................ 5.37
s 69 ................................ 5.37
s 70 ................................ 5.30
s 70(1) ............................ 5.32
s 70(3) ..................... 5.33, 5.34
s 72(1) ............................... 5.6
s 72(1)(a) ........................... 5.6
s 72(1)(a)(ii) ...................... 5.11
s 72(1)(b) .................. 5.6, 5.13
s 72(1)(c) .................. 5.6, 5.13
s 72(2)(a)–(b) ..................... 5.5
s 72(5) ............................ 5.13
s 72(7) ............................ 5.12
s 73 ................................ 5.14
s 73(1) ............................ 5.14
s 73(1)(b) ........................ 5.14
s 73(1A) ............................ 5.2
s 73(8) ............................ 5.14
s 73(9)(a)–(b) ............ 5.5, 5.14
s 73(12) .......................... 5.14
s 73(14) .......................... 7.57
s 75 .................................. 5.2
s 77(1)(a) ........................ 11.13
s 77(2)(a) ........................ 11.14
s 77(2)(b) ........................ 11.14
s 77(2)(c) ........................ 11.14
s 77(5)(a) ........................ 11.13
s 77(11) .......................... 11.13
s 94(3) ............................ 3.10
s 99 ................................ 3.10
s 100 .............................. 3.10
s 101 .............................. 3.10
s 103(6) .................. 3.13, 3.14
s 104(1) .......................... 3.17
s 105(1)(a)–(b) ................ 3.18
s 106 ...... 3.19, 3.20, 3.21, 3.22, 3.23
s 108(6) .......................... 3.12

**Social Security Contributions and Benefits Act 1992** – *contd*
s 115(2) .......................... 3.4
s 117 .......................... 3.4
s 124 .......................... 7.17
s 124(1)(a) .......................... 7.16
s 124(1)(d) .......................... 7.15
s 124(1)(e) .......................... 7.10
s 131(1)(a) .......................... 7.47
s 131(3)–(5) .......................... 7.47
s 134(1) .......................... 7.5
s 136(1) .......................... 7.3
s 138(5) .......................... 7.57, 7.58
s 151 .......................... 6.1
s 151(4) .......................... 6.1, 6.2
s 151(6) .......................... 6.5
s 152(3) .......................... 6.3
s 153(2)(d) .......................... 6.3
s 153(3) .......................... 6.1, 6.3
s 153(7) .......................... 6.3
s 154 .......................... 6.3
s 154(2) .......................... 6.3
s 155(1) .......................... 6.3
s 155(4) .......................... 6.3
s 162 .......................... 6.3
s 163(2) .......................... 6.1
s 171A(2A) .......................... 6.9
s 171B(3) .......................... 6.8
s 171B(2) .......................... 6.8
s 171B(3) .......................... 6.8
s 171C(5) .......................... 6.9
s 171E(1)(a) .......................... 6.11
s 171F .......................... 6.10
s 171F(1)(b) .......................... 6.11
Sch 3, para 2 .......................... 6.7
Sch 3, para 5 .......................... 11.9
Sch 3, Part 1, para 4 .......................... 11.8
Sch 6, para 1(a) .......................... 3.13
Sch 7 ...... 3.19, 3.20, 3.21, 3.22, 3.23
Sch 11 .......................... 6.1, 6.3
Sch 11, para 2 .......................... 6.1
Sch 11, para 4 .......................... 6.1
Sch 12, para 1 .......................... 6.6

**Social Security Contributions (Transfer of Functions, etc) Act 1999**
s 8 .......................... 6.5
s 11 (2)(a) .......................... 6.5

**Social Security (Recovery of Benefits) Act 1997** .... 10.9

**State Pension Credit Act 2002**
s 1(2)(a) .......................... 7.50
s 2(2) .......................... 7.50
s 3 .......................... 7.50
s 3(2) .......................... 7.50
s 4(2) .......................... 7.50
s 9(4) .......................... 7.54
s 15(2) .......................... 7.6, 7.50

## T

**Tax Credits Act 2002**
s 3(3) .......................... 7.33
s 3(3)(a) .......................... 7.33
s 3(8) .......................... 7.33
s 6(3) .......................... 7.33
s 23(2) .......................... 2.15
s 28 .......................... 2.16
s 32(3) .......................... 7.33
s 39(1) .......................... 2.15

## U

**Unfair Contract Terms Act 1977**
s 6(1) .......................... 9.12

## V

**Vaccine Damage Payments Act 1979** .......... 1.5, 10.9
s 1(1A) .......................... 8.23
s 1(2) .......................... 8.19
s 1(3) .......................... 8.19
s 1(a)(i) .......................... 8.21

**Vaccine Damage Payments Act 1979** – *contd*
s 2(b) ................................ 8.20
s 2(c) ................................ 8.20
s 2(5) ................................ 8.21
s 6(1) ................................ 8.22
s 6(2) ................................ 8.22

**Vaccine Damage Payments Act 1979** – *contd*
s 6(3) ................................ 8.22

**W**

**Welfare Reform and Pensions Act 1999** ........ 5.37

# Table of Statutory Instruments


**C**

**Council Tax Benefits (General) Regulations 1992**
(SI 1992 No 1814) .... 7.46
Reg 3(1) .... 7.48
Reg 8(1)(b)–(e) .... 7.3
Reg 28 .... 7.47
Reg 51(1) .... 7.48
Reg 62(16) .... 2.7
Reg 84(2) .... 2.16
Sch 4, para 13(6) .... 7.27

**D**

**Discretionary Financial Assistance Regulations 2001**
(SI 2001 No 1167)
Reg 2(1) .... 7.45

**H**

**Housing Benefit (General) Regulations 1987**
(SI 1987 No 1971)
Reg 5(5)(e) .... 7.36
Reg 5(8) .... 7.36
Reg 5(8B) .... 7.36
Reg 6(1) .... 7.35
Reg 7 .... 7.36
Reg 7A(4)(e) .... 7.12
Reg 7(5) .... 7.12
Reg 11(3A) .... 7.38
Reg 12A(1), (8) .... 7.38

**Housing Benefit (General) Regulations 1987** – *contd*
Reg 16(1)(b)–(e) .... 7.3
Reg 37 .... 7.35
Reg 72(15) .... 2.7, 7.44
Reg 99(2) .... 2.16
Sch 3 .... 7.41
Sch 4, para 13(6) .... 7.27

**I**

**Income Support (General) Regulations 1987**
(SI 1987 No 1967)
Reg 4ZA .... 7.10
Reg 4ZA(2) .... 7.15
Reg 4ZA(3) .... 7.15
Reg 4(1)–(2) .... 7.12
Reg 5(1) .... 7.14
Reg 5(2)(a) .... 7.14
Reg 6(1) .... 7.14
Reg 6(4) .... 7.14
Reg 13 .... 7.15
Reg 15(1)A) .... 7.3
Reg 16(1) .... 7.3
Reg 21(3) .... 7.12
Reg 21(3F) .... 7.12
Reg 44(5) .... 7.3
Reg 47 .... 7.3
Reg 48 .... 7.24
Reg 49 .... 7.7
Reg 51(1) .... 7.8
Reg 51A .... 7.8
Reg 52 .... 7.7
Reg 53 .... 7.6
Sch 1B .... 7.10, 7.12

**Income Support (General) Regulations 1987** – *contd*
Sch 2 .............................. 7.20
Sch 2, para 1A .................. 7.19
Sch 3 .............................. 7.21
Sch 7, para 17 .................. 7.12
Sch 8 .............................. 7.26
Sch 8, para 6 .................... 7.26
Sch 8, para 9 .................... 7.26
Sch 9 ...................... 7.24, 7.25
Sch 9, para 15(5)(a) .......... 7.27
Sch 10 .............................. 7.9
Sch 10, paras 1,4 ................ 7.4
Sch 10, para 12 .................. 7.9
Sch 10, paras 26–28 ............ 7.4
Sch 10, para 44 .................. 7.9

N

**National Health Service (Charges for Drugs and Appliances) Amendment Regulations 2000**
(SI 2000 No 620) ....... 7.61, 7.65

**National Health Service (Dental Charges) Regulations 1989**
(SI 1989 No 394) .............. 7.62

**National Health Service (General Opthalmic Services) Regulations 1986**
(SI 1986 No 975) .............. 7.64

**National Health Service (Optical Charges and Payments) Regulations 1997**
(SI 1997 No 818) ....... 7.63, 7.64

**National Health Service (Travelling Expenses and Remission of Charges) Regulations 1988**
(SI 1988 No 551) ...... 7.61, 7.62, 7.65, 7.66

**Naval, Military and Air Forces etc. (Disablement and Death) Service Pensions Order 1983**
(SI 1983 No 883)
Art 3 ................................ 4.1
Art 4 ................................ 4.1
Art 4(1)(a)(ii) .................... 4.2
Art 4(b) ............................ 4.4
Art 4(3) ............................ 4.1
Art 5, para 5(2) .................. 4.1
Art 5(1)(b) ........................ 4.4
Art 6 ................................ 4.2
Art 55 .............................. 4.6
Art 62 .............................. 4.5
Art 63 .............................. 4.5
Sch 1
Sch 1, part III ...................... 4.3
Sch 1,part V ........................ 4.3
Sch 3 ................................ 4.5
Sch 4, item 22 .................... 4.1

R

**Regulatory Reform (Carer's Allowance) Order 2002**
(SI 2002 No 1457) ............ 5.34

**Regulatory Reform (Vaccine Damage Payments Act 1979) Order 2002**
(SI 2002 No 1592) ............ 8.24

S

**Social Fund Maternity and Funeral Expenses (General) Regulations 1987**
(SI 1987 No 481)
Reg 7 .......... 11.17
Reg 7(1) .......... 11.17
Reg 7(1)(a) .......... 11.17
Reg 7(1)(e) .......... 11.17
Reg 7A(1) .......... 11.17
Reg 8(1) .......... 11.17

**Social Security and Child Support (Decisions and Appeals) Regulations 1999**
(SI 1999 No 991)
Reg 3(1) .......... 2.12
Reg 3(5–7) .......... 2.13
Reg 4(3) .......... 2.12
Reg 5(c) .......... 2.13
Reg 6(2) .......... 2.14
Reg 11 .......... 6.9
Reg 31(1) .......... 2.15
Reg 32 .......... 2.15
Reg 33(1) .......... 2.15
Reg 36 .......... 2.15
Reg 39 .......... 2.15
Reg 53 .......... 2.15
Reg 57 .......... 2.15
Reg 58
Sch 2
Sch 2, para 5 .......... 2.7
Sch 2, para 14(a) .......... 3.18
Sch 2, para 23 .......... 7.57

**Social Security (Attendance Allowance) Regulations 1991**
(SI 1991 No 2740)
Reg 2(1) .......... 5.21
Reg 2(2) .......... 5.21
Reg 3 .......... 5.24
Reg 5 .......... 5.23

**Social Security (Attendance Allowance) Regulations 1991** – *contd*
Reg 8BA .......... 5.7

**Social Security Benefit (Persons Abroad) Regulations 1975**
(SI 1975 No 563)
Reg 4(2B) .......... 11.8
Reg 9(7) .......... 3.20
Reg 10C(5)(6) .......... 3.4
Reg 11 .......... 3.4

**Social Security (Claims and Payments) Regulations 1979**
(SI 1979 No 628)
Reg 24 .......... 3.11
Reg 25 .......... 1.2, 3.11

**Social Security (Claims and Payments) Regulations 1987**
(SI 1987 No 1968)
Reg 4(1) .......... 2.7
Reg 4(1A) .......... 2.7
Reg 4(1B) .......... 2.7
Reg 4(3) .......... 7.2
Reg 6(1)(a) .......... 2.7
Reg 6(8) .......... 2.7
Reg 6(9) .......... 2.7
Reg 7(1) .......... 2.7
Reg 8(2) .......... 2.7
Reg 10 .......... 2.7
Reg 19(2) .......... 2.7
Reg 19(3) .......... 2.7
Reg 19(4) .......... 2.7
Reg 19(5) .......... 2.7
Reg 19(6) .......... 2.7
Reg 19(7) .......... 2.7
Reg 22 .......... 2.8
Reg 28(1) .......... 2.9
Reg 28(2) .......... 2.9
Sch 4 .......... 2.7, 3.14
Sch 4, para 9 .......... 11.17

**Social Security (Disability Living Allowance) Regulations 1991**
(SI 1991 No 2890)
Reg 2(1) .......... 5.3
Reg 2(2) .......... 5.3
Reg 7 .......... 5.12
Reg 8(1) .......... 5.25
Reg 10(c) .......... 5.8
Reg 12 .......... 5.14
Reg 12(1) .......... 5.14
Reg 12(7) .......... 5.15

**Social Security (Employed Earners' Employments for Industrial Industries Purposes) Regulations 1975**
(SI 1975 No 467)
Sch 1, part 1 .......... 3.3
Sch 3 .......... 3.3

**Social Security (General Benefit) Regulations 1982**
(SI 1982 No 1408) .......... 3.13
Reg 2 .......... 3.20
Reg 3 .......... 3.20
Reg 11(6) .......... 3.13
Sch 2 .......... 3.13

**Social Security (Guardians Allowance) Regulations 1975**
(SI 1975 No 515)
Reg 2(2)(b) .......... 11.13
Reg 3(1) .......... 11.14
Reg 4 .......... 11.14
Reg 5(2)(a) .......... 11.14
Reg 5(6) .......... 11.14
Reg 6(1) .......... 11.13

**Social Security (Incapacity Benefit) Regulations 1994**
(SI 1994 No 2946)
Reg 4 .......... 6.11
Reg 6 .......... 6.11

**Social Security (Incapacity for Work) Regulations 1995**
(SI 1995 No 311) .......... 6.8
Reg 5 .......... 6.8
Reg 6(1)(a) .......... 6.9
Reg 6(1)(b) .......... 6.9
Reg 7(1) .......... 6.9
Reg 8 .......... 6.9
Reg 8(2) .......... 6.11
Reg 9 .......... 6.9, 6.11
Reg 10 .......... 6.8
Reg 10A .......... 6.10
Reg 11 .......... 6.8
Reg 12 .......... 6.8
Reg 13 .......... 6.8
Reg 13A .......... 6.8, 6.11
Reg 14(a) .......... 6.8
Reg 14(b) .......... 6.8
Reg 16(2) .......... 6.10
Reg 16(4) .......... 6.10
Reg 17 .......... 6.10
Reg 17(1)(b) .......... 6.10
Reg 17(1)(c) .......... 6.10
Reg 18(1)(a) .......... 6.11
Reg 18(1)(b) .......... 6.11
Reg 18(1)(c)(i) .......... 6.11
Reg 27 .......... 6.8

**Social Security (Industrial Injuries) (Prescribed Diseases) Regulations 1985**
(SI 1985 No 967)
Reg 2(c) .......... 2.7, 3.12
Reg 2(d) .......... 3.12
Reg 2(e) .......... 3.12
Reg 6(2)(b) .......... 3.12
Reg 6(2)(c) .......... 3.14
Reg 20(4)(a) .......... 3.14
Reg 25 .......... 2.7
Reg 25(2) .......... 3.12
Reg 26 .......... 2.7
Reg 27 .......... 3.12
Reg 36(1) .......... 3.12
Sch 1 .......... 3.12

**Social Security (Invalid Care Allowance) Regulations 1976**
(SI 1976 No 409)
Reg 4(1) .......................... 5.31
Reg 4(2) .......................... 5.35
Reg 9(1) .......................... 5.28
Reg 9(2) .......................... 5.28
Reg 9(3) .......................... 5.28

**Social Security (Medical Evidence) Regulations 1976**
(SI 1976 No 615)
Reg 2(1)(a) ........................ 6.8

**Social Security (Overlapping Benefits) Regulations 1979**
(SI 1979 No 597) ....... 5.36, 5.37

**Social Security (Unemployment, Sickness and Invalidity Benefit) Regulations 1983**
(SI 1983 No 1598)
Reg 17(1)(d)(ii) ................ 6.11

**State Pension Credit Regulations 2002**
(SI 2002 No 1792)
Reg 2 .............................. 7.50
Reg 3 .............................. 7.50
Reg 4 .............................. 7.50
Reg 4(3)(b) ...................... 7.53
Reg 6 .............................. 7.40
Regs 10–12 ...................... 7.54
Reg 15(1) ........................ 7.51
Reg 15(6) .................. 7.6, 7.51
Sch 1, para 1(2)(b) ............ 7.53
Sch 4, para 10 .................. 7.51
Sch 4,para 11 ................... 7.51
Sch 4, para 13 .................. 7.51
Sch 4, para 14 .................. 7.51

**Statutory Sick Pay and Statutory Maternity Pay (Decisions) Regulations 1999**
(SI 1999 No 776)
Reg 3 .............................. 6.5

**Statutory Sick Pay (General) Regulations 1982**
(SI 1982 No 894)
Reg 2 .............................. 6.2
Reg 3 .............................. 6.3
Reg 3(3) .......................... 6.3
Reg 5(2)(3) ...................... 6.3
Reg 7(1) .......................... 6.4
Reg 7(2) .......................... 6.4
Reg 7(4) .......................... 6.4
Reg 7(5) .......................... 6.4
Reg 9A ............................ 6.5
Reg 16 ............................ 6.1
Reg 16(2) ........................ 6.1
Reg 19 ............................ 6.3

**Statutory Sick Pay (Mariners and Persons Abroad) Regulations 1982**
(SI 1982 No 1349)
Reg 5 .............................. 6.3

**Statutory Sick Pay (Medical Evidence) Regulations 1985**
(SI 1985 No 1604)
Reg 2(2) .......................... 6.4

## T

**Tax Credits (Appeals) (No 2) Regulations 2002**
(SI 2002 No 3196)
Reg 6 .............................. 2.15
Reg 12(2) ........................ 2.15
Reg 21 ............................ 2.15
Reg 25 ............................ 2.15
Reg 27 ............................ 2.15

**Tax Credits (Claims and Notifications) Regulations 2002**
(SI 2002 No 2014)
Reg 7 .................................. 2.7
Reg 21 ............................. 7.33

**V**

**Vaccine Damage Payments Regulations 1979**
(SI 1979 No 432)
Reg 5 ............................... 8.21
Reg 5A ............................. 8.19

**W**

**Welfare Reform and Pensions Act 1999 (Commencement No 9, and Transitional and Savings Provisions Order 2000**
(SI 2000 No 2958) ............ 5.37

**Working Tax Credits (Entitlement and Maximum Rate) Regulations 2002**
(SI 2002 No 2005)
Reg 3 ............................... 7.32
Reg 3(3) ........................... 7.31
Reg 4 ....................... 7.31, 7.32
Reg 5 ............................... 7.32
Reg 13 ............................. 7.31
Reg 17 ............................. 7.31
Sch 1 ............................... 7.31

# Index


**A**

Accident
  employment, in course of **3.10**
  industrial **3.7**
  loss of faculty, causing **3.13**
  notification **3.11**
  personal injury, claimant suffering
    causation **3.9**
    course of employment, out of and in **3.10**
    requirement **3.7**
  process distinguished **3.8**
Accident book
  details recorded in **1.2**
Animals
  damage by, liability for **1.11, 9.15**
Appeals
  Appeals Service **2.15**
  benefit decisions, against **2.2, 2.9, 2.15**
  criminal injuries compensation, as to
    consideration of **8.15**
    oral hearing **8.16**
  industrial disablement benefit, relating to **3.15**
  war pensions, decisions concerning **4.7**
Asbestos, exposure to
  armed force, claim by member of **12.9**
Attendance allowance
  care home, people in **5.25**
  claiming **5.24**
  entitlement to **2.19**

Attendance allowance – *contd*
  hospital, people in **5.25**
  immigration status condition **5.22**
  other benefits, effect on **5.26**
  people aged over 65, for **5.20**
  qualifying conditions **5.23**
  residence condition **5.21**
  terminally ill people, for **5.20**

**B**

Bereavement benefits
  bereavement allowance **11.10**
  bereavement payment **11.8**
  child dependent, increases for **2.5**
  entitlement to **2.20**
  nature of **11.7**
  polygamous marriage, not payable to survivor of **11.7**
  widowed parents allowance **11.9**
Bullying
  stress, causing **1.3**

**C**

Carer's allowance
  claimant
    age limit **5.34**
    breaks, taking **5.35**

Carer's allowance – *contd*
claimant – *contd*
employment, not be in **5.32**
full-time education, not be in **5.33**
claiming **5.36**
entitlement to **5.27**
extent of care **5.31**
immigration status condition **5.29**
other benefits, effect of **5.36**
person cared for, benefits received by **5.30**
residence condition **5.28**

Charities
payments by **8.29**

Child tax credit
entitlement to **7.30, 7.32**
payment of **7.33**

Community care
assessment, duty to carry out **8.1**
carers, provision for **8.4**
disabled persons, for **8.2**
temporary disablement **8.3**
services **8.1**
obtaining **8.6**
payment for **8.5**
statutory provisions **8.1, 8.2**

Community Care Grants
social fund, from **7.58**

Compensation
criminal injuries, for *see* Criminal injuries compensation
fault, not referable to **9.1**
financial support by **2.1**

Constant attendance allowance
entitlement to **3.17**

Consumer protection
statutory provisions **9.13**

Contributory negligence
damages, reduction of **9.9, 12.7**

Coroner
role of **11.2**

Council tax benefit
backdated claims **2.7**
calculating **7.48**
conditions of entitlement **7.47**
income based benefit, as **7.1**
rebate of council tax, as **7.46**
regulations **7.46**
second adult rebates **7.49**

Criminal injuries compensation
appeals
consideration of **8.15**
oral hearing **8.16**
Authority **8.8**
award
level of **8.10**
review **8.15**
withholding **8.16**
care, for **8.12**
criminal injury, definition **8.9**
deductions **8.14**
eligibility for **8.9**
family violence, in relation to **8.17**
fatal injuries, in case of **8.13**
loss of earnings, for **8.11**
Scheme **8.8**
time limit **8.9**

Crown proceedings
asbestos, liability for disease caused by **12.9**

## D


Damages
aim of **10.1**
assessment **10.2**
awards **10.2**
benefits, recovery of **10.9**
contributory negligence, effect of **9.9, 12.7**
expenses, claiming **10.7**
fatality, in case of **11.4**
Fatal Accidents Act, claims under **11.6**
heads of **11.5**
financial support by **2.1**
future loss, for **10.5**
general, levels of **10.8**
income support, effect on capital for purposes of **7.9**
loss of earning capacity, for **10.6**
pain, suffering and loss of amenity, for **10.3**
past loss, for **10.4**
structured settlements **10.10**
Defective equipment
employers' liability for **9.14**
Defective premises
damage suffered, cause of action **9.16**
statutory liability for **1.9**
Defective products
defences **9.12**
liability for **9.12**
meaning **9.12**
statutory provisions **9.12**
Dental treatment
free, entitlement to **2.21, 7.62**
Department for Work and Pensions
role of **2.2**
Disability
benefits for **2.18, 2.19**
Disability – *contd*
specific causes of **2.18**
Disability living allowance
age limit **5.2**
care components
attention, requiring **5.7**
bodily functions, meaning **5.8**
children and young persons **5.11**
continual supervision, interpretation of **5.9**
lower **5.10**
renal dialysis, people receiving **5.12**
statutory provision **5.6**
terminally ill people **5.13**
children and young persons, attention or supervision requirements **5.11**
claiming **5.18**
components of **5.1**
entitlement to **2.19**
immigration status condition **5.4**
mobility components
circumstances for payment **5.14**
fluctuating condition of claimant **5.16**
higher rate **5.14**
lower rate **5.15**
Motability scheme **5.19**
nature of **5.1**
other benefits, effect on **5.17**
qualifying period **5.5**
renal dialysis, people receiving **5.12**
residence condition **5.3**
terminally ill people, for **5.13**
Disabled facilities grants
eligibility for **8.7**

Disabled facilities grants – *contd*
mandatory **8.7**
statutory provisions **8.7**

E

Eileen Trust
payments from **8.27**
Employed earner
exclusions **3.3**
meaning **3.3**
Employment
accident in course of **3.10**
Exceptionally severe disablement allowance
entitlement to **3.18**

F

Family Fund
payments from **8.28**
Fatalities
bereavement benefits *see* Bereavement benefits
Fatal Accidents Act, claims under **11.6**
inquests **11.2**
survivor, actions by
claims **11.3**
damages, for **11.4**
heads of **11.5**
deceased's right to sue, inheritance of **11.5**
Fatal Accidents Act, under **11.6**
Funeral expenses
assistance with **2.20**
Social Fund, payment from **2.20, 11.17**

G

Glasses
free, entitlement to **2.21, 7.63**
Guardian's allowance
age limits, absence of **11.15**
claiming **11.16**
entitlement to **2.20, 11.13**
meaning **11.12**
qualifying children **11.14**

H

Harassment
stress, causing **1.3**
Health and safety
statutory duties **1.2**
Health benefits
charges, exemption from **7.60**
Health records
access to **1.4**
Highways
maintenance of **1.7**
repair of **12.1**
tripping in **1.7**
Hospital
travel to, assistance with **2.21, 7.66**
Hospital treatment allowance
former entitlement to **3.23**
Housing benefit
age limits **7.35**
amount payable **2.6**
backdated claims **2.7**
calculating
eligible rent and applicable amount **7.40**
income **7.41**
income compared to applicable amount **7.42**

Housing benefit – *contd*
calculating – *contd*
non-dependants, deduction for **7.43**
rules for **7.39**
capital for purposes of **7.35**
claiming **7.44**
conditions of entitlement **7.35**
discretionary housing payments **7.45**
income based benefit, as **7.1**
other benefits, effect of **7.44**
payment of **7.44**
person on income support claiming **2.17**
rent
eligible **7.37**
restrictions on **7.38**
helping with **7.34**
liability to make payments in respect of **7.36**
standard rent allowance **2.6**

## I

Illness
industrial diseases *see* Industrial diseases
stress, based on **1.3**
work, at **1.3**
Incapacity benefit
contribution rules **6.7**
disqualification **6.11**
entitlement to **6.6**
incapacity for work
own occupation test **6.8**
personal capability assessment procedure **6.9**

Incapacity benefit – *contd*
incapacity for work – *contd*
tasks **6.8**
tests of **6.8**
increases for dependants **6.11**
payment of **6.11**
permitted work **6.10**
rate of **2.3**
adult dependent, increases for **2.4**
child dependent, increases for **2.5**
Income support
applicable amount **2.6, 7.18, 7.22**
backdated claims **2.7**
calculating
applicable amount **7.18, 7.22**
calculation **7.29**
housing costs **7.21**
personal allowances **7.19**
premiums **7.20**
capital for purposes of
cut-off **7.5**
damages, effect of **7.9**
meaning **7.4**
notional **7.8**
tariff income **7.6**
valuation **7.7**
claiming **2.7**
cohabitees claiming **7.3**
conditions of entitlement
age limits **7.16**
education, receipt of **7.15**
immigration status **7.13**
presence in GB **7.12**
remunerative work, as to **7.14**
residence in UK **7.12**
dependent children, for **7.3**
family, claim for **7.3**

Income support – *contd*
- incapacity for work, on **2.17**
- income based benefit, as **7.1**
- income for purposes of
  - completely disregarded **7.24**
  - fully taken into account **7.28**
  - part-time earnings **7.26**
  - partly disregarded **7.25**
  - personal injury compensation awards **7.27**
  - taking into account **7.23**
  - tariff **7.6**
- other benefits, relationship with **7.17**
- persons entitled to claim, categories of **7.10**
- widow or widower, entitlement of **11.11**

Independent Living Funds
- financial assistance from **8.26**

Industrial death benefit
- entitlement to **3.21**

Industrial disablement benefit
- additions to
  - constant attendance allowance **3.17**
  - exceptionally severe disablement allowance **3.18**
- amount of **3.14**
- appeals **3.15**
- assessments **3.13**
- claiming **2.7, 2.18**
- decision making **3.15**
- other benefits, effect on **3.16**
- physical damage or mutilation, for **3.13**

Industrial diseases
- illnesses recognised as **1.3**
- industrial injury benefit, claiming **3.12**
- loss of faculty, causing **3.13**
- occupation specified for **3.12**
- onset **3.12**
- pneumoconiosis, byssinosis and miscellaneous benefits scheme, entitlement under **3.24**

Industrial injury benefit
- basis entitlement **3.2**
- claiming
  - conditions **3.2**
  - employed earners, by **3.3**
  - personal injury, claimant suffering **3.5–3.11**
  - residence condition **3.4**
- loss of faculty, requirement of **3.13**
- personal injury, claimant suffering
  - accident, by **3.7–3.11**
  - see also Accident
  - causation **3.9**
  - course of employment, out of and in **3.10**
  - nature of **3.6**
  - process, by **3.8**
  - psychological **3.8**
  - requirement **3.5, 3.6**
- prescribed diseases **3.12**
- scheme **3.1**

Inquest
- Coroner, role of **11.2**
- duty to hold **11.2**
- jury **11.2**

Insurance
- compulsory **1.12**

J

Jobseekers allowance
  claiming 2.7

L

Limitation period
  relevant date 9.17

M

Macfarlane Trusts
  payments from 8.27
Medical conditions
  private provision for 8.29
Medical negligence
  clinical judgment, error of 9.4
  complexities of claims 1.4
  duty of care 1.4, 9.4
  hospital records, access to 1.4
  standard of care 9.4
Motability scheme
  vehicle, payment for 5.19
Motor Insurers Bureau
  insurer of last resort, as 8.18

N

Negligence
  causation 9.6, 12.4, 12.5
  contributory 9.9, 12.7
  criteria for claim 9.2
  defective products, liability for 9.12
  duty of care 9.2
    requirement of 1.4
  fatalities, application of principles to 11.1
  foreseeability 9.2, 9.3
  medical *see* Medical negligence
Negligence – *contd*
  mesothelioma, cause of 12.5
  principles of 9.1, 9.2
  proximity principle 9.2
  remoteness of damage 9.6, 12.4, 12.5
  road accident, causing 1.6
  secondary victims 9.3, 12.2
  sports injuries 9.8, 12.6
  stress, claim for 9.5
  vicarious liability 9.10
  volenti non fit injuria, principle of 9.7

O

Occupational pensions
  long-term sickness, payment in case of 8.29
Occupational sick pay
  contractual provisions 8.29
Occupiers liability
  care, degree of 1.9
  occupier, meaning 9.11
  statutory provisions 9.11
  trespasser, claim by 12.8
  visitors, duty to 9.11

P

Pensions
  long-term sickness, payment in case of 8.29
Personal injury
  actions for 1.12
  animals, caused by 1.11, 9.15
  benefits
    death, on 2.20
    incapacity for work, for 2.17

Personal injury – *contd*
benefits – *contd*
specific causes of disability 2.19 **2.18,**
circumstances of **1.1**
home, in **1.8**
income support, awards taken into account for **7.27**
premises under control of another, on **1.9**
road accident, in **1.6**
tripping, caused by **1.7**
Pneumoconiosis, byssinosis and miscellaneous benefits scheme
entitlement under **3.24**
Prescriptions
free, entitlement to **2.21, 7.61**
war pensioners **4.14**
wigs and fabric supports, for **7.65**
Product liability
defences **9.12**
statutory provisions **9.12**

**R**

Reduced earnings allowance
entitlement to **3.19**
replacement **3.20**
withdrawal of **3.19**
Retirement allowance
entitlement to **3.20**
Road accidents
damages, claim for **1.6**

**S**

Severe disablement allowance
abolition **5.37**
claiming **5.37, 5.38**
Severe disablement allowance – *contd*
entitlement to **2.19**
Sight tests
free, entitlement to **2.21, 7.54**
Social fund
budgeting loans **7.56**
Community Care Grants **7.58**
crisis loans **7.57**
discretionary grants and loans from **7.55–7.58**
mandatory grants from **7.59**
payments
entitlement to **2.21**
funeral expenses, for **2.20, 11.17**
Sports injuries
litigation concerning **1.10**
negligence, and **9.8, 12.6**
standard of care **9.8**
State benefits
backdated claims **2.7**
claiming **2.7**
appointees **2.8**
contributory
adult dependent, increases for **2.4**
rates of **2.3**
damages award, recovery from **10.9**
decisions
adjudication officers **2.9**
appeals **2.2, 2.9, 2.15**
Department for Work and Pensions, responsibility of **2.2**
papers, on **2.9**
revision **2.10–2.13**
supercessions **2.10, 2.14**
Department for Work and Pensions, responsibility of **2.2**
entitlement to **2.2**

State benefits – *contd*
- financial support by **2.1**
- income based **2.6, 7.1**
- overpayments **2.16**
- personal injury, for
  - death, on **2.20**
  - incapacity for work **2.17**
  - specific causes of disability **2.18, 2.19**
- rate of **2.3**
  - adult dependent, increases for **2.4**
  - child dependent, increases for **2.5**
- statutory provisions **2.2**
- statutory, rates of **2.3**
- system of **2.2**

State pension credit
- claiming **7.54**
- entitlement to **7.50**
- guarantee credit **7.50, 7.51**
- hospital, effect of going into **7.53**
- introduction of **7.1**
- savings credit **7.52**
- scheme **7.50**

Statutory sick pay
- decision, challenging **6.5**
- incapacity for work, on **2.17, 6.2**
- notification of incapacity **6.4**
- payable, where **6.3**
- payment of **6.4**
- period of entitlement **6.3**
- qualification for **6.1**
- scheme **6.1**

Stress
- bullying and harassment, caused by **1.3**
- cases on **12.3**
- claims based on **1.3**
- workplace injury, as **9.5**

**T**

Tax credits *see also* Child tax credit, etc
- amount of **2.6**
- claiming **7.33**
- conditions of entitlement **7.33**
- system of **7.30**

**U**

Unemployability supplement
- former entitlement to **3.22**

**V**

Vaccine damage payments
- age limits **8.20, 8.24**
- amount of **8.23**
- claiming **8.22**
- disability threshold **8.24**
- other benefits, effect on **8.25**
- place of vaccination **8.21**
- qualification for **8.19**
- statutory scheme **1.5**
  - scope of **8.19**

Vicarious liability
- principle of **9.10**

Volenti non fit injuria
- principle of **9.7**

**W**

War pensions
- appeals **4.7**
- basic benefit **4.3**
- claiming **2.18**
- claiming **4.5**
- conditions for entitlement **4.1**
- disability caused by military service, for **4.1**

War pensions – *contd*
injury attributable to or aggravated by service, in respect of **4.2**
medical evidence, obtaining **4.5**
overlapping provisions **4.6**
payment **4.5**
pensioners, medical treatment and care for
appliances **4.8**
convalescence **4.9**
free prescriptions **4.14**
home nursing equipment **4.10**
hospital travelling expenses **4.11**
house adaptation grants **4.12**
priority **4.15**
private **4.16**
skilled nursing care **4.17**
treatment allowance **4.13**

War pensions – *contd*
Royal Prerogative, paid under **4.1**
supplementary allowances **4.3**
widow or widower, for **4.4**

Widowed parents allowance
entitlement to **11.9**

Working tax credit
disabled claimants **7.32**
employer, paid by **7.33**
entitlement to **2.17, 7.31**
low earnings, topping up **7.1**

Workmen's Compensation Scheme
entitlement under **3.25**

Workplace injuries
details, recording **1.2**
how arising **1.2**
stress **9.5**